DECODING CHALLENGING
CLASSROOM BEHAVIORS

ABOUT THE AUTHOR

Ennio Cipani is a full professor at National University in Fresno, California. Prior to his current position, he performed a faculty role at the California School of Professional Psychology in the child clinical emphasis. Prior to that position, he was a faculty member in the department of special education at the University of the Pacific. He graduated from Florida State University with a Ph.D. in educational psychology. He has written many articles, chapters, and books on behavior management, including *Punishment on Trial* (2004, free at www .ecipani.com/PoT.pdf) and *Functional Behavioral Assessment, Diagnosis, and Treatment* (2011, Second Edition). He has conducted workshops, continuing education, and training programs on topics involving classroom behavior management, discrete trial training, functional behavioral assessment, and behavioral intervention at the local, state, and national level.

For inquiries about possible on-site workshops and training systems, please contact Doctor Cipani at ennioc26@hotmail.com.

DECODING CHALLENGING CLASSROOM BEHAVIORS

What Every Teacher and Paraeducator Should Know!

By

ENNIO CIPANI, Ph.D.

National University
Fresno, California

CHARLES C THOMAS • PUBLISHER, LTD.
Springfield • Illinois • U.S.A.

Published and Distributed Throughout the World by

CHARLES C THOMAS • PUBLISHER, LTD.
2600 South First Street
Springfield, Illinois 62704

© 2011 by CHARLES C THOMAS • PUBLISHER, LTD.

ISBN 978-0-398-08674-9 (paper)
ISBN 978-0-398-08675-6 (ebook)

Library of Congress Catalog Card Number: 2011015695

With THOMAS BOOKS *careful attention is given to all details of manufacturing
and design. It is the Publisher's desire to present books that are satisfactory as to their
physical qualities and artistic possibilities and appropriate for their particular use.*
THOMAS BOOKS *will be true to those laws of quality that assure a good name
and good will.*

Printed in the United States of America
MM-R-3

Library of Congress Cataloging-in-Publication Data

Cipani, Ennio.
   Decoding challenging classroom behaviors : what every teacher and
paraeducator should know! / by Ennio Cipani.
      p. cm.
   Includes bibliographical references.
   ISBN 978-0-398-08674-9 (pbk.) -- ISBN 978-0-398-08675-6 (ebook)
   1. 373.12/913.2. School children–Psychology. 3. Claswsroom management. I. Title.

   LB1060.2.C567 2011
   371.102'4–dc22

                                                    2011015695

PREFACE

In many teacher training programs, future teachers are told that student problem behavior is a function of many factors outside their purview and sphere of influence. Challenging behaviors and poor student performance are often attributed to many of society's ills. As a result of the presence of such factors in some students' lives, changing these students behavior in the classroom is seen as futile unless one can change their nonschool environment.

I feel differently. Challenging behavior problems can be understood in the same manner one understands why other child behaviors occur. Once you understand that behavior occurs for a reason, and that the reason for behavior is embedded in the **current social context** of the problem behavior, solving behavior problems is "doable." One does not have to wait for society to ameliorate the level of violence portrayed in the popular media to be effective. A four-decade history of applied research using behavioral interventions in homes and classrooms successfully supports my contention. Such efforts have empirically demonstrated that behavior change occurred as a result of what teachers did inside their classroom!

The current text provides sufficient background in understanding why behavior occurs to facilitate the reader's capability to develop intervention strategies that make functional sense. In order to design and implement effective intervention strategies, the ability to decode the function of challenging behavior is a requisite. To acquire such skills requires a comprehensive approach to skill development. Too often, classroom personnel are taught a few tricks and then encouraged to go and try them. Changing behavior is not a matter of a few tricks! Rather, the professional repertoire needed requires a thorough understanding and analysis of the role of the social environment, both before and after the behavior. Therefore, I have taken painstaking efforts to make sure that this text is not a "cookbook" of menus to try. In contrast, this text provides a conceptual basis for understanding why certain behaviors occur under specific conditions. After reading this material, I am sure you will have a finer appreciation for the role of a behavior's antecedent and consequent conditions.

A SELF-CONTAINED INSTRUCTIONAL APPROACH

I wanted to design a set of materials that would make you feel like you are taking a course from me.[1] To accomplish this goal, I had to advace past offering words on a page to be consumed by the reader. Imagine you are enrolled in a course that I am teaching on the topic of behavioral intervention in classrooms. As a student, you would (hopefully) attend my lectures, where I attempt to impart my knowledge to you. The pages in this book supplant that medium. Realize that presenting lectures is just part of the mechanism I would use in shaping your behavioral repertoire. As your course instructor, I would also want to assess the degree to which you comprehend the content I delivered. In that regard, I would give you tests, and then grade them and provide you feedback on your skill acquisition. To that end, there are two sets of objective measures when you finish reading and studying each chapter: fill-in-the-blank (see Appendix A) and true/false test items that follow the chapter summary. The answers to both these measures are provided in files on the attached CD.

Additionally, I might ask you to discuss how a certain behavioral interaction is indicative of some principle I just lectured about. With your exposition, I would then point out how your discussion addresses (or does not completely address) the principles involved. It is this interactive manner that allows a teacher to effectively impart his (or her) knowledge to students.

I hope a unique feature of this text will accomplish that phenomenon of an on-site course. Since Chapters 1 and 2 form the heart of the decoding behavior approach, I selected them for this unique instructional text approach. Within these chapters, after reading a short section, between one and three short answer discussion questions appear. Subsequent to providing your response to each question, you can listen to the desired answer in a narrated presentation in the attached CD. The labeling system I used in the text for these questions allows you to go directly to the narration needed, e.g., my answers to discussion questions 1a can be found on PowerPoint file labeled 1a, and so forth. When you run these PowerPoint files in slide show, you can listen to my discussion of the answers. You will find seven separate PowerPoint files in the Chapter 1 folder that correspond to the seven sets of discussion questions in Chapter 1. In that same vein, there are nine corresponding files in the Chapter 2 folder. After listening to my response to the discussion questions, you may find the need to review that previous section of the text before proceeding with the next section. This unique instruction-

---

1. This intention is for students taking a course where this text is used as well as classroom personnel studying this material as part of their professional development.

al component should greatly facilitate your comprehension of this material in the first two chapters. To further self-assess your capability in decoding behavior, Appendix B provides performance tasks for several of the chapters for your consideration.

OVERVIEW OF TEXT

The first two chapters provide the basic conceptual knowledge for decoding student classroom behavior. With these two chapters, you will see that decoding student behavior requires that you examine and analyze the antecedent as well as consequent conditions of the student's behavior. Behavior just doesn't happen; it happens for a reason. Once you realize this, you will be able to solve behavior problems by addressing their environmental function. In the first chapter, a number of hypothetical examples[2] are used to illustrate that challenging problem behavior does **make sense** when looked at from a functional perspective. An analysis of a student's behavior from its actual surroundings provides the teacher with a greater understanding of why that particular behavior occurs. In Chapter 2, six behavioral functions are delineated and many examples are used to illustrate how behavior can serve such a purpose. The scenarios under which adult attention, peer attention and access to preferred items and events are the function or purpose of the behavior are clearly explicated. Additionally, some challenging behaviors are the result of escaping or avoiding aversive events or activities. Three common factors within classroom environments are offered and examples are portrayed.

The next two chapters present basic principles of behavior. These basic principles undergird the content in Chapters 1 and 2. Chapters 5 and 6 deal with methods of collecting information and data, and are essential skills for classroom personnel in their efforts to decode student behavior. Chapter 7 addresses how to intervene with challenging behavior problems by providing an intervention that enables an appropriate behavior to effectively and efficiently produce the identified function. The final chapter involves a discussion of challenging behaviors that occur in classroom contexts which are not socially mediated.

I hope you find the following pages informative and enjoyable to read. Once you have developed skills in decoding student behavior, you become a resource and mentor to others who may be struggling. Many teachers and

---

2. Hypothetical cases, an amalgam of real-life cases I have served during my 30 years in applied behavior analysis.

paraeducators leave the field because they become disillusioned with the challenging problem behaviors they face day after day. Let's not lose good people because they were not taught how to be effective behavior change agents!

CONTENTS

DECODING CHALLENGING
CLASSROOM BEHAVIORS

Chapter 1

DECODING CHILD BEHAVIOR

W hy does he or she do that? If you are a paraeducator, it is likely that on any given day, some of the behaviors they see in the classroom will bewilder you. Why are some children aggressive in school? Why do some children fail to follow classroom rules? Why do some children engage in oppositional behavior during class assignments and instruction? Perhaps such inappropriate behavior serves a purpose in the student's social environment (Bailey & Pyles, 1989; Cipani, 1990; Cipani & Trotter, 1990; Cipani & Schock, 2007, 2011; Iwata, Vollmer & Zarcone, 1990; LaVigna, Willis & Donnellan, 1989; Lennox & Miltenberger, 1989).

For example, let us say a hypothetical nine-year-old child named Peter, who is verbally aggressive, has been diagnosed by a school psychologist as having severe emotional disturbance. You subsequently hear school personnel explain to you that this child acts aggressively because he has a disorder; severe emotional disturbance. When Peter engages in verbally aggressive behavior, the disorder made him do it. Peter is expected to exhibit such inappropriate behavior from time to time, irrespective of context and consequences.

In contrast, the functional approach I am advocating would explain Peter's verbal tantrum episodes from an analysis of the inherent social context (Cipani, 1994; Cipani & Schock, 2007, 2011). Suppose we find the following. Peter often engages in such behavior when presented with an instructional activity that holds no interest for him. He indicates his displeasure of the instructional task and his desire to terminate his involvement. His teacher obviously is determined to keep him from leaving the instructional activity. Peter will initially complain and argue about the assignment to his teacher.

"Why do we have to do this?" His teacher becomes more assertive in her demand that he finish his assignment and tries to deflect these arguments. When Peter sees that his mild arguments are not helping his cause, i.e., getting out of the assignment, he tries another tactic. He states, "This is stupid. I do not need math in my life. I am going to throw this book on the floor! I won't do my work!" He follows through on his promise and then proceeds to run around the classroom until the teacher calls the principal. He then sits in the office, missing math period and reading that day while he calms down.

With this information about the social context, what is a more plausible explanation for Peter's behavior? He does this because he is emotionally disturbed. Or he does this because it "works" for him when he wants to get out of the instructional activity. If you examine the sequence of events, what happens after the episode provides significant information in **decoding** Peter's behavior. The verbal tantrum and disruptive behavior in the classroom resulted in terminating the instructional activity. If such behavioral episodes from Peter continue to terminate his engagement with the task, the function of behavior is one of escaping the instructional task. Decoding child behavior requires that you identify the behavioral function of the problem behavior in the given context. The catch phrase, *Behavior just happens* is not accurate or valid!

Questions to Answer Before Proceeding (1a)

1. If you had to bet money, when would you predict that Peter would engage in tantrum behavior? Why would you think this bet would pay off for you?
2. Is the social environment enabling Peter's behavior? How?

Here is another illustration of decoding behavior with a very bizarre example. People diagnosed with mental illness are ascribed to behave in ways that make no sense, due to "faulty brain mechanisms." If you visit a hospital for psychiatric patients and observe what transpires, you would probably conclude that some of the clients' behavioral episodes you observe are indeed bizarre and seem to be maladaptive. To you, their behavior might also seem to make no sense. Moreover, I believe you would often be wrong. Here is an illustration. What would you say about a man who spins with arms outstretched when people approach him? Is his behavior beyond logic and understanding? The following case illustrates a traditional approach to determining why the behavior occurs and contrasts it with a functional perspective.

THE CASE OF THE SPINNING TOP

A middle-aged man, diagnosed with schizophrenia, in a locked psychiatric unit, engaged in an unusual behavior (see Cipani & Schock, 2007). He would spin around with his arms outstretched. When medical staff would approach him to interact, he would simply stretch out his arms and begin to spin in circles. Anyone within arms' distance is struck. The medical staff apparently surmises that such behavior is the result of his mental disorder, thus dismissing an analysis of its behavioral function. Here is a hypothetical conversation between an attending nurse on this patient's unit and a psychiatrist assigned to this patient that portrays the traditional explanation.

Nurse: Dr. Des-Order, as you probably know, we are having some difficulty with your patient, Mr. Smith. As part of his therapeutic treatment, the nursing staff and some of the physicians attempt to interact with him, hoping to bring him "out of his shell." At some point, as you know, he begins spinning in circles, right when you are attempting to engage him in conversation. I am not sure why he does this. Perhaps if we understood what internal process or delusion is creating this response to interaction, we could set up a therapeutic milieu.

Dr. Des-Order: Yes, Nurse Seaver, I have experienced that reaction myself. I believe it is part of his pathology because he suffers from schizophrenia. Mr. Smith becomes involved in some delusion with you and your staff being representative of some feared experience. When he rejects our attempts to break into his world by spinning like that, he is not rejecting us. His paranoid delusion views us and others as people he cannot trust. Therefore, his behavior does not make sense because his thought processes are not logical due to his schizophrenia. His brain mechanisms allow this break from reality, which relieves him of responsibility for his actions.

Nurse: So what should we do? Do we continue to attempt interaction with him? When we try to interact, he begins that spinning top routine.

Dr. Des-Order: By all means, we should try. Nevertheless, do not force it.

Nurse: Dr. Des-Order, what do you mean by, "don't force it."

Dr. Des-Order: When he begins the spinning routine as you have referred to it, nursing staff and other people should back away from him, and "give him space." He is too emotionally fragile at this point to push it. Again, this is his delusional state putting up a defense so that his fragile ego can cope with his underlying emotional turmoil. If we persist in attempts to interact, his fragile state may go into complete psychotic break. Neither you nor I want such a thing to happen!

Nurse: Yes, I see your point. I will instruct my staff to continue to try to interact with him, but when he starts the spinning routine, we will back away until the next opportunity.

Dr. Des-Order: I see you are an astute mental health professional.

Do you buy this analysis? If you believe the patient in the above scenario is *driven* to spin around, then the approach to "back away" seems plausible. However, suppose people with mental illness, like this real patient, behave in a manner that makes sense, when you view how such behavior affects their environment. Let us examine more closely the effect this client's spinning behavior has on his immediate social environment.

What would you guess is the immediate effect on his social environment when he begins to spin around with his arms outstretched? If you were approaching him, would you try to "shoot the breeze" or deliver "talk" therapy? My guess is that such a behavior would have a halting effect on your intentions. This behavior was quite successful in getting not only the doctors and nurses, but also the other patients to avoid him. The environmental result of such behavior on his social environment was profound. Further, one can see that the treatment regimen to "back off" during such episodes enables such a behavior rather than treats it. The hypothetical conversation below depicts a functional perspective of the spinning behavior.

Nurse: Dr. Context, as you probably know, we are having some difficulty with your patient, Mr. Smith. As part of his therapeutic treatment, the nursing staff and some of the physicians attempt to interact with him, to bring him "out of his shell." This is proving very difficult. He often begins spinning in circles just as you are attempting to engage him in conversation. Several of my nurses have been hit in the shoulder in attempting to "break through" this barrier. However, we were told that we should not push the issue, since pressing this client at this time could result in a complete psychotic breakdown.

Dr. Context: Yes, Nurse Seaver, Thank you for bringing this to my attention. Let me get some idea of what is going on. You seem to indicate when you attempt to interact with him, that he will often initiate this behavior. You also indicated that sometimes you are interacting with him and after a short period of time, he then starts this behavior. Consequently, when he does this, people back away from him as prescribed by medical personnel.

Nurse: Yes, that is it. Why do you think he does this? Could he be delusional?

Dr. Context: Since a phenomenon such as delusions is a private event (therefore not verifiable), no one can say for sure. Let me offer an alternative explanation. It seems plausible that in these circumstances, he may not want to interact with you. I am sure that sometimes you do not feel like conversing with people at a particular moment. You might excuse yourself to get out of continued conversation with someone at that time. Maybe Mr. Smith is a little different from us in that he hardly ever seems to enjoy "shooting the breeze" with you or others. For some reason, his method of getting people to leave him alone is to spin around. As you can see, spinning around in circles is effective in getting people, both staff and other clients, to back away and leave him alone for a while. This seems to be particularly true since staff back off because they are under the impression that to persist might engender a "psychotic break." Possibly, in prior placements, other attempts (e.g., "Please leave me alone") to get people to leave him alone were unsuccessful. People did not honor such a request. Nevertheless, they certainly get the picture when he starts spinning around!

Nurse: Well, you sure are right there. After getting whacked a few times, who would want to attempt an interaction with him? We keep trying because we were told that this is part of his disorder, and that once he trusts us, he will "open up." At least that is the theory we were given.

Dr. Context: OK, how's that (*misguided*) theory working for you?

Nurse: Not well, as you surmise. But what can we do? We were told that it might take years of therapy before we see even the slightest breakthrough.

Dr. Context: Let us treat this problem behavior by changing the way we respond to this client. I want to develop an alternate manner for him to terminate or avoid social interactions when he is uncomfortable engaging in them at the time. With the aid of you and your staff, we can prompt him to say, "Please, not now. I would like some time alone." We would then honor that verbal request.

Nurse: Great, I will meet with all the staff and inform them of the new plan.

Dr. Context: Great, I will be on the unit the first several days to work with your staff as they deploy this strategy of dealing with him.

In the real case (Keven Schock, BCBA), identifying this as a behavior that served a purpose, i.e., one of escaping social situations, led to successful intervention (see Cipani & Schock, 2007, p. 91). This client was taught to indicate verbally that he did not want to engage in any social interaction at that time by stating, "Leave me alone." Staff members at the inpatient unit were told to honor such a request. Subsequently, the spinning behavior ceased, while the frequency of appropriate requests occurred at a reasonable level. Given the success of this approach, which was the more helpful explanation of this person's spinning? Explanation #1: He spins around because he is schizophrenic and delusional. Explanation #2: He spins around because such a behavior is successful in terminating or avoiding social interactions when he cares not to be involved in such. As you can see, decoding this behavior's function makes changing it possible. In contrast, failing to decode the function of behavior can sometimes lead to the implementation of ineffective or disastrous treatment efforts.

Questions to Answer Before Proceeding (1b)

1. How does the explanation of the spinning behavior and the derived treatment from Dr. Des-Order exacerbate the problem?
2. Why was the functional treatment for this behavior to develop the patient's verbal request "Leave me alone" directed to staff or patients approaching him? Why was it essential for staff and others to honor such a request?
3. Explain what is entailed when you *decode behavior*.

BASIC PRINCIPLES OF DECODING CHILD BEHAVIOR

Child behavior is viewed as functional (i.e., purposeful) for certain antecedent contexts because of the environmental result such behavior produces. The function of behavior is derived by examining these contextual factors and decoding the purpose of the behavior. Decoding a child's behavior does not include the age-old practice of asking; "why did you do that?" as the following hypothetical scenario illustrates.

Parent: Johnny, why did you hit your sister?
Johnny (eight years old): She made me mad.
Parent: Do you think that is a good reason?
Johnny: I don't know. She makes me mad.

Very often adults feel compelled to ask children why they engage in certain inappropriate behaviors. Unfortunately, such an interrogation rarely leads to an analysis of why the behavior occurs. One cannot decode children's behaviors by asking them to provide "insight" into why they did what they did. It often leads nowhere. In contrast, observing the phenomenon in action is more productive. Such observations may determine that Johnny hits his sister when she picks up one of his toys. When she is hit, she drops the toy. Johnny thereby gets the toy from her. Now which explanation is better? (1) He hits because he is mad, or (2) he hits because it "works" in getting the toy back.

Decoding child behavior rests on the teacher's ability to discern the function or purpose of the behavior by examining the temporally contiguous antecedent and consequent conditions to the behavior. I call this the "action frame," which is equivalent to the A-B-C (antecedent-behavior- consequence) model referred to in other texts and materials. The action frame will form the basis for decoding child behavior.

THE ACTION FRAME

I use the term *action frame* to represent the temporal relationship between operant behavior (herein referred to as behavior) and its antecedent and consequent conditions (Table 1.1). The antecedent conditions (A), which are present prior to the behavior occurring, are comprised of motivating conditions and discriminative stimuli. Given these two conditions, a behavior occurs (B). The result is some consequence (C) that makes the behavior more probable in the future under the same or similar antecedent conditions.

How does an action frame provide an explanation of the function or purpose of behavior? A hypothetical child with autism desires potato chips. She has not had them in quite some time. She cannot reach the cabinet where they are. Therefore, she needs to get the potato chips by having someone else become involved. When her older sister enters the room, she whines and pleads for potato chips. Such behavior has been successful in the past with her sister in procuring items. Her sister has been discriminative (think of this as cue for a certain behavior) for reinforcing such behavior (whining and pleading) in the past. Reliably, within some duration of pleading, the sister delivers the potato chip bag. The action frame of that interaction appears in Table 1.2.

Table 1.2 illustrates that when the sister is available, pleading behavior results in potato chips. The action frame explains why the girl pleads for potato chips when her sister is around. However, the behavior that is functional with her father in the room (see Table 1.3)

Table 1.1
ACTION FRAME

Antecendent Conditions (A)		Behavior (B)	Consequent Conditions (C)
Motivating conditions	Discriminative stimuli	Behavior	Consequent events

Table 1.2
ACTION FRAME FOR POTATO CHIPS

Antecendent Conditions (A)		Behavior (B)	Consequent Events (C)
Motivating conditions	Discriminative stimuli		
Deprived of food (potato chips in particular)	Presence of sister	Pleads for potato chips for about 20 seconds	Gets potato chip

is different. When her father is present, pleading is not successful, i.e., it does not produce the desired reinforcer. However, tantrum behavior in the form of throwing herself on the floor and kicking everything in the immediate area is eventually effective. This action frame portrays tantrum behavior as an effective means of getting potato chips when she: (a) desires potato chips and (b) Dad is in the kitchen area. The analysis of a child's behavior involves both the antecedent conditions as well as the consequences that follow behavior. Such conditions are important in explaining why a child engages in certain behavior.

Here is another example of decoding behavior using the action frame. A hypothetical child with traumatic brain injury occasionally throws his papers and books on the ground during writing assignments in his fifth grade class. Why does he do this? Again, an easy explanation that is void of understanding the role of the environment is that his brain injury makes him do these things. However, an analysis of the following sequence of events is more illuminating in discerning the

Table 1.3
DECODING CHILD BEHAVIOR'S FUNCTION WITH FATHER PRESENT

Antecendent Conditions (A)		Behavior (B)	Consequent Events (C)
Motivating conditions	Discriminative stimuli		
Deprived of food	Presence of father	Pleads for potato chips	Does not get potato chips
		Tantrums	Eventually gets potato chips

Table 1.4
ACTION FRAME FOR COLORED PEN WITH FEATHER

Motivating Conditions	Discriminative Stimuli	Behavior	Consequent Events
Desires special pen (state of deprivation)	Presence of instructional aide	Requests colored pen with feather multiple times	Does not get favored pen
		Initiates desk clearing incident and tantrum behavior	Eventually gets favored pen

immediate cause. We observe the child during one of these incidents. This child asks the instructional aide if she can have the colored pen that has a pink feather at the end. The instructional aide tells her that she must use the regular pencil first and that the assignment is not appropriate for a colored pen. After a short time, the child makes a second request. The second request is also not honored. Subsequently the child gets incensed and begins throwing the materials on the floor. We observe that after several minutes, the persistence of tantrum behavior in various forms produces the preferred colored pen with the feather for the remainder of the writing task. Table 1.4 presents the action frame.

The analysis of the action frames within this social context allows one to decode the function of behavior. In this case, requesting the desired pen was ineffective. However, engaging in disruptive behavior with this particular person does produce the desired event (i.e., positive reinforcement). Whether such a behavior becomes functional in the presence of other personnel remains a question. If other personnel provide a better *rate of return* for disruptive behavior over appropriate requests, such will be the case.

In an action frame, there are several variables to understand in relation to why behavior occurs. A discussion of the role of motivation is essential and follows in the next section. The discussion of discriminative stimuli appears under the consequence variable, detailing the function of behavior.

Questions to Answer Before Proceeding (1c)

1. How does the action frame differ with the potato chip example with the sister present versus father present?
2. Explain why the child who wanted the colored pen resorted to the desk-clearing incident with tantrum behavior. If you were in his shoes and really wanted the pen, what behavior is more likely to assist you in your quest?

THE ROLE OF MOTIVATION

"What motivates him to do that?" The question regarding motivation is more aptly phrased in the following manner: Why would a child exhibit a particular behavior that has a history of resulting in a specific reinforcer (e.g., food) at a specific time?

The motivating condition, or MC, makes the individual more prone to engage in behaviors that more reliably produce certain consequences over other consequences. This condition is temporally antecedent to the behavior that produces a specific reinforcer (Hesse, 1993; Laraway, Snycerski, Michael, & Poling, 2003). Motivating conditions (MCs) for operant behavior consist primarily of either of two conditions: (1) a relative deprivation of some event, item or activity, or (2) a presence (or impending presence) of a relative aversive state.

First, a demarcation of the term *relative* in both operations is necessary. *Relative* requires that the state of deprivation or aversive stimuli is defined with respect to the individual child or person being assessed. *Relative* typifies the opposite of absolute. For example, where is the point of hunger (i.e., food deprivation)? For some people it is four hours after they just finished eating lunch. For other people, the state of hunger[1] does not occur until the end of the day. One cannot say a state of hunger is achieved by denying access to food for a 10-hour period (absolute value). Hunger and, therefore, food deprivation is relative to the individual under consideration. Therefore, the point in time when a given individual will engage in behaviors that make access to food highly likely is different, hence relative.

---

1. Also realize, we cannot observe someone being hungry, we only infer it when we observe certain behaviors ("Can I please have a sandwich?") that result in food ("Oh, he must be hungry").

We can also be deprived of a particular food. Deprivation in this circumstance is relative to the individual and relative to a particular type of food. For example, let us say you have had ham and eggs for the past ten days because you are a guest at a relative's house. When you get home, you make waffles, having reached the satiation point with ham and eggs. At what point in the ten days of constant indulgence in ham and eggs made eating waffles in a deprived state? What is clear is that this individual was not sufficiently "motivated" to engage in a chain of behaviors that would have led to waffles for breakfast instead of the usual while at her relative's house. Perhaps if the access to waffles was made easier, e.g., a choice offered by his host, she may have selected waffles on day four. But apparently, the state of deprivation with respect to getting waffles was not sufficient enough to cause her to pursue more actively such a desired event.

Let's say an adolescent child is used to being on her computer (playing games, viewing blogs, visiting popular sites) between one and two hours per day. Unfortunately, her computer develops a system problem, and her mother has to take it to a technician for repair. Would you say her motivation is greater on the first day it is absent or the seventh day? The answer is obvious. What is equally true is the following correlation. The greater her state of deprivation (with respect to computer time), the greater the chance she will engage in a variety of behaviors to get access to computer time. She may call her friends, and if that does not work out, she may call acquaintances. Finally, on the seventh day, really wanting to get on a computer, she calls a boy who likes her (but not vice versa), asking if she can come over (to get on his computer). Stooping this low was not a behavior that she considered on day one (because motivation was not strong enough). However, by day seven, the state of deprivation has become too severe for her that such a lower probability behavior occurs. Note that the greater the level of deprivation is with respect to a given item or event, the greater the variability in exhibited behaviors that might possibly ameliorate such an motivating condition.

Table 1.5 below presents the relationship between the relative deprivation of an event and the value of an event or stimulus to act as a reinforcer under such a condition of deprivation.

People also exhibit behavior to escape or avoid aversive events. Again, there are MCs that are built in as stimuli that produce an aver-

Table 1.5
RELATIONSHIP BETWEEN MCs AND REINFORCER

Motivating Condition		Reinforcing Event
1. Deprived of computer time	⟶	Getting on computer
2. Deprived of toy	⟶	Getting toy
3. Deprived of swimming time	⟶	Getting into pool to swim
4. Deprived of attention (wants attention	⟶	Getting attention
5. Deprived of TV (wants TV)	⟶	Getting TV

sive state at some level relative to the individual (Michael, 2007). Painful stimulation, physical discomfort, inflicting physical blows, and similar events provide the conditions for humans to engage in behaviors that escape such stimulation. The aversive value of these stimuli can vary between individuals. In contrast to many of us, professional boxers can tolerate a certain level and intensity of punches to the body without it creating an aversive condition. However, there is a point at which even their tolerance "breaks down," and terminating such a condition becomes reinforcing.

Table 1.6 depicts two examples that illustrate how relative aversive events create the conditions for escape. In the first example, the teacher may present a relatively difficult task to the child. Because the child is not capable of performing such a task or demand, the child develops an aversion to the task or demand Therefore, a behavior or set of behaviors in the repertoire of this child that results in its removal becomes strengthened. Realize that what is difficult for one child may be easy for another; hence, *difficult task* is a relative term.

Table 1.6
ANTECEDENT AVERSIVE CONDITIONS

Antecedent Condition: MO	Negative Reinforcer
1. Presence of difficult task Creates state of aversion to engage in task for that child	Removal of task
2. Person acting in an obnoxious manner Creates state of aversion to be in that area	Terminating engagement in social situation

In example two, a behavior that terminates the presence of a person's obnoxious behavior becomes stronger under conditions involving the presence of the noxious conditions. Let us say this person's obnoxious behavior is the use of foul language. A behavior that results in getting the obnoxious person to cease such verbal behavior will become functional. Such a behavior will be more probable in future situations when faced with this person's foul language. But let us say that nothing seems to perturb this individual, and he goes right on with his rude language. In fact, he ignores requests to "tone down" his language. Because of these requests to produce the desired change, leaving the area then becomes probable. Why? Because leaving the area directly terminates the aversive condition, i.e., having to listen and put up with such language. Leaving the area becomes a more probable manner of responding to this unpleasant situation in the future.

The following conditions can be aversive and thus create the conditions for escape behaviors: (1) Presence of difficult instructional tasks, (2) Presence of demands/commands, (3) Presence of requests, (4) Noisy environment, (5) Quiet environment, (6) Many people in physical area, (7) Presence of attention to individual, (8) Presence of a specific activity, and (9) Presenting an undesirable consequence (punishment) for behavior.

Questions to Answer Before Proceeding (1d)

1. A child plays on the swings every day for about 20 minutes after she comes home from school. Describe what might happen if the time on the swings for two straight days is reduced to just five minutes per afternoon.
2. What do you think she might do on the third day when someone signals it is time to leave the swing area after five minutes?

THE ROLE OF FUNCTION

Given the effect that motivating conditions have on altering the value of certain reinforcers over others at a given point in time, how does one behavior become more probable than another behavior in that circumstance? The answer: Environmental function! For example, a child whines for potato chips when her older sister is present.

What explanation is there for why she whines for potato chips instead of asking nicely? Obviously, whining is functional when this child wants potato chips. Further, asking nicely is probably less effective or efficient at those times for this child than whining. Given these environmental reactions to whining and asking nicely, what behavior would you perform if you were in this child's shoes? You would become a whiner when the sister is present! When Dad is around, it is a different story.

So what makes whining a functional behavior to access potato chips? In one word—people! Child behavior often produces a *socially mediated* result. As is evident from the prior example, whatever behavior is more likely to produce potato chips is the behavior more likely to occur. Nevertheless, **people decide** the behavior (or behaviors) that become functional. Potato chips do not just drop out of the sky when this child whines! The adult produces the chips, contingent upon some level and intensity of whining behavior (i.e., socially mediated). How do you explain why the child resorts to tantrums instead of asking nicely when her Dad is present? A view of a hypothetical scenario would give the explanation.

Child: Can I please have some potato chips? I am hungry.
Dad: No, you cannot. They are not healthy snacks. Go clean your room. That will keep you busy.
Child: (goes to clean room thinking that may serve her well in getting potato chips afterward.)

Fifteen minutes later (repeat above scenario, same ineffective result (from child's standpoint), 30 minutes later, the following ensues:

Child: (in a pleading whiny voice) Dad, I want some potato chips. I really do.
Dad: You know the rules. We only eat fatty foods on the weekends.
Child: (in a real whiny tone) But I am hungry now! (Falls on the floor screaming, crying and flailing her feet wildly)
Dad: Stop acting like a baby. If you can act your age, maybe you can have a few just this one time.
Child: Straightens up.
Dad: Here are just a few, just this time.

Under these conditions, Dad becomes discriminative for tantrum behavior to produce potato chips. Concurrently, Dad is not discriminative for another type of behavior. The sister was discriminative for another set of behaviors: whining. Given the sister's presence, whining produces reinforcement. She is a discriminative stimulus for whining behavior.

Questions to Answer Before Proceeding (1e)

1. Explain why deprivation of attention is an MC that is relative to each individual. Can some people desire more frequent attention than others?
2. In general, what is the MC condition for escape behavior? Can you list some?

Remember that there are two basic motivating conditions (MC): (1) relative deprivation of some event or stimulus, and (2) presentation of a relative aversive stimulus. There are two corresponding types of socially mediated functions: socially mediated access and socially mediated escape.

SOCIALLY MEDIATED ACCESS (OR SMA FUNCTIONS). Functions that are existent under deprivation states are termed **access** functions. Access functions involve a behavior that produces an event (activity, object) that subsequently strengthens the occurrence of that behavior in the future. There are two requirements for identifying an access function. First, the probability of the behavior increases because the behavior reliably produces the desired reinforcer. Second, the existent deprivation state lessens with the delivery of that event. Perhaps an example will illustrate better.

A five-year-old hypothetical child named Sarah, who has mild disabilities, is reported to complain incessantly and tantrum in her afternoon kindergarten program. Such tantrum behavior occurs often when she asks for some desired activity while everyone else is engaged in storytime. Let us look at the scenario as it unfolds to examine how such tantrum behavior is functional at that time.

Sarah: (in a pleading whiny voice) Teacher, can I go play with the picture puzzles?

Mom: Sarah, you will have to wait until after storytime. See how everyone is listening to the story about the red fox. Would you like to
come and sit next to me?

Sarah: (in a pleading whiny tone) But I want to play now. (Sarah continues to whine until the teacher finally gives in and lets her leave
the group early and play with the picture puzzles). As soon as
Sarah begins playing with the picture puzzles, the level of disruption in the room becomes tolerable again; thus, everyone is
happy, at least for now.

Let us examine the result of the entire chain of events. Did the initial complaint result in getting her favored activity? No. However, what
happened after the teacher refused the first request? Sarah "upped the
ante." What resulted from Sarah's persistent whining and pleading?
Getting a play activity much sooner than waiting until the storytime
was finished. Let me pose a question: What do you think Sarah will do
the next time she wants to switch activities to a more preferred event?
Wait patiently or begin a barrage of demands and requests?

A four-year-old hypothetical child named Miranda, diagnosed
with autism, hits herself (termed self-injury) multiple times during the
day. Many people will explain such behavior by referring to her developmental disorder. They will proclaim, "Miranda hits herself because
she is autistic. Her autism is the cause of this behavior." Is this really a
good explanation? Does such behavior differentiate children with
autism from other developmental or mental disorders (i.e., only autistic children hit themselves)? Do all children with autism engage in
such behavior? Maybe back in the 1970s, this explanation was somewhat accepted. In the year 2011, we know far too much about the role
of environmental variables!

By examining the conditions upon which Miranda engages in self-
injury, we might be able to decode the function of the behavior. After
multiple observations, it becomes apparent that self-injury frequently
produces adult attention. This is particularly the case with the more intense forms of self-injury. Self-injury and tantrums become more probable when Miranda desires attention. Does self-injury occur at random? No! Self-injury often occurs under certain antecedent conditions. Through observation of the context and analysis of behavioral
function, we can deduce several factors involved in self-injury. First,

self-injury is more likely when the teacher is away from her, hence a relative deprivation state exists. Second, an adult or adults in her immediate social environment are discriminative for self-injury to produce the desired consequence: adult attention. The production of attention for some level and duration of screaming and self-injury maintains such behaviors as a functional response class. It works! Once she begins receiving sufficient attention, the probability of self-injury goes down considerably (unless it also serves another function). Miranda's teaching staff are discriminative for the delivery of attention contingent upon some level of self-injury. When she wants attention, hitting yourself does the trick.

Socially Mediated Escape (or SME Functions). Not all problem behavior functions to access some desired event. **This is an important point for teachers, because numerous problem behaviors in the classroom can be traced to the conditions involving escape functions**. In escape functions, the effect of behavior is to terminate the existence of, or postpone (for some time) the presentation of an aversive event (Cipani, 1994; Iwata, 1987; Cipani & Spooner, 1997; Cipani & Schock, 2007; 2011). Such an event is commonly referred to as aversive. Again, aversive is a relative term. What is aversive to one person may not be to another; and what is aversive to you today may be less aversive next week.

How is this escape function different from the access function delineated earlier? First the MC is not a deprivation state. Rather, it is the presence of an event (state) deemed aversive. For example, many children often find task demands, compliance situations, instructional conditions, or chores/work a relatively aversive event. Hence, such aversive events set up the context for escape behaviors. All that the child needs is a social environment that differentially selects aggressive behavior as the act that efficiently and effectively produces escape from that condition (or avoidance).

How does aggressive behavior function to escape circumstances such as compliance situations? We can take the hypothetical case of Miranda, who hits herself to get attention. Let us suppose that self-injury also occurs within a different context as well (we term this a multifunctional behavior). Miranda's teachers sometimes ask her to match numbers from a field of three. The teacher places one number (1-5) on an index card and provides three other cards from which to select.

The teacher asks Miranda to match the numbers. Miranda protests by screaming. The teacher then provides mild physical guidance by picking up Miranda's hand and moving it toward the correct selection. This event results in Miranda slapping herself in the face with the other hand. The teacher backs off immediately. She says, "I'll try again when you are in a better mood." What is the result of face slapping? Getting out of the task for the time is the socially mediated result.

Question to Answer Before Proceeding (1f)

1. Explain how the function of Miranda's self-injury was different as a socially mediated access function from a socially mediated escape function.

SELECTIVELY REINFORCING DANGEROUS BEHAVIOR. In some cases, individuals with developmental disabilities engage in very destructive forms of behavior, such as self-injury. With some children who engage in self-injury, the form of their response and intensity defies one's sensibilities. Such episodes of protracted hitting to their face and body of severe intensity perplex both lay people and professionals. In watching such a severe and extended episode of self-injury, it is not uncommon for even professionals to claim that the child is biologically driven to such episodes. The overriding contention made is that any learning environment cannot explain such behavior.

How can severe forms of aggression and self-injury develop over time? Under certain aversive conditions, a hypothetical child engages in minor forms of self-abusive behavior, which produce the desired result. However, the social environment unsystematically begins to ignore these minor forms. This ignoring (extinction) of minor forms is the first step in unintentionally exacerbating the form of self-injury over time. Over the course of several or many months, the severity of the child's self-injury (e.g., head hitting) may intensify because of the adult's ability to tolerate and thereby ignore the minor forms of self-abuse. The child hits himself once on the shoulder and nothing changes. He does so again, and still nothing happens. He slaps himself in the face, and this "ups the ante." He achieves the desired result; termination of the instructional activity. The ante has increased in favor of hits to the face over hits to the shoulder. Consequently, a cycle of reinforcement for more extreme forms and concurrent ignoring of lesser episodes of self-injury develops.

Let us illustrate this cycle using the hypothetical case of Miranda. Perhaps when Miranda was only a preschool child, she would just hit her thigh under instructional demand conditions. In the beginning, such a form of behavior would catch the parents and teachers off guard, and they would remove the task demand contingently. As a result, Miranda avoided having to comply with the demand. However, over time the adults in her life became more tolerant of these minor forms of protest. They noted that no physical damage occurred and their reaction to such forms of behavior changed incrementally. They would continue pressing Miranda to comply with the instructional demand or house chore. However, when the adults ignore this minor form of self-injury, it leads to results that are more disastrous. Miranda is intent on getting out of undesirable demands and requests made by her social environment. She, therefore, intensifies her self-injury on some occasions when the leg slapping incidents do not impress the parents or teachers. She initiates a quick and harder slap to her face. As you can imagine, these more severe incidents makes the adults produce escape for that incident. Thus, Miranda has now "upped" the ante on what is needed to escape task demands. Because of the differential ability of severe forms to produce avoidance of task demands, she becomes more adept at such intense forms. Further, the amount of pain she perceives from such incidents lessens; much the way martial artists can hit boards many times without flinching (whereas most people stop after the first one or two intense strikes). Such a process coincides with a progressive alteration of the form of behavior that produces escape.

The severe forms of self-injury have become even more powerful in their ability to alter the environment, as it now reduces the likelihood of making such demands. Now, months or years later, Miranda's repeated self-injury has left some scars and has become too difficult for her parents and teachers to handle. As she engages in this behavior when she encounters or faces instructional demands, the educational staff members are unable to treat such a behavior effectively. She has her educational placement change multiple times during her school years, but to no avail in stopping such behavior. As Miranda gets older, she becomes more capable of inflicting greater intense forms of physical abuse on herself. Further, the environment becomes more respectful of such a performance so that very few, if any, demands are placed on her. Now, if you simply observed Miranda after years of "practice" altering her environment, you might conclude that she is driven by some innate mechanism to abuse herself.[2] Nevertheless, what you would be unaware of is the progressive shaping of such an intense form and duration of self-injury over time.

The same case applies to severe and horrendous forms of aggressive behavior, e.g., severe incidents of property destruction or aggression to others. Possibly throwing small items initially produced the desired adult reaction, whether it be accessing a preferred event or escaping an aversive condition. As minor forms of behavior are ineffectual, other more severe forms occur and produce reinforcement. Some children develop additional ancillary behaviors that co-vary with aggressive and destructive episodes such as a cold stare, spewing hateful remarks, etc.

Questions to Answer Before Proceeding (1g)

1. Who decides if a behavior produces a socially mediated reinforcer?
2. What is the difference between a socially mediated access behavior and a socially mediated escape behavior?

SUMMARY

Designing effective management strategies in school settings requires an understanding of why students engage in problem behaviors such as noncompliance, failure to follow rules and other more severe disruptive classroom behaviors. Is it helpful to have someone tell you that he behaves like that because he is behavior-disordered? For classroom personnel who are content with that explanation, changing behavior is seen as something that is highly improbable. If he has this disorder, then it must be that he cannot help himself. Any efforts will probably be in vain. One must simply learn to accept such behaviors from time to time.

---

2. There is a disorder (Lesch-Nyhan syndrome) that is hypothesized to automatically produce self-injury.

You are a different breed of teacher or paraeducator. Something must be driving his inappropriate behavior, in terms of its purpose. You start to decode this behavior by looking for the situations where he is more likely to engage in these problem behaviors. You carefully observe him over a period of several days in your classroom, noting the times when he becomes more likely to exhibit such behaviors. Your observations and analysis reveal that these behaviors often occur when he is asked to read a passage aloud during language arts. He initially refuses to read when called upon. As you move closer to "coax" him, he starts throwing a verbal tantrum. You recall that in those situations you were taken aback and often left him alone, calling on someone else. By understanding that these behaviors have an environmental function, a successful intervention strategy can address both of them as the same entity. Further, one may be able to determine why such a task generates escape behavior with this child!

Being a classroom teacher or paraeducator does not require that you become numb to problem behavior. I believe that when you begin to decode student behavior successfully you will see that the following credo applies: **What I do in the classroom matters!** The remaining chapters will provide detail on how your understanding of motivation and behavioral function can help you change student's behavior.

CHAPTER 1 SUMMARY TEST

(Answers on CD)

True or False

1. A behavioral frame consists of an antecedent condition and a behavior.
2. The two variables in the antecedent condition are the MC and consequence.
3. A deprivation state or aversive condition can be an antecedent condition for a student's behavior.
4. When a behavior does not result in a reinforcer, the MC remains or possibly even gets stronger.
5. All students will be in a deprivation condition if they went 4 hours without playing outside.
6. The deprivation condition makes a behavior that is effective at abating it more likely.
7. The MC for SMA behaviors is an aversive condition, relative to the individual.
8. The MC for a behavior maintained by socially mediated access is a relative state of deprivation.
9. A socially mediated behavior is one in which the reinforcer is delivered through a person, such as an adult.
10. People are discriminative for certain behaviors under certain MC's.
11. A deprivation state with respect to attention is a discriminative stimulus for socially mediated behavior.
12. If a father gives his child attention when his child cries, under a condition of the child wanting attention, we say that the father is discriminative for crying behavior.
13. If a father gives his child attention when his child cries, under a condition of the child wanting attention, we say that crying behavior is functional in any circumstance.

A short, fill-in-the-blanks test can be found in Appendix A.

Chapter 2

SIX FUNCTIONS OF
CLASSROOM PROBLEM BEHAVIOR

Decoding a child's behavior translates to developing a hypothesis about its environmental function. The collection of evidence regarding the behavioral function of a problem precedes a hypothesis about the purpose of behavior (Bailey & Pyles, 1989; Carr, Taylor, Wallender, & Reiss, 1996; Cipani, 1994: Cipani & Schock, 2007; Iwata, Dorsey, Slifer, Bauman, & Richman, 1982). Determining the behavioral function of specific problem behavior requires the collection and examination of functional behavioral assessment data (to be discussed in chapter 6). With a hypothesis about the current function of problem behavior, an intervention designed for that problem will alter the function, i.e., a functional treatment (DuPaul & Ervin, 1996; Blair, Umbreit, & Boss, 1999).

One caveat requires mentioning. Venturing a hypothesis regarding the current function of the problem behavior does not mean that you have identified the original factor in the genesis of the behavior (Cipani & Schock, 2007, 2011)! The reason for the maintenance of a behavior could be quite different from its original cause. Your focus is on the *current* function of the behavior.

My colleague, Keven Schock, and I have developed a diagnostic categorical function-based system applicable to many diverse settings (Cipani & Schock, 2007, 2011). A function-based classification system allows a user to entertain possible functions of a referred problem behavior within the social environment. This chapter presents six common functions of problem behavior in classrooms. These six socially mediated functions are derived from the two major socially mediated

Table 2.1
SOCIALLY MEDIATED FUNCTIONS

Socially Mediated Access	*Socially Mediated Escape*
• Adult attention	• Escape from unpleasant social situations
• Peer attention	• Escape from lengthy instructional tasks
• Tangible reinforcers	• Escape from difficult instructional tasks

categories given in Table 2.1. I have selected the six functions or categories from our original text that appear to have the most relevance for classroom settings. The assessment methods for determining which functional category a specific problem behavior falls into and what the functional intervention strategy would involve will be covered in several later chapters of this text.

SOCIALLY MEDIATED ACCESS (SMA) CATEGORIES

In relative states of deprivation, behavior that produces an event or item that abates (lessens) that state or condition becomes functional. Table 2.2 illustrates how a target problem behavior becomes more likely under states of deprivation (see second row). This function develops due to the effectiveness of the target behavior at producing the desired event under conditions of deprivation. Usually, the target problem behavior is made even more powerful as a result of other more appropriate behaviors being rendered (by social environment) less effective or not at all effective in producing the desired event (Horner & Day, 1991). The last row illustrates the relative ineffectiveness of the alternate behavior to produce the desired reinforcer. Hence, alternate behaviors that are more appropriate fail to recruit the functional reinforcer. Such behaviors, therefore, fail to occur; or if at some level from prior environments, decrease in probability within these contexts.

Let us say you have a six-year-old child with mild mental retardation in your special day class for students with communicative handicaps. He engages in a series of behaviors to get to play on the computer during class time. He sees the computer in the corner of the room. He points to it and says, "Computer please." The instructional

Table 2.2
MC AND BEHAVIORAL FUNCTION

MC	*Behavior (engaged in)*	*Environmental Result*
Deprivation state (relative)	Target problem behavior	Someone delivers the event or item addressing deprivation
Deprivation state (relative)	Alternate appropriate behavior	Item or event not delivered, motivating condition remains

staff person "re-directs" him to his desk to trace and then copy the numbers 1–10 on a sheet of paper. As the social environment fails to produce reinforcement of his request, he tries another tactic. He gets out of his seat and points to the computer vociferously. He tries even harder to get the instructional staff to turn it on. This attempt also meets with nonreinforcement as the staff person brings him back to his desk again. He then finishes the writing assignment. After he completes the assignment, the instructional staff person then directs him to another instructional activity, in which he must put the correct number of blocks under designated numbers on a page. Obviously, finishing his work did not result in getting computer time either. After five minutes of a minor level of whining during the new instructional activity and without accomplishing much on the new task, he gets up, screams, and cries. This continues, with staff unable to stop this display of behavior. At that point, the teacher says he can go on the computer for a while if he can calm down. Do you see what happened (see Table 2.3)?

It is important to note that a number of behaviors were ineffective in accessing time on the computer (see all but last row of Table 2.3). However, the last row shows that tantrum behavior, in the form of screaming and whining, which is probably the least preferable behavior, was unfortunately functional and effective. The child's access to the computer contingent upon this behavior makes it more probable in the future when he wants computer access. The relationship between the level of tantrum and computer access forms a maintaining contingency, given a relevant level of deprivation.

Table 2.3
BEHAVIOR ANALYSIS OF COMPUTER ACCESS

Deprivation State (relative)	Behavior	Effect in Getting Desired Item	Future Probability of Behavior Under MC
Computer access in a deprived state	Asks computer please	Not effective	Less likely
Computer access in a deprived state	Attempts to turn it on	Not effective	Less likely
Computer access in a deprived state	Finishes one assignment	Not effective	Less likely
Computer access in a deprived state	Whines and screams for several minutes	Not effective	Less likely

There are three categories of SMA functions for classroom problem behaviors: adult/staff attention, peer attention, and tangible reinforcers. Problem behaviors that are at unacceptable levels often are functional under conditions of relative deprivation of these events or items.

Questions to Answer Before Proceeding (2a)

1. Explain in general what function problem behaviors serve under the category of SMA or socially mediated access.
2. In the above example of the child's wanting to play on the computer, why are tantrums a more probable behavior in the future under conditions of wanting computer time? Why is asking nicely or finishing the initial assignment not functional and less probable under those same conditions?
3. How would this teacher make finishing an assignment functional given the child's desire to get on the computer?

ADULT ATTENTION

How many times have you heard someone proclaim, "He does it for my negative attention!" While attention is not always the purpose or function of problem behavior, it can be a powerful (and misplaced) contingency (reference studies). Adult attention can be the maintaining contingency in circumstances in which such attention is not often available for other more appropriate behaviors, and the student desires such, i.e., he or she is in a relative state of deprivation. If minor or major disruptive classroom behaviors receive an adult's attention reliably, what does that imply about the selective nature of adult attention? The social environment provides a schedule of reinforcement for such behaviors with attention being the consequent event. Unfortunately, other behaviors in the child repertoire are apparently less effective or efficient in producing the desired attention. Table 2.4 illustrates the nature of this function.

The first two rows of Table 2.4 illustrate the role of the MC in generating a behavior as functional. Note that when the MC for attention is high, the probability of a given behavior is a function of its effectiveness and efficiency to produce attention. When the target problem behavior is more capable (i.e., more effective and efficient) than other behaviors in producing attention when attention is desired, the probability of such behavior is greatly enhanced (first row).

In contrast, when a more appropriate behavior is more effective at producing attention, then the probability of the student's exhibiting the problem behavior is low (see second row). Concurrently, the likelihood of the appropriate behavior is high. In the last row, when the MC for attention is nonexistent, both sets of behaviors become less probable. The functional relationship no longer exists. Attention is no longer desired; hence its ability to function as a reinforcer for any behaviors is diminished at that time.

Table 2.4
ANALYSIS OF BEHAVIOR UNDER MOTIVATING CONDITIONS FOR ATTENTION

MC for Attention	Efficiency to Produce Attention: Target Behavior	Efficiency to Produce Attention: Appropriate Behavior(s)	Probability of Target Behavior
high	high	low	high
high	low	high	low
low	n/a	n/a	low

Table 2.5
QUESTIONS FOR ESCAPE FUNCTION OF UNPLEASANT SOCIAL SITUATIONS

1. Is the existing motivating condition for that child one of relative deprivation of attention from the adult(s)?
2. Is there a reliable, somewhat frequent relation between the child's problem behavior and adult attention? What is the form of the behavior?
3. Is the problem behavior more likely to produce adult attention than acceptable appropriate behaviors under the MC for attention?

In this function, there are three existent factors (see Table 2.5). First, the child is in a relative state of deprivation with respect to attention. What may be a sufficient amount of attention for some children may constitute a deprivation state for other children. Most kindergarten students need more frequent and longer durations of adult attention when compared to high school students. Also, some kindergarten students require teacher attention more frequently than their classmates.

Second, the problem behavior(s) should reliably produce teacher attention, and this temporal relationship should be observed consistently. For example, in the context of a child wanting attention, the problem behavior reliably produces attention over many observed incidents. The third factor is extremely important to examine. Is the problem behavior more effective and/or efficient at getting the adult's attention than other behaviors, either desirable or undesirable? Posing these questions can reveal the functional capability of the target problem behavior over other behaviors. Your observation should reveal that such behaviors occur when the child desires attention but are ineffective at getting such. On the other hand, when the child engages in the problem behavior, adult attention quickly follows.

HITTING GETS YOUR ATTENTION. A hypothetical parent has several young children. As she attends to one child by picking him up, one of her other children wants to be picked up. This child, Robert, who does not have his mother's attention, now desires it even more than just a minute ago, when his baby sister was not in her arms (existence of MC for attention). He whines and pleads to be picked up, but his mother redirects him to play with his brother (other behaviors are in-

Table 2.6
QUESTIONS FOR HITTING SIBLING SCENARIO

1. **Is the existing motivational condition for Robert one of relative deprivation of attention from the adult?**

   Answer: Yes, particularly when his sister is receiving his mother's attention, he deserves it even more.

2. **Is there a reliable, somewhat frequent relation between the child's problem behavior and adult attention?**

   Answer: Yes, particularly under these conditions of deprivation of mom's attention, hitting his siblings is more likely to get attention.

3. **Is the problem behavior more likely to produce adult attention than acceptable appropriate behaviors under the MO for attention?**

   Answer: Yes, other behaviors that attempt to recruit attention are ineffective. However, hitting his brother brings his mother to pick him up after a short admonishment.

effective). In other words, such minor behaviors are not fruitful (functional) in ensuring that he is picked up. When appropriate behaviors are ineffective, what can a child resort to? You guessed it, hit someone. He hits his baby brother, and after a short admonishment, he gets picked up (reliable contingency). What looks like a good response in the short run is disastrous in the end. Hitting his siblings under the conditions of minimal attention will become a pattern (i.e., a maintaining contingency). Because the parent fails to realize this misdirected contingency, she will report that the child's aggressive behavior problem came out of nowhere. Incidentally, such a context can exist anywhere adult attention is desired, and the ratio of adults to children is lean, e.g., in schools, playgrounds, etc. The answers to the questions in Table 2.6 reveal the reason for Robert's behavior becoming functional.

What is the chance of this child stopping such a behavior if the parent's response continues to be the same? It will not abate unless getting picked up by mom becomes a less potent reinforcing event over time (as the child grows older). Of course, hitting would probably generalize to other motivating conditions, as a functional (generalized) response in this social ecology.

Questions to Answer Before Proceeding (2b)

1. If the child desires adult attention, what makes a behavior functional in that circumstance?
2. When the efficiency to produce teacher attention is high for an appropriate behavior such as being on-task, what will be the result on the probability of that behavior under an MC for attention?
3. What happens to disruptive behaviors when the child recruits attention via appropriate behavior?

PEER ATTENTION

As children become older, peer attention becomes a more prized reinforcer. Probably you would immediately think of the class clown in junior high school as a great example of behavior maintained by peer attention. Getting other students to laugh produces attention from many students in the classroom. It can become a desirable event more often by the class clown as he or she experiences its effects. While some people have made a career out of making people laugh (e.g., Jim Carrey), unfortunately such behavior often has deleterious educational results when performed in the classroom. Table 2.7 illustrates the functional relationship between peer attention and two sets of behaviors: (a) target problem behaviors and (b) appropriate behaviors. When the MC for peer attention is high, the probability of any given behavior is a function of its effectiveness and efficiency to produce peer attention. When the target problem behavior is more capable than other behaviors of producing attention when attention is desired, the probability of such behavior is greatly enhanced.

If peer attention was available only for an appropriate behavior, then the target problem behaviors would decrease in level (see first row). However, such is not often the case in junior high schools where clowning around and making fun of the teacher result in peer attention. In contrast, doing one's classwork does not result in peer attention. When was the last time you heard students in the hallway give each other the high five because they accurately completed their classwork? Note that when the MC for peer attention is nonexistent (see last row), both sets of behaviors become improbable because peer

Table 2.7
ANALYSIS OF BEHAVIOR UNDER MO FOR PEER ATTENTION

MO for Peer Attention	Efficiency to Produce Peer Attention: Target Behavior	Efficiency to Produce Peer Attention: Appropriate Behavior(s)	Probability of Target Behavior
high	high	low	high
high	low	high	low
low	n/a	n/a	low

attention is no longer desired. Removing the audience for peer attention renders the repertoire of the class clown irrelevant. Unfortunately, that describes a classroom of one!

The function of peer attention requires three existent factors (see Table 2.8). First, the child is in a relative state of deprivation with respect to peer attention when the behavior occurs. Second, the problem behavior(s) should reliably produce attention, and the practitioner or parent should repeatedly observe this temporal relationship. For example, in the context of a child wanting peer attention, the problem behavior consistently produces peer attention. Third, the problem behavior is more effective or efficient at getting peer attention than other behaviors (point 3 in Table 2.8). These alternate behaviors can be either desirable or undesirable behaviors.

THE CLASS CLOWN. An example of problem behavior maintained by peer attention is a hypothetical high school special day class (SDC) student, Geraldo. He frequently makes jokes and comments during the teacher's lecture. He is a Jim Carrey in the making. Unfortunately,

Table 2.8
QUESTIONS TO CONSIDER FOR A PEER ATTENTION FUNCTION

1. Is the existing motivating condition for that child one of relative deprivation of peer attention when the problem behavior occurs?

2. Is there a reliable, somewhat frequent relation, between the child's problem behavior and peer attention? What is the form of the behavior?

3. Is the target problem behavior more likely to produce peer attention than other (acceptable) appropriate behaviors?

such comments disrupt the lesson presentation, as classmates get a laugh at the expense of the instructional objective of the lesson. Below is a sample of what transpires during an incident of inappropriate comments during a math skills class.

Teacher: Who can tell me what a mixed fraction is?
Geraldo: (Somewhat covertly, although within earshot of other students.) This is lame!
Teacher: Geraldo, do you have something to contribute to this discussion?
Geraldo: I said, this reminds me. I have to go to the bathroom! (Other students start giggling.)
Teacher: Perhaps you would like to spend the period in the principal's office?
Geraldo: Does she have a bathroom in there? (Class breaks out laughing, the teacher sends Geraldo to the principal's office.)

It is not difficult to surmise that such inappropriate comments result in peer attention. While the teacher's comments seem to produce an even bigger stage for Geraldo, her attention to this incident is not the reason for its display. If Geraldo's teacher chose to ignore his comments, he would continue to make such inappropriate comments as his classmates look forward to the next "smart" remark from him. Simply removing her attention from him will not lessen his entertainment of the peers in the class. If peer attention is mediating the behavior, then only the removal of that contingency would markedly alter the rate of Geraldo's comments.

A PINCH MEANS "HELLO, LET'S PLAY." If you talk to kindergarten or early elementary teachers, they will tell you that some boys have unique ways of getting the attention of girls at recess time. What looks like an aggressive response, e.g., pinching or pushing, actually serves as an attention-getting function.[1] Such behaviors can result in the clique of girls screaming and running away, generating the game of "chasing each other." It would be better if the boy(s) who want to play with the girls would make a simple verbal request, such as "let's play

---

1. This has probably become far less frequent with a zero tolerance for sexual harassment in recent years.

chase." However, such is not generally the mode in which these co-ed games get started.

For those readers who are playground supervisors, the bigger concern is how to deal with such an incident. Zero tolerance has probably cut down drastically on such behaviors, but in rare cases where such behavior happens, two contingencies would seem indicated. First, the discipline doled out for such behaviors should be followed, irrespective of the offender's intent. It is important to ensure that the desired reinforcer does not occur; hence, immediate termination of this game for all participants should be effected. However, it is also essential to set the conditions under which a teacher can assess peer play in an appropriate manner. The adults need to take a more active role in prompting the play activity. Perhaps during recess the playground supervisor can set up a designated time for an activity called the "Chase Game." The playground supervisor might say, "Okay, it is time for the Chase Game. Whoever wants to play come here. Here are the rules (then states rules). Ready, go." This would facilitate access to this fun activity, without entailing an undesirable behavior to produce it.

VERBAL ARGUMENTS WITH THE TEACHER. How can verbal arguments with the teacher be maintained via peer attention? Arguing with the teacher brings about peer social attention and notice. Concurrently, other behaviors do not bring peer attention. A hypothetical teacher of a class for children with behavior disorders directs the class to do an activity. Some students shout out, "Why do we have to do that. It is stupid." The teacher retorts, but peer attention has already been delivered for such. In some classes with children with severe behavior problems, the form of argument takes on a more unacceptable topography, e.g., I won't do that! You can #^*##@!" Irrespective of

Table 2.9
ANALYSIS OF VERBAL AGREEMENTS

MC for Peer Attention	Efficiency to Produce Peer Attention: Arguing with Teacher	Efficiency to Produce Peer Attention: Complying with Teacher Request	Probability of Target Behavior
high	high	low	high
high	low	high	low

what verbal response the teacher provides, the reinforcer is delivered. Let us examine and explain this unacceptable behavior (see Table 2.9).

The second row in Table 2.9 illustrates that arguing behavior is efficient and effective at deriving peer attention, while other behaviors are less efficient at producing peer attention. This is a common scenario in many classrooms. Therefore, arguing with the teacher in older grades is highly probable when a student seeks peer attention in these classrooms. With problem behaviors maintained by peer attention, teacher or adult attention often cannot compete with such a powerful maintaining contingency. Providing teacher attention for appropriate behavior in this scenario will probably not result in a long-term change in arguing behavior. A derivative of this analysis is that ignoring the behavior will prove ineffective. In fact, ignoring the behavior provides a context for such behavior to flourish. If arguing behavior is under strong control of peer reinforcement, and there are few (if any) contingencies to inhibit such behavior, such children will continue the behavior. Of course, attributing such behavior to the behavior disorder also does little to shed light on the role of the function of such behavior in the classroom environment.

What should the teacher of children who engage in such problem behaviors do? Construct the social environment so that incidents of arguing do not result in peer attention. In contrast, following teacher directives should produce peer attention and social reinforcement (last row). Following directives would increase in level, and arguing would be very infrequent. How to accomplish such will be covered in the subsequent chapter on Functional Intervention Strategies in this text. As a preview, I offer the following: group-oriented contingencies (Hayes, 1975; Holland & McLaughlin, 1982).

Questions to Answer Before Proceeding (2c)

1. When the efficiency to produce peer attention is high for a target behavior such as inappropriate and rude comments, what will be the result on the probability of that behavior, given the relevant audience?
2. In the case involving arguing with the teacher, with such a behavior maintained by peer attention, what would you suspect to happen if the teacher worked with this student in the absence of the relevant audience?

WHAT REALLY HAPPENED IN THE "GOOD OLE DAYS"?[2] In 1965, I was in seventh grade in a brand new junior high school in Lake Ronkonkoma, New York. The wrestling coach, who also was the industrial arts teacher, was in charge of the cafeteria during my lunch period. There were several hundred students who ate lunch at each shift, and prior to each lunch shift's being dismissed to go back to classes, Mr. Felser (not his real name) would signal the students via microphone that "quiet time" had ensued. During quiet time, students were to sit quietly, put their tray up, and not utter a peep to their neighbor.

The consequences for being caught talking during quiet time were a function of one's previous number of infractions. The first time you were caught, Mr. Felser broadcast your infraction to everyone: "Mr. Sundin, please stand. You have just been awarded cleaning duty." You then were assigned to clean up the cafeteria. With your second incident, you received the above consequence as well as a scheduled spanking with a paddle (actually you could choose either a paddling or a detention). The third time you got all three.

When quiet time began, the cafeteria became noticeably quiet. This obviously made it easier for Mr. Felser to identify the guilty parties. A few people talked on occasion, including yours truly. The first time I got caught by Mr. Felser, I, along with a few other select individuals, picked up paper around the cafeteria. The second time, I picked up paper and also scheduled a paddling for later that day. Mr. Felser knew me because I was in his industrial arts class. On that day, upon command (i.e., "Mr. Cipani, assume the position"), I got ready. Mr. Felser remarked, "Well, Mr. Cipani, you are fortunate today; my wrist is a little weak." (*Thinking to myself: well, please by all means hit me while you are weak. In fact, if you want to try to paddle me with just your pincer grasp around the paddle, I am all for innovation in discipline techniques Mr. Felser.*) The blow came and it pushed me forward. Boy was I glad he was a little weak. I would have hated to catch him when he had his Wheaties for breakfast! The paddling left no marks, but the hit was so hard that it jerked several tears from my eyes immediately upon contact. I went back to the next period. I never violated quiet time again for the remainder of the year. Once was enough for me.

---

2. Taken with permission from Cipani, 2004, free at www.ecipani.com/PoT.pdf (make sure to use capitals where indicated).

However, what was apparent to me at that time was that there was a small but distinct group of boys who violated this rule constantly. I can remember the name of one of them, Mr. Leonard Tortellini (not his real name). It seemed like it was every other day that Leonard was talking or doing something that would gain the attention of Mr. Felser. One of his more devious ploys was to dump the contents of his tray before it reached the disposal area (i.e., food and plates were on the floor). What was also apparent to everyone was that Leonard did not try to violate the rule in a stealth fashion. He actually looked like he wanted to be caught. Was he not playing with a full deck?

Based on my personal experience, I wondered how he could handle such a paddling multiple times per week. Leonard had long hair and wore extremely tight pants, which was the style back then. I also knew that he and several of his fellow quiet-time violators were quite popular with the girls. Do you see why Leonard and his band of brothers acted they way they did? They weighed physical pain versus later pleasure. I chose lack of pain and lack of pleasure. The "bad" boys saw this as a mark of honor, and they were lining up in droves for the paddling, and subsequently collecting phone numbers right after receiving their "punishment." I would also surmise that calling Mr. Tortellini by name in front of the entire lunch shift was not a wise move either on the part of Mr. Felser.

Questions to Answer Before Proceeding (2d)

  1. Explain why some students in my junior high school *loved* to get hit by Mr. Felser.

TANGIBLE REINFORCERS

This category of behavioral function involves the maintenance of problem behaviors as a result of their ability to obtain tangible reinforcers under conditions of mild to severe deprivation of items or events (see Table 2.10). Tangible reinforcers can be certain food or drink items, specific toys, or items. Tangible reinforcers also include activities such as free time, playing on the swing, playing tetherball, structured games, and other similar preferred activities.

Table 2.10
ANALYSIS OF BEHAVIOR UNDER MC FOR TANGIBLE REINFORCERS

MO for Tangible Reinforcer	*Efficiency to Produce Tangible Reinforcer: Target Behavior*	*Efficiency to Produce Tangible Reinforcer: Appropriate Behavior(s)*	*Probability of Target Behavior*
high	high	low	high
high	low	high	low
low	n/a	n/a	low

It is important to note that when the child's motivation for a particular item or activity is high, the probability of a given behavior is a function of its effectiveness and efficiency to produce the reinforcer. When the target problem behavior is more capable than other behaviors in producing the tangible item or activity desired, it greatly enhances the probability of such behavior (see first row). Unfortunately, other behaviors in the child's repertoire are less effective or efficient in producing the desired tangible item or event. In contrast, when the appropriate behavior is more effective at producing the item or activity, then the probability of the student's exhibiting the problem behavior is low. The last row shows that when the MC for an event is nonexistent, both sets of behaviors become improbable. When the item is no longer in a state of desire, behaviors that are capable of producing such are not likely to occur due to lack of desire of the event.

The factors to examine when considering a tangible reinforcer hypothesis are the same as previously delineated. First, the child is in a relative state of deprivation with respect to the desired item or activity. Second, the problem behavior(s) should reliably produce such an item or activity, and the teacher should repeatedly observe this temporal relationship. Third, the problem behavior is more effective or efficient at getting this reinforcer at the times when the MO is higher than other behaviors. These can be either desirable or undesirable behaviors. The target problem behavior is more effective and efficient at getting attention than other behaviors.

IT'S COMPUTER TIME. Some students in special day classes, due to the nature of the problem behavior, are sent to work on the computer or other preferred activity when disruptive behavior reaches unac-

Table 2.11
ANALYSIS OF BEHAVIOR UNDER MC FOR COMPUTER TIME

MO for Peer Computer Time	Efficiency to Produce Computer Time: Target Behavior	Efficiency to Produce Computer Time: Appropriate Behavior(s)	Probability of Target Behavior
high	high	low	high

ceptable levels. Of course, once the child goes to the computer, thus leaving the less preferable class assignment, he or she ceases the boisterous behavior and becomes intent on focusing on the computer game. The analysis of the action frame appears in Table 2.11. Unfortunately, computer time is not contingent on appropriate behavior such as finishing one's classwork. The long-term result of failing to decode the function of this problem behavior is to exacerbate its probability under these classroom conditions for the near future.

HEAD START AND THE TRIKES. I was a behavioral consultant to Head Start in the early 1990s (Cipani, 2004). I provided specific strategies to deal with problem behaviors of the children attending the particular site. Often, the referral was for a child who was aggressive (overwhelmingly boys). One of the referrals for aggression was a boy who exhibited such behavior during and outside playtime. The catalyst for such behavior revolved around the desire of many children to ride the three-wheeled tricycles. If six children want three tricycles, all at once a conflict situation arises. The children argued and pushed each other away from the bike in order to establish themselves as the bike riders. Once a child landed in the seat, she or he usually went unchallenged (kind of like *King of the Mountain*). As you might guess, my client was quite good at getting the bike and keeping it. It is quite easy to see that any problem in this context would be driven by the behavior's ability to get the tricycle instead of someone else. So why was aggression serving that function?

As is evident, aggression in this context is a behavior that produces access to the trike and maintains such engagement. In comparison to other behaviors, aggression, when performed adeptly is far more effective and efficient than other behaviors, such as pleading, whining or crying. However, what the teachers did (or did not do) explained also why aggression was functional. They did not resolve such disputes

Table 2.12
QUESTIONS FOR A TANGIBLE REINFORCER FUNCTION

1. **Is the existing motivational condition for that child one of relative deprivation of that item or activity?**

   Answer: Yes, three tricycles and many children desiring them sets up the MO for such an activity. In fact, if there were ten tricycles, with no need to wait for a tricycle to become available, the MO would be low, since the desired event is freely available.

2. **Is there a reliable, somewhat frequent relation between the child's problem behavior and accessing certain items or activities? What is the form of the behavior, and what items or activities are produced?**

   Answer: Yes, aggressing against other children in a profound manner resulted in this child's getting the tricycle on a regular basis (or any other item/toy he wanted).

3. **Is problem behavior more likely to produce the tangible reinforcer than acceptable appropriate behaviors?**

   Answer: Yes, Absolutely. By not designating who initally gets the tricycles and for how long he or she gets the tricycles, the teacher ensures that aggression will become a functional behavior among children.

when some children complained to them. Instead, the complainers were told to go back and work things out for themselves. I asked one of the teachers why none of the staff mediated the disputes with the bike (until someone is hit). She remarked, *Our philosophy here is that we want the children to learn to work out their problems on their own. If we solve their interpersonal squabbles and problems, they will never learn to develop self-control and personal responsibility to themselves and their fellow human being!*

Let us examine what the contextual conditions are for this case by answering the three questions to pose for a tangible reinforcer hypothesis (see Table 2.12).

In this case, the failure of the social environment to mediate other behaviors to facilitate getting the tricycles was a major factor in the continued utility of aggressive behavior. Treatment would have to significantly alter the manner in which the teachers intervened in this context. Aggression had to become less functional. I accomplished this by designating a contingency for aggression to be his removal from the play area for a brief time and loss of any tricycle time during that recess period. An additional component would have to strengthen the alternate more acceptable form for getting the tricycle. I decided to reward complaining to the teacher by making children accept a "plea deal from the teacher." The plea deal meant the parties involved in the complaint would all get a shorter allotment of time on the tricycle. The teacher would announce the following: "You get the tricycle for 3 minutes, then she gets it for 3 minutes," and so forth.

With this approach, aggressive behavior dropped dramatically, including the child referred to me. The removal of the opportunity to ride the tricycle whenever a child aggressed made such a behavior unproductive in this context. The teachers remarked that the children were now bringing their complaints surrounding toys and bikes to them frequently. These functional treatment contingencies produced a more acceptable way for children to work out their impulsive behavior. What was also an interesting finding in this program was that many of the children who needed the tricycle right away learned one of two things. Sometimes they waited for the tricycle to become available to them. More frequently, they would find something else interesting to play with that was not in as great a demand as the bikes. Can children actually learn to refrain from aggression? This finding does not settle with the old adage "boys will be boys." Perhaps we adults have a lot more to do with child aggression than scholars portend.

Questions to Answer Before Proceeding (2e)

1. Why is it not a good idea to use the computer time to "de-escalate" a behavior problem?

YOU NEED TO "COOL OFF."[3] How you react to student behavior matters! In the 1990s, a ten-year-old boy with mild mental retardation attended a special education day class with 12 other students. Roberto had a history of engaging in problem behavior, including disruptive and aggressive behavior. He also had progressively lower rates of work completion as his aggressive and disruptive behavior increased each year. In past years, the teaching staff had used time-out when he became aggressive or engaged in what they described as agitated behavior. However, at his current weight of 140 pounds, using time-

---

3. Taken from Cipani (2004) with permission, book is free at www.ecipani.com/PoT.pdf

out was no longer feasible, given the ensuing aggressive struggle. At the time of our intervention,[4] the teaching staff had used a "cool off" program for him. When he appeared agitated (as well as avoiding aggression against them), the teaching staff asked him if he wanted to go outside and "cool off." He would assent to that, take his matchbox cars outside, and play for a while. While such a response certainly lessened his agitation at the time, you can see that this plan has some flaws. While Roberto certainly does calm down, this plan generates two undesirable events. First, agitated behavior allows him to escape his instructional program. Second, such escape from instruction is enhanced with a play period! In spite of that misguided plan, school staff members called Roberto's mother one to two times per week to pick him up for his unruly behavior. It was at this point that we got involved with a referral from the developmental disabilities agency. This situation was rendering havoc on the child's education, the classroom, and the child's mother. The work supervisor (at the mother's place of employment) told Roberto's mother that she could not continue leaving during the day if she wanted to be an employee of the company.

It was not difficult for my behavioral specialist, Steve Taylor, to decipher Roberto's behavioral pattern. If he does his work, he gets more work until it is time to go to recess. In other words, behaving appropriately means that he has to wait up to one hour and a half to get recess. What happens if he becomes agitated and begins throwing objects around when he enters the classroom? Bingo, he is outside with toys! Now which behavior pattern is more profitable from Roberto's viewpoint? My behavioral specialist would obviously have to make a significant change in the way the teaching staff would handle Roberto. The response of the staff (although seemingly the "right" thing to do) was actually "feeding" into agitated and aggressive behavior. When Roberto wanted to go outside, he engaged in behaviors that signaled to staff that aggression was impending. The staff headed this off by "capitulating," e.g., allowing him to leave his work assignment and the classroom and go outside to play. Aggression probably occurred when someone decided not to let him out as quickly and served to immediately access playtime. In other words, engaging in the be-

---

4. Steve Taylor (now a BCBA) was the behavioral specialist working under my direction at the time.

haviors interpreted as agitated and aggressive behavior served a function under the MO of wanting to play outside the classroom.

How can anyone straighten out a situation such as this? Steve Taylor decoded his problem behavior as serving to get a play period. He then rearranged the teaching staff response to both his problem and appropriate behavior. Instead of allowing him to play when he misbehaved, Roberto could quickly earn play periods with his matchbox cars if he did a short amount of work. Do you see the difference? The results of this plan were outstanding. His compliance to task requests no longer included oppositional and aggressive behavior, and the student study team did not receive any more referrals. Further, school staff did not call his mother once in the three-month follow-up period to pick him up. What adults do in response to child behavior matters! In order to intervene successfully in this case, we changed the contingencies for both appropriate and agitated behavior. Outside playtime was now a contingent event for finishing a smaller part of his work. Agitated behavior would not result in getting to go outside. When the consequence of agitated behavior changed, problem behavior dropped.

SELF-INJURY PRODUCES FOOD. Children with severe disabilities can often be incapable of producing vocal behavior that communicates their desires. When we are hungry, we can ask for food. If one does not have vocal behavior that conveys the meaning as wanting food, other behaviors have to fill the void. In a small percentage of these children, self-injury becomes a problematic behavior pattern. At some point such an incident may bring the child the desired food item. Unfortunately, the lack of communicative capability gives rise to such a behavior becoming functional in getting food when desired. If self-injurious behavior exists for several years, it often generalizes to situations involving MCs for other tangible items. Such a child hits his face with his hand not only when he desires a cookie, after refusing to eat the healthful food prepared by his caregiver, but also when he wants to go out, get a preferred toy, or turn on his TV or radio. Self-injury becomes a generalized behavior across many different motivational conditions involving relative deprivation states. Many children with autism and other similar severe disabling conditions who lack the ability to communicate their needs develop other behaviors that serve an access function to food and other tangible reinforcers.

NO, YOU CANNOT WATCH THE NEWS. My behavioral specialist, Ron Pekarek, and I had a case in which the presenting problem was tantrums and aggression to parents. The child (about four years old) with developmental disabilities literally dictated the agenda in the home. He watched his TV programs constantly. If the parent(s) attempted to turn off the TV or even switch to another (adult-relevant) channel like the local news, he would scream vociferously and occasionally hit his parent if nearby. Such a tantrum episode continued until the parents changed the channel back to the cartoons or child show. The parents reported they rarely were able to watch any TV program of their choosing. In some practical sense, they were banned from their own TV. It is obvious that turning the channel back to the desired station contingent upon his tantrum behavior was not effective in the long term since it made such behaviors functional. How do you stop such a cycle?

We initiated a program of more frequent channel changes, starting with the turning off the TV. In the first few days of the behavioral program, the length of time we would turn the channel off was extremely short (about five seconds). If the child did not throw a tantrum, the parents switched the TV back to the desired channel after that short interim. If a tantrum did start, the parents turned the TV on only when the tantrum ceased. In the short five-second period, the child engaged in some brief compliance request, e.g., go pick up the book, and give it to me. This scenario occurred multiple times during the day for the first phase of the intervention.

This program readily achieved success. We then progressively increased the length of time that the TV remained off. The length added was just a few more seconds in the beginning. Fortunately, it was not long before the TV channel was off for up to a minute without generating a tantrum. The second phase of the behavioral program involved progressively longer periods of turning off the channel. The child and his parent would engage in an alternate activity while the TV was off for minutes at a time. The intervention was developing the child's capability to handle a small disappointment and switch to another entertaining activity. In the last phase of the intervention, the parents turned the TV channel off and then set the channel to an adult program. Finally, these parents could watch the evening news. While that may not seem like a wonderful outcome for some people, it was a treat for these parents to watch TV news together.

Questions to Answer Before Proceeding (2f)

1. Explain how self-injury can function to get food for children with severe disabilities.
2. What was the maintaining contingency for aggression in the Head Start tricycle case example?
3. How was aggression rendered nonfunctional with the intervention?

SOCIALLY MEDIATED ESCAPE (SME) CATEGORIES

In some cases, child behavior produces escape or avoidance of a relatively aversive event. These functions are termed socially mediated escape (which includes avoidance functions as well). Someone mediates the termination of the aversive event contingent upon aggressive behavior. It is important to reiterate that the term *relative* requires one to consider each circumstance as unique in determining what constitutes an aversive condition. For some children, having to eat broccoli for dinner creates an aversive situation. For others, broccoli is a favorite food. One child may like to do math problems and would select that activity over a reading assignment. The opposite could be true for another child.

Table 2.13
NEGATIVE REINFORCEMENT CONTINGENCIES

MO	*Behavior*	*Environmental Result*	*Maintaining Contingency*
Aversive condition (relative)	Target problem behavior	Someone terminates aversive condition (or postpones it for some period of time	Socially mediated negative reinforcement
	Alternate appropriate	Aversive condition remains	Appropriate behaviors not functional in terminating or postponing aversive event

Table 2.14
ACTION FRAMES FOR ESCAPE BEHAVIOR

MO: Presence of Aversive Condition (relative)	Behavior	Effect in Avoiding the Aversive Event	Future Probability of Behavior Under MO
Unpleasant social interaction with staff or other patients	"I don't want to talk" and turing his head away from intruder	Not effective	Less likely
Unpleasant social interaction with staff or other patients	Spinning around with arms outstretched	Effective immediately	More likely

The depiction of temporally ordered environmental events in Table 2.13 illustrates how the target problem behavior becomes more likely (see first row). Note that the target behavior is effective at terminating the aversive event. Unfortunately, other more appropriate behaviors become less effective in terminating the aversive event (see last row). If the alternate appropriate behavior occurs, it does not act on the social environment in a manner that terminates the aversive event.

Remember the case of the spinning top? Such a behavior occurred under conditions of attempted interaction from medical staff. This apparently set up an aversive social condition for that man. What behavior avoided or terminated social interaction? When this man spun around in circles with arms outstretched like an airplane propeller, anyone attempting to get close got cut off. Identifying this behavior's function as escaping social situations led to the successful intervention. To illustrate the function of the spinning behavior, let us make some hypothetical assumptions. Let us say that we found out that other prior attempts at getting people to leave him alone via request ("I don't want to talk") were not successful (see first row in Table 2.14). The person attempting to engage in a social interaction with this client ignored his plea and continued the intrusion. One can see why he resorts to spinning like a top in those situations (see second row).

The treatment confirmed the suspicion that the spinning behavior served an escape (actually avoidance) function for impending social interaction. When the social environment honored his request to leave him alone, the spinning behavior stopped occurring. Concurrently, the behavior involving a request to leave him alone increased in frequency due to its newly established function.

An adult often produces the maintaining contingency; hence, the term socially mediated escape (SME). There are three subcategories of SME problem behaviors that are relevant for school settings: (a) unpleasant social situations, (b) relatively lengthy tasks or assignments, and (c) relatively difficult tasks or assignments. Problem behaviors that are at unacceptable levels often are functional under such conditions of relative aversion of these events or activities.

Questions to Answer Before Proceeding (2g)

1. When the efficiency to escape an aversive event is high for a target problem, what does that imply for an alternate more acceptable behavior leading to escape?
2. What are three categories of escape behaviors that are socially mediated?

ESCAPE OF UNPLEASANT SOCIAL SITUATIONS

Have you recently been in a social situation that you dreaded and could not wait to leave? Very often, we have verbal behaviors that produce an acceptable manner of leaving such situations. You might excuse yourself from the interaction by saying, "I have to go. I have an appointment" or some other nicety. The presence of a relative aversive social situation sets up the motivational condition to engage in a

Table 2.15
QUESTIONS FOR ESCAPE FUNCTION OF UNPLEASANT SOCIAL SITUATIONS

1. Is the existing motivating condition for that child one of relative aversion to the current or impending social situation?

2. Is there a reliable, somewhat frequent relation between the child's problem behavior and escape from the social situation that is mediated by an adult? What is the form of the behavior?

3. Is the problem behavior more likely to produce escape than acceptable appropriate behaviors (i.e., quicker or on a denser schedule of escape)?

Table 2.16
ANALYSIS OF BEHAVIOR WITH ASSEMBLIES' SCENARIO

Presence of Aversive Condition (relative)	Behavior	Effect in Terminating the Aversive Event	Future Probability of Behavior Under MO
Lengthy assemblies	Sitting for two minutes quietly	No effective	Less likely
Lengthy assemblies	Disruptive behavior	Effective immediately	More likely

behavior that is successful in producing escape (and or avoidance). If other more appropriate behaviors are unsuccessful at producing escape, then it is possible that disruptive or aggressive behavior will result in someone removing the child from the context.

One needs to pose the following questions in Table 2.15 to determine if escape from an aversive social situation is the behavioral function for the target problem behavior.

For this category of SME functions, the presence or impending advent of a relatively unpleasant social situation is existent (question 1). Such a condition is necessary for some behavior to function as an escape or avoidance behavior. There is a reliable relation between problem behavior and the escape/avoidance of the unpleasant social situation (question 2). In other words, there is a history of such a behavior reliably producing escape under the designated aversive social situation. The termination of the aversive event occurs via an adult mediating such behavior. Contingent upon the problem behavior occurring at some level, an adult removes the event or activity from the child and substitutes something else. Unfortunately, the target problem behaviors are more successful at terminating the undesired social situation than other more acceptable behaviors (question 3).

AN EXAMPLE INVOLVING ASSEMBLIES. A hypothetical 11-year-old student with learning disabilities in an elementary special day class is reported to engage in disruptive and aggressive behaviors. Such behaviors often occur during assemblies. The problem has gotten to such a point that staff must frequently remove him from the assembly within the first 10–15 minutes for behavior. He has not managed to remain in an assembly for the entire length in the last five assemblies. If the latency to removing him has shortened over the school year, what effect is removal from assembly having on disruptive behavior? Removing this child from assemblies contingent on disruptive behavior is exacerbating the problem.

The analysis of behavioral function in Table 2.16 shows that appropriate behavior does not produce escape from the assemblies (see first row). However, as the assembly drags on, the motivating condition for escape increases, and disruptive behaviors become more probable. Their effect on the social environment, one of producing termination of the assembly for that child, is the maintaining contingency (see last row).

What can staff do to alleviate such a problem without completely removing him from such activities unconditionally? Perhaps some form of shaping greater tolerance to length of assemblies might work, along with a sufficient additional consequence for removal (e.g., loss of recess time that day to practice how to sit still).

RELATIVELY LENGTHY TASK OR INSTRUCTION

Imagine you hate cutting your lawn. It takes about 45 minutes on a Saturday morning. Now imagine that your property line extends by a factor of four! That means a lot more lawn mowing. In addition, for the next three weeks, for some strange reason, your grass grows so fast that you have to cut it every third day. You should see that cutting the lawn has just become even more distasteful, due to the increased amount required. Every third day, you are going to get up feeling unhappy, dreading the impending lengthy activity for the day. The increase in the length you have to engage in this activity is providing a significant MC for escape and avoidance behaviors. There are days when you put off cutting the lawn, claiming some other household activity needs your attention. On days when you do begin, you find that you need more breaks in between the lawn-cutting activity. If only you could go back to your smaller lawn and one that takes weeks before needing mowing.

The aversive state occurs because the task or chore is lengthy in duration. *Lengthy* is a relative term. What may be lengthy to you may be of short duration to me. While some of us may not mind cutting the front lawn if it takes 15 minutes, we may not be comfortable with a lawn that is four acres (that is why riding lawn mowers have a certain market share). In this sub-category, the child is capable of performing the assignment or task, but the duration of the instructional activity required is too long. Under this motivational condition, aggressive behavior occurs and produces the child's removal from the lengthy task. This diagnostic category encompasses behaviors that postpone or terminate the child or client's engagement with an instructional task, chore, or demand.

For some children math periods that last 50 minutes are 40 minutes too long! If the period lasted for only ten minutes, there would be no problem. If minor forms of protest or disruption are unsuccessful in getting an adult to change or terminate the assigned task, then more severe and unacceptable forms may rise to the forefront. If hitting someone results in leaving the classroom, then hitting somebody is effective when the situation reaches an intolerable level. The first hit may be tentative, but as its socially mediated effect becomes apparent, future incidents become more probable.

For this category of socially mediated escape behaviors, the presence or impending advent of a relatively length instructional task, lesson, or assignment is existent. Such a condition is necessary for some behavior to function as an escape or avoidance behavior. The social maintaining contingency for this category involves a reliable relation between problem behavior and the escape/avoidance of the relatively aversive instructional task. In other words, there is a history of such a behavior reliably producing escape under the designated aversive event. The termination of the aversive event happens via an adult's mediating such behavior. Contingent upon the problem behavior occurring at some level, an adult removes the event or activity from the child and substitutes something else. In some cases, the adult removes the activity and replaces it with a more preferable one. For example, a child who hates to work on math drill sheets disrupts the class, and the teacher subsequently puts him on the computer to play math games. Disruptive behavior then ceases which makes it more likely the teacher will resort to this strategy the next time. Unfortunately, other more acceptable behaviors are less likely to result in escape. The target problem behaviors are more successful at terminating the lengthy task than other more acceptable behaviors (question 3).

HOW MUCH DO I HAVE TO DO? A student in a classroom for children with learning disabilities receives a task, which she completes. She is about to get out of her seat, but she is directed to work on another task. She reluctantly complies with this request. She finishes part of it, and then attempts to leave her seat for a short break. As she leaves her seat, the aide admonishes her to finish. She hits the desk at this point, and the aide comes over to her and tells her to stop. As the aide presses her to return to work, she pushes a chair over and proclaims, "I am tired of this place." The aide then moves her to another area of the room with a different activity. Of course, this activity change results in the student stopping the destructive behavior toward furniture. She contentedly settles down to work on this different task. The aide may believe she did the right thing, as evidenced by the change in the student's emotional state. However, the long-term effect of this mediation is not appreciated. If you were this child, what would you do the next time you felt you did enough work on a particular task or activity? Ask nicely for a different activity? Or destroy property?

Obviously allowing a change in instructional activities contingent upon property destruction is not recommended! What is the solution to this type of problem? The rearranged contingencies would include the following: (1) Finish one assignment of reasonable length (e.g., 12 minutes,) and a change in tasks occurs, and (2) engage in destructive behavior prior to finishing the task, and a change in activities is postponed until task completion. As this student becomes adept at achieving a change in activities with this new contingency arrangement, one can progressively employ a more stringent requirement for task completion. Perhaps she now must finish two assignments of about 12 minutes in length in order to get a change in activities. One can progressively alter the standard for reinforcement as a function of performance. In that manner, this student may eventually achieve a level of task completion with the assigned task(s) prior to a switch to a more desired activity.

I'LL HIT MYSELF. Students with severe disabilities such as severe mental retardation, autism, and traumatic brain injury have extreme difficulty with lengthy periods of instruction. Some of these students with severe disabilities also engage in problem behavior during lengthy assignments. However, the length they can tolerate may be even shorter than the above scenario. Some teachers report that a hypothetical child starts hitting himself in the face and head area as soon as he or she faces the work task at his table. Contingent upon the self-injury the teacher comes over to try to stop him, which of course terminates instruction at that point in dealing with the behavior. If attempts to get him to stop are unsuccessful, what do you think happens? The teacher moves the student to another area, where either no task or possibly a different, more preferred activity is provided. Of course, once the activity becomes one of preference, the motivating condition for self-injury is removed, and the self-injury stops. But what happens in the long term?

My consulting firm was involved with many children with such problems. A particular child that we served in the 1980s had severe rates of self-injury. Such self-injury occurred right at the start of the instruction at school. The school program reported that teaching him could no longer take place due to this behavior. One of my behavioral specialists began serving him at home under the auspice of a behavioral program to treat his self-abuse. We began with minimal requirements for allowing escape from instruction, such as following one to two commands to place something in a tin can. This escape contingency continued throughout the training session. This part of the plan had two outcomes. First, there was a reduction in the aversive nature of instructional tasks due to the decreased amount of task compliance required. Second, we designed a contingency that allowed him to leave the instructional setting when he finished a fixed, defined amount of work.

As the program proceeded in the coming weeks, we progressively altered the criterion level for escape over time. Once he was readily compliant with one to two commands, we increased the escape requirement to complying with four or five requirements. At the end of the program, while he was still at home, he was capable of working for about 45 minutes on a variety of tasks without any self-injurious behavior occurring. He also acquired some sign language and was proficient at a number of tasks.

It is Time to Clean Up. This scenario plays out across households with young children in America (and the world). The toy room is full of toys on the floor, perhaps a result of several days of not picking up after the play activity is ending.

Parent: Billy, it is time to clean up.

Billy: No, I don't want to.

Parent: Come on. I will help you.

Billy: I do not want to.

Parent: Let us do this together.

Billy: He falls on the floor kicking and screaming, knocking over toys, small chairs, etc.

Parent: Okay, if you are going to act that way, I will not let you play with your toys again. (Results in even greater level of tantrum and property destruction as parent picks up toys. Of course, the next day we find Billy playing with ten toys strewn throughout the playroom. Can anyone say "inconsistent.")

What does not happen when Billy goes into a tirade? He does not pick up any toys. What also happens? His parent does that for him. Would you say such behavior is a function of a mental disorder? It was there lying dormant for eight years, and then voila! Do you think it would matter if this parent stops cleaning up the toys when this child has a meltdown? Suppose, the child has to pick up three toys before the parent picks up the rest, and he stays in the room until he completes that task. Obviously, such a contingency postpones engaging in any other activity until he picks up three toys. If someone would do your child's homework for him if he threw himself on the floor, what do you think we would see more frequently?

Questions to Answer Before Proceeding (2h)

1. Why would time-out work during recess time for most children and not during instructional periods that last too long?
2. What can one do for escape behaviors where the MC is a relatively lengthy instructional task or lesson? Why not do this more often?

RELATIVELY DIFFICULT TASK OR INSTRUCTION

A prescription for problem behavior is the following: Place students who are functioning at the third-grade level in reading or math, and provide a curriculum that is based on having competence in reading and math at the ninth-grade level. When you present them with material that is above their current reading or math level (particularly several grade levels above), you create an "instructional mismatch" (Cipani & Belfiore, 1999). An instructional mismatch occurs when a teacher asks someone to perform instructional tasks that are beyond his or her current capability. Some students repeatedly face this condition. They begin to look for ways to escape such assignments. Hence, they become disruptive and create management problems for you.

If you doubt the potential for this instructional mismatch to create an environment for problem behavior, ponder the following scenario. Suppose I give you an assignment to write a piece of software that does invoicing for accounts payable at an agency. To accomplish this task, I give you an instructional manual on how to develop computer software. Sounds doable? Well, let us say that you are a novice, and it was just last week that you figured out how to use the mouse to click on icons. What would you predict would happen? What would your motivational state be? If you are unable to comprehend even the first few pages without guided help, will you stay at the task long? Alternatively, will you look for other things to do? How long would it be before you look for another job?

Now imagine you are a student that faces difficult material every day because you are in a grade that is several levels above your reading or math level. You cannot quit because you are not old enough. Every day and every week, you fall farther and farther behind until every assignment begins to take on the role of "mission impossible." If this image strikes you, you can now empathize with some of the students in your classroom. They face the prospect of failure with every class assignment without any hope of succeeding. Maybe just once they would love to get something that they look at and say, "Holy mackerel! I can do this!" This scenario plays out every day with all too many students. They cannot do the work, and they begin to look for other things to do. Unfortunately, many of those things they find to occupy their time violate class rules, hence the genesis of disruptive behavior.

This diagnostic subcategory encompasses problem behaviors that terminate the task or chore with such escape responding motivated by the difficulty of the task or chore. What may be difficult to you may be easy to me and vice versa. Under this condition, the problem behav-

Table 2.17
QUESTIONS TO CONSIDER

1. Is the existing motivational condition for that child one of relative aversion to the difficult instructional task or assignment? Are there any data to indicate that such material is significantly above his or her level of achievement in that area?

2. Is there a reliable, somewhat frequent relation between the child's problem behavior and escape from the aversive task, choare, or assignment? What is the form of the behavior?

3. Is the problem behavior more likely to produce escape than acceptable appropriate behaviors?

ior occurs. As with all socially mediated behaviors, the adults involved in the situations produce the desired condition, e.g., termination of task difficulty.

Researchers demonstrated this functional relationship in a landmark study (Weeks & Gaylord-Ross, 1981). The participants in the study were students with severe disabilities. The target behavior involved disruptive behavior. The researchers showed that presenting tasks to the individual student that were easy for him or her resulted in lower rates of disruptive behavior. In contrast, presenting difficult tasks produced the opposite effect on disruptive behavior.

What constitutes a difficult task? When the child is incapable of performing the task accurately or fluently, a level of difficulty exists. This lack of skill sets the stage for escape from or avoidance of those instructional situations and conditions. Of course, the degree to which this constitutes an aversive condition is relative for each individual student. In many special and general education classes, teachers present students with material they are incapable of completing accurately. Daily exposure to material that the child has very little chance of succeeding with will create an aversive state. In these cases, the child may engage in the problem behaviors to avoid all schoolwork because such work is often something she or he is unsuccessful in completing.

One can use the following questions to determine this function (see Table 2.17).

For this category of socially mediated escape behaviors, the presence (or impending advent) of a relatively difficult instructional task, lesson, or assignment is existent (question 1). Such a condition is necessary for some behavior to function as an escape or avoidance behavior. There is a reliable relation between problem behavior and the escape/avoidance of the relatively aversive instructional task (question 2) due to the task's difficulty. In other words, there is a history of such a behavior reliably producing escape under the designated aversive event. The termination of the aversive event occurs via an adult mediating such behavior. Unfortunately, other more acceptable behaviors are less likely to result in escape (question 3). The target problem behaviors are more successful at terminating the lengthy task than other more acceptable behaviors (question 3).

The material may be difficult if the child lacks the prerequisites. For example, a student with disabilities (or any student for that matter) attends an Algebra class where the week's lesson is on factoring second-order polynomials (e.g., $y = 4x^2 + 20x + 21$). How well will he perform at this objective if he cannot add and subtract negative numbers to mastery (let alone be able to solve a simple linear equation)? It is evident that such a task is difficult and will create an aversive condition. This may be a more common phenomenon with many special education programs fostering a mainstream-at-all-costs approach to the education of students with special needs (a detailed analysis of this phenomenon can be found in the Cipani and Schock text (2011).

SELF-INJURY OFTEN ESCAPES INSTRUCTION. Very often problem behaviors such as self-abuse can function to remove instructional tasks or materials by the teacher's stopping instruction to "deal with" the behavior. A student with autism hits herself repeatedly when faced with a task demand. At that point, the teacher attempts to hold her hands, preventing her from hitting her face. Concurrently, instruction stops! Because of the ability of the child's self-abuse to terminate instructional demands, hitting her head becomes more probable in the future when she faces the same or similar tasks.

Questions to Answer Before Proceeding (2i)

1. Describe how an instructional format like a relatively difficult instructional assignment might present the MC for escape behaviors.
2. Explain how self-injury can become a socially mediated escape behavior when a student with severe intellectual disabilities is given a task above her language comprehension.

Table 2.18
MULTI-FUNCTION PROBLEM BEHAVIORS

MC	*Functional Behavior*	*Result*	*Likelihood in the Future Under MO*
Desires toy	Hits peer	Gets toy as peer runs away crying	Increased
Presence of lengthy morning circle time	Hits peer	Placed in time-out	Increased

MULTIFUNCTIONAL BEHAVIOR PROBLEMS

One cannot examine the form or topography of problem behavior and determine its function. It is very possible that the same (or similar) form of behavior will serve different functions (Kennedy, Meyer, Knowles, & Shulka, 2000). For example, a student with severe disabilities may engage in self-injury when she wants to go outside, indicating a tangible reinforcer SMA function. Self-injury may also occur under conditions involving difficult tasks, such as any task in which she is required to speak in sentences. Her current level is one of one to two words at a time, and such a requirement sets the conditions for an SME function of the self-injury.

Table 2.18 illustrates aggression toward others as a multifunctional behavior. Note that the child will hit under two different motivating conditions. Because this behavior produces the desired consequence, it becomes functional in both sets of circumstances. Functional intervention would have to derive separate contingencies for each context.

SUMMARY

This chapter examined the action frame for two major categories of socially mediated functions: (1) Socially mediated access (SMA), and (2) socially mediated escape (SME). In addition, the chapter included the sub-categories within each major function and delineated the analysis of the action frame with respect to the MC and function of behavior. It should now be evident to you that most student problem behavior is maintained by a current environmental purpose or function. Further, decoding that function can lead to the solving of the behavior problem. It is important to have a thorough grounding of the basic principles of behavior, as evidenced by the material presented in these first two chapters. The next chapter will provide a basic grounding in behavioral principles.

CHAPTER 2: SUMMARY TEST

(Answers on CD)

True or False

1. Deprivation is an absolute state, its level is pretty much the same for all humans.
2. If attention from an adult is in a relatively deprived state, a behavior that is functional is one that produces a reinforcer that exacerbates (heightens) that deprivation state.
3. If attention from an adult is in a relatively deprived state, a behavior that is functional is one that produces a reinforcer that ameliorates (lessens) that deprivation state.
4. The three SMA categories are peer attention, relatively unpleasant events, and adult attention.
5. The three SME categories are relatively unpleasant events, relatively lengthy tasks or assignments and relatively difficult tasks or assignments.
6. A problem behavior becomes functional as an SMA when it reliably produces a functional reinforcer that abates the deprivation state effectively than other behaviors.
7. Teacher attention is a function that involves escape from the teacher's presence.
8. If aggression is effective in terminating an unpleasant social situation than another behavior, it will be functional under that aversive condition.
9. Socially mediated access functions involve behaviors that terminate aversive events.
10. SME functions occur to deprivation conditions as an antecedent to behavior.
11. The three SME categories are relatively difficult tasks or assignments, relatively lengthy tasks or assignments and extremely difficult tasks or assignments.
12. A behavior that reliably and effectively terminates a social activity is an example of an SMA function.
13. A relatively lengthy instructional task sets up an antecedent condition for a behavior that serves an SME function.

14. An undesirable behavior such as aggression can only be functional under antecedent conditions of relative deprivation of tangible items.
15. A behavior that is multifunctional can be highly probable under two different motivating conditions.
16. A behavior that serves one function could be an SMA under one context and an SME under another.
17. A behavior that is multifunctional can produce two different contingencies under two different motivating conditions.
18. A relative deprivation state constitutes an absolute value for the particular deprived item.

A short, fill-in-the-blanks test can be found in Appendix A.

Chapter 3

BASIC PRINCIPLES OF BEHAVIOR

W hat are operant behaviors? Operant behaviors are behaviors that operate on the environment (Catania, 1979). In "old writings," the term *instrumental behavior* was often used. *Instrumental* referred to the ability of the behavior to produce certain effects or consequences on the environment (e.g., behavior was *instrumental* in achieving a certain outcome). The production of these specific consequences made operant behaviors more or less likely. Researchers found that they could alter the level of operant behaviors (probability of occurrence) by presenting a specific environmental consequence. This ability to change the rate of behavior was initially demonstrated in animal laboratories, followed by demonstrations in applied settings.

As Chapters 1 and 2 illustrate, understanding that classroom problem behaviors are a function of their environmental result allows classroom personnel to explain why children engage in some behaviors over time, i.e., decode child behavior. Table 3.1 illustrates hypothetical examples of operant behaviors and their relation to the environmental consequence that alters the future probability of behavior.

Note that the behaviors of the two children are altered in their probability of occurrence by the environmental consequence. In the first row, the tantrum of Child A resulted in getting cookies. Such a behavioral consequence for tantrums strengthens the probability of tantrums in the future given the MC of desiring cookies. In the second row, leaving the grocery store immediately upon child B's tantrum weakens tantrum behavior in the future. Therefore, because the consequence is different for each child, the effect on the future probability of behavior is different. For Child A, tantrums will be more likely

Table 3.1
EXAMPLES OF OPERANT BEHAVIOR

Behavior	*Consequence Produced*	*Effect of Consequence on Behavior*	*Probability of Future Occurrence*
Child A throws a tantrum in grocery store	After 5 minutes of tirade, gets cookies with Indiana Jones sticker	Strengthens tantrum behavior's function under those antecedent conditions	Increased
Child B throws a tantrum in grocery store	Parent leaves store immediately, not getting any cookies	Weakens tantrum behavior's function under those antecedent conditions	Decreased

to occur. For Child B, tantrums will be less likely in the future. This analysis of operant behaviors allows the user to explain why Child A will continue to throw tantrums in the store in subsequent visits. As long as the consequence of such is the access to the desired item (while other behaviors are less successful), one could predict that Child A will continue to engage in such behavior. One need not resort to a personality assessment or make claims that Child A was born to be a menace.

However, not all behaviors are operant behaviors. The contrast is respondent behaviors. An environmental stimulus elicits respondent behaviors that do not change (for the most part) as a result of the consequences of such an occurrence. Reflexes are subsumed under respondent behaviors. For example, shooting a puff of air into your eyes will elicit an eye blink. What happens after the behavior will not alter the future probability of such behavior's occurring again with the eliciting stimulus, i.e., the puff of air to the eyes. Eye blink rate is not a function of what happens after, but rather is a result of the antecedent presenting eliciting stimulus. Similarly, hitting a specific part of the knee (Patella) with an object will result in the knee jerk reflex. Provided there is no injury to the femoral nerve, such a response will occur irrespective of what happens after the reflex. One cannot modify this response by providing a consequence following the knee jerk response. The determinants of whether this response occurs are whether one strikes the patella at a correct angle as well as principles of respondent conditioning.

As teachers and paraeducators, you most often deal with operant behaviors. You are change agents. Understanding that operant behaviors can be changed by altering the consequences that are produced allows you to become effective change agents.

BEHAVIOR-CONSEQUENCE RELATIONS: POSITIVE REINFORCEMENT

What is a Contingency?

A contingency is a *reliable* relation between a behavior and a consequence. The term *reliable relation* requires that the temporal pairing of behavior and the consequence occur regularly. Contingencies are often referred to as the, If _____, Then _____ statement. Some examples are:

- If you finish your homework, you can go outside to play.
- If you speed in the presence of a police officer, you will get a ticket when she catches up to you.
- If you bang your arm hard against a solid object, you will get a swelling or contusion in that area.
- If you jump into the lake, you will get wet.
- If you miss the bus, you will have to use another mode of transportation that time.

A contingency specifies two conditions: (1) what happens when the behavior occurs, and (2) what happens when the behavior does not occur (i.e., the absence of specified consequence). Note that the contingencies stated above also imply what happens when the behavior does not occur.

- If you do not finish your homework, you cannot go out to play.
- If you do not speed in the presence of a police officer, you will not get a ticket.
- If you do not bang your arm hard against a solid object, you will not get a swelling or contusion in that area.

- If you do not jump into the lake, you will stay dry.
- If you do not miss the bus, you will not have to find another mode of transportation.

Understanding that already existing contingencies in a student's life exert their effect on his or her behavior allows a teacher to decode a child's behavior. A teacher who understands the role of everyday contingencies on child behavior is not mystified by the exhibition of problem behavior by some students. If a teacher understands that there are already existing contingencies maintaining problem behavior, then the solution to the problem becomes more straightforward. That the teacher realizes her ability to alter such existing contingencies in favor of acceptable behaviors is the behavioral solution. Chapters 1 and 2 have already introduced you to contingencies via the delineation of functions for behavior.

A behavior that is maintained by a particular contingency is termed a *maintaining contingency.* It is simply another term to express a reliable relation between behavior and a consequence under a given MC. There are two types of maintaining contingencies: (1) positive reinforcement, and (2) negative reinforcement.

What is Positive Reinforcement?

It is not candy! It is not your attention! Many people have a misunderstanding about what constitutes positive reinforcement. When asked if they think positive reinforcement is effective, they will ascribe teacher or adult attention as a positive reinforcer for children. However, their answer belies a technical misunderstanding and one that can have ramifications for their effective use of consequences.

Reinforcement is not an inherent property. It is always defined in terms of a specified contingency's effect on the behavior it follows (Williams, Howard, Williams, & McLaughlin, 1994). Reinforcement requires two conditions: (a) a temporal contingent relationship between two events, one's behavior and some event subsequent to it, and (b) the effect of such a contingency is one of making the behavior more probable in the future. Reinforcement, *by definition,* is a process that always serves to increase the future probability of the behavior (or maintain it at heightened levels) through the contingency. This is not to say that certain applications of contingencies in certain situations are not successful in increasing behavior. However, in those situations, reinforcement did not occur, but rather some other phenomenon occurred.

Given this definition of reinforcement, examples of reinforcement must meet two requirements: (1) there is a consistent contingent relationship between behavior and a subsequent environmental event, and (2) such a relationship serves to produce and maintain a high level of that behavior over time. If saying, "You're a nice person" after your aunt opens the door increases the future probability of your aunt's opening the door for you, by definition, reinforcement has occurred. Can saying "thank you" contingent upon your aunt opening the door for you over a several-week period not be an example of positive reinforcement? Yes, if the long-term result of your behavior is her failing to open the door for you as much as she used to.

Many people think of candies for children as a positive reinforcer. In fact, early behavioral intervention efforts were often called M & M therapy by its critics. Do M & M candies always constitute a positive reinforcer? Suppose a parent asks for your help with her child. She cannot get her to walk in the house. Rather, her child frequently runs throughout the house, and on occasion falls and scrapes her leg. Unfortunately, such natural results of this behavior have not affected the running behavior. You believe that you can help and set up the following contingency: Every time the child walks from one room to another, she gets two M & M's. Is this an example of the use of positive reinforcement? It will be an example of positive reinforcement only if its effect is to increase the rate of walking in the house. Does the child walk more frequently in the house? If the answer is yes, then positive reinforcement has occurred. Additionally, candy functioned as a positive reinforcer. However, if such a contingency has no effect on the rate of walking between rooms, then candy is not a positive reinforcer in this context. I will explain the reasons why such a contingency may not function as a positive reinforcer in a section of this chapter called "factors affecting the potency of reinforcers."

Here is another incorrect usage of the term *positive reinforcement.* You often hear people say, "I want to reinforce your idea on _____." Ideas cannot be reinforced! One can say, "I would like to state my approval of your idea." Only behavior can be reinforced and made more probable in the future under relevant MCs. Also, saying that you want to reinforce someone is also technically incorrect for the same reason. Teachers should keep in mind that behavior becomes more or less probable in the future, not people.

WHAT IS THE RELEVANCE FOR PRACTICE IN EVERYDAY CLASSROOMS? An understanding of the causal relationship between behavior and reliable consequences is crucial in changing behavior. In many areas of education, factors and variables that are not under the control of the teacher are posited as major contributors to problem behavior. Further, many educators are taught in university training programs that solving such societal ills is a prerequisite to effective teaching or intervention with such afflicted children. In contrast, the reliance on behavioral principles has led to many successful demonstrations of changing behavior with such afflicted children. *My belief is that classroom personnel need not wait for society to become less violent or children to watch less TV to be effective with children at risk.* I believe that changing academic and social behaviors in the classroom requires a specific and distinct set of behavioral skills. Teachers and paraeducators who want to be able to solve behavior problems and increase desirable, appropriate behavior have to learn how to decode child behavior and manipulate consequences effectively to achieve such behavior change. Teachers and paraeducators who learn basic principles will analyze why certain existing contingencies may not be effective. Instead of giving up, blaming the child's home life, alcoholism in society, or a host of other factors, they will hunt for a more effective plan. The following hypothetical example depicts this capability.

A junior high teacher manipulates a contingency that she believes will function to increase behavior. She believes she is using positive reinforcement. Unfortunately, the introduced contingency fails to increase the appropriate target behavior. This teacher realizes this application did not work, and the contingency used was not effective. The consequence used turned out not to be a positive reinforcer for that child under that context. A consequent event that serves as a reinforcer for one child's behavior may not have the same effect for another child. This teacher makes this distinction. She subsequently hunts for a new potential positive reinforcer. While some people "give up" on changing behavior, other astute teachers take up the challenge with renewed vigor.

USING A POSITIVE REINFORCEMENT CONTINGENCY. As pointed out

above, teachers need to restructure or manipulate the existing contingencies to produce desired changes in student behavior. This requires the teacher to examine the current contingency. The teacher needs to identify what currently happens after the behavior, and what consequent event(s) could be changed to set the conditions for an alternate behavior to occur.

For example, a teacher has a class of students in a junior high setting who often arrive late to class. Currently, the sole contingency for being late to class is a reprimand from the teacher. Each day she records the students who arrive late and sums these numbers weekly. She plots this data on a bar chart. Figure 3.1 depicts the number of students that are late over the five weeks, with the data labeled "Reprimand." During this period of time, the number of students arriving late ranged from a low of 11 to a high of 20 students on week 4 (see Figure 3.1). This reprimand contingency is not resulting in the desired effect on student tardiness. This is still of a level too high to be acceptable for this teacher.

She decides to enact a different contingency plan. She institutes the following new contingency. First, she stops giving a reprimand when they come in late. She merely notes who arrives on time on the blackboard. At the end of the week, she gives five minutes of early release for lunchtime for those students who came to class on time each day for that week.

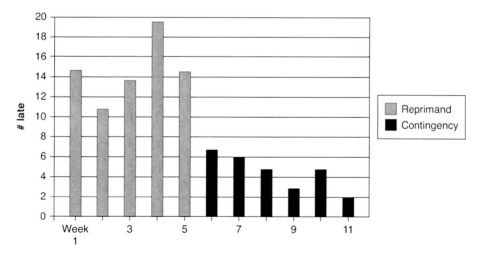

Figure 3.1. Reprimand vs. early release contingency.

She evaluates the effectiveness of this new contingency plan on tardiness. She continues to record the number of students coming late to class each day. She sums up the total for each day of the week and plots it on the same bar graph (Figure 3.1). She compares the first six weeks of this new plan (data labeled "Contingency") against the weekly totals for the reprimand condition. The question posed: "Is early lunch release on Fridays a positive reinforcer for on-time attendance?" As is evident from viewing Figure 3.1, tardiness decreased from the reprimand condition. The worst day in the early release contingency was seven, which was better than the best day in the reprimand condition. Therefore, early release is a positive reinforcer for this class as a whole, and the operation was that of positive reinforcement. However, if such a contingency did not result in a decrease in the number of students coming late, then the teacher did not find positive reinforcement contingency. If this contingency were ineffective, this teacher would continue to hunt for an alternate contingency that could have the desired effect. Due to its effectiveness, I would advise this teacher to continue using early lunch release as a contingency for on-time arrival until the data demonstrates that it is not functioning as a reinforcement contingency.

What is the Premack Principle?

The *Premack Principle* (Premack, 1959) is an invaluable tool for a teacher who is hunting for an effective reinforcement contingency. The Premack Principle states that a behavior of high probability can be used to reinforce (i.e., increase) a behavior of lower probability. Premack (1959) found that he could increase one behavior simply by allowing the animal access to a higher probability behavior following the completion of the lower probability behavior. This ingenious finding allows a teacher to change a student's behavior by doing two actions. First, she identifies what behavior she wants to make more frequent, usually a class task(s) or assignment. She then makes its occurrence result in the immediate access to a higher probability behavior. This resulting special contingency has applications in a variety of educational contexts. You may have heard this referred to as Grandma's Rule: You do not get your dessert (high probability event for most children) until you eat your vegetables (lower probability event during mealtime).

A hypothetical parent reports difficulty getting her child to complete homework. She asks for your help. You ask her what the routine is when she comes home. The parent says, "Well, when she comes home, she is pretty hungry, so I have a snack for her. Then her friends come over, and she goes out to play. She comes home for dinner. After dinner and some TV, we try to get her to do her homework, but she is usually oppositional. She is stubborn, just like her dad." You see the error in the arrangement of the routine and apprise the dad that he is off the hook! You tell the child's mother that you suggest altering the routine upon her arrival at home from school. She now has to complete a designated portion of the homework (lower probability behavior) before getting a quick snack (higher probability behavior). The child does not receive the snack until the small amount of homework is completed. Once she consumes the snack, she must finish another designated portion (depending on the length) in order to go outside to play (higher probability behavior). Because of this Premack arrangement, the rate of doing homework improves to the point at which the parent no longer identifies this as a problem.

The following case in point is a real-life example of the utility of the Premack Principle. I had a graduate student in the 1980s. In the graduate course she was taking, she was working with a child with profound mental retardation at a public school development center. This course required each graduate student to provide discrete trial instruction under my immediate supervision. Reinforcer sampling is one of the initial tasks required of each graduate student. After a period of time on the first day with her assigned child, she finds me in the room and says, *Dr. Cipani, I have tried everything. This child does not want food items, drink items, music, praise, tickles,[1] activities or anything else. He is not interested! He just wants to lay his head down on the table! What should I do?*

While the novice graduate student was perplexed, I knew the Premack Principle would "save the day." The low probability behavior is complying with the small number of instructional requests. The high probability behavior at that time was putting his head down on the table. Can you see a Premack Contingency? Let the student put his head down on the table (high probability behavior) once he complies with a fixed number of requests (low probability behavior).

---

1. Back in the 1980s, this was not deemed to be inappropriate, perhaps a teacher would be wise today not to use such a reinforcer.

Here are some other Premack examples that one can apply to everyday life:

- When <u>you eat your vegetables</u>, then *you can get dessert.*
- When <u>you finish washing the dishes</u>, then *you can watch TV.*
- When <u>you clean off the top of your desk</u>, then *you go to lunch early.*
- When <u>you finish mowing the lawn</u>, then *you can go to the swimming pool.*

Here is a hypothetical example involving the use of a Premack contingency for a student with mild mental retardation. The low probability behavior for this student is completing a worksheet containing math drill problems. A computer math game played with other children is a higher probability behavior. Using that information one can set up the following Premack contingency: If you accurately complete your math drill sheet, you can then have 15 minutes of computer game time. Note that the higher probability activity is made contingent upon the lower probability event occurring.

The Premack contingency has great application for students with severe disabilities. Some students with autism will engage incessantly in the same repeated behavior pattern; called stereotypic behavior. Some students weave their hand in a circle-eight pattern many times an hour. Some students engage in floor touching in a repeated pattern for a short interval followed by the same behavior just moments later. High rate stereotypic behavior interferes with instructional delivery and attending in students with severe and profound skill deficits.

However, a Premack contingency making stereotypic behavior as contingent events for instructional compliance has been a great demonstration of the power of such a contingent relationship with students with severe disabilities and autism (Charlop, Kurtz, & Casey, 1990: Wolery, Kirk, & Gast, 1985). Contingent upon completing the instructional task, the student receives unimpeded access to engage in stereotypic behavior for a designated period. By using stereotypic behaviors as the contingent event for performing an instructional task, the results are twofold. First, greater student compliance with instruction is achieved, particularly in cases where the stereotypic behavior was frequently interfering with the task. Second, stereotypic behavior

Table 3.2
PROCEDURES FOR USING PREMACK PRINCIPLE
WITH STEREOTYPIC BEHAVIORS

(1) Identify stereotypic behavior(s), and label them as high probability behavior.

(2) Select the task(s) or the number of compliant behaviors to instructions required for authorized access to stereotypic behavior for a short designated length.

(3) Present the task(s) or instruction (low probability behavior).

(4) Immediately interrupt (and stop) any attempt to engage in stereotypic behavior during a task, but provide enough prompts to effectively engage the student in task compliance.

(5) Authorized access to stereotypic behavior for a designated interval as an earned activity is contingent upon completion of task or compliance to task instructions. An oven timer set for several minutes denotes earned activity time.

(6) When timer goes off, re-present additional instructional task(s) with same contingency stipulated.

is brought under temporal and stimulus control of authorized access. This makes the student's instructional compliance more likely since the teacher will not attempt to deprive the student of this activity.[2] Rather, there is a time and a place for such.

Here is an illustrative hypothetical example. Mrs. Ramirez is concerned that Joey's behavior interferes with her delivery of instruction to Joey. Joey engages in toe touching behavior frequently (touches tips of shoes). She decides to utilize it as a reinforcer by requiring Joey to follow two simple instructions, one right after the other, and then allow him to engage in stereotypic behavior for a one-minute period during the training session. She might ask Joey to clap his hands upon command and then put two blocks in a small box. If Joey fails to perform the requested behaviors, he does not get one minute of time to engage in stereotypic behavior. If he engages in stereotypic behavior during the task presentation, the teacher would stop him from continuing such stereotypic behavior immediately. The teacher then issues both instructions for compliance again. Gradually, the number of instructional requests increases with the same contingencies in effect. By using stereotypic behavior as a reinforcer and restricting access to

---

2. As many teachers of students with high rate stereotypic behavior will report, such an attempt at complete elimination is often unsuccessful, unless other instructional behaviors are developed.

it during the task presentation, Mrs. Ramirez is able achieve two goals: (1) She brings stereotypic behavior under stimulus control of the absence of an instructional task, and (2) increases student engagement in learning environment when direct instruction is present. Table 3.2 details the procedures to use this specialized form of the Premack Principle for students with autism who frequently engage in repetitive behaviors, as well as other students with severe disabilities.

What is Extinction?

What happens when you withhold a reinforcer for a designated behavior? If a behavior is increased in level as a result of a positive reinforcement contingency, then the removal of such a previous reinforcement contingency reduces that level of behavior. The process called *extinction* involves the removal of a previously contingent reinforcer for a specified behavior (Iwata, Pace, Cowdery, & Miltenberger, 1994). Chapter 2 provided many examples of a behavior's function, illustrating that such behaviors are maintained by a specific consequence. What happens if that function is eliminated by removing the temporal reliable relation between that behavior and the consequence? The target problem behavior decreases in probability, which is a good thing! Removing the identified maintaining contingency when the behavior occurs is the use of *extinction* in the classroom.

Suppose an undergraduate student majoring in psychology and hoping to get into graduate school is motivated to earn great grades in her undergraduate classes, (i.e., contingency for such grades is inherent). She earns points toward her grade for completing the workbook exercises in her research methods psychology course. In this course, she completes all the exercises and receives maximum points toward her grade. However, completing the workbook exercises in her linear algebra class is recommended but optional, with no points given for this activity. If the exercises in the book have little or no relation to the exam questions in the linear algebra class, her diligence in completing the algebra workbook activity will decline markedly. Removal of the reinforcer will result in a lower level of such behavior over time. Only if completing the exercises is fruitful in terms of doing well on the exams will such a behavior still occur at high levels in linear algebra. However, that continued workbook activity on the part of the student is not a function of points. Rather, engaging in the workbook activity is maintained because of its relation to performing better on the exams. The behavior of completing the algebra workbook would then only be under control of a more inherent reinforcer, i.e., grades in the course.

The above hypothetical example brings up a side issue. Unfortunately, in building new behaviors, if other more natural reinforcers do not "support" the newly acquired behavior in the social environment, contrived reinforcement may have to be deployed until such begins to occur. I would point out that the first goal is to build appropriate behaviors, even if one needs to utilize contrived reinforcers. You do not finish the race if you do not get started! Once the behavior develops, one can gradually implement interventions that could fade the reinforcer. Transferring the control of the behavior to inherent reinforcers in the environment needs to occur.

What Factors Affect Reinforcer Potency?

Four factors affect the potency of a reinforcer.

1. Deprivation-satiation
2. Magnitude of reinforcer
3. Immediacy (in some cases)
4. Schedule of reinforcement

An item or event that functions as a positive reinforcer for one child might not function as a positive reinforcer for another child. Further, the potency of any consequent event or item to function as a reinforcer for a given child is not constant across time. In reading Chapter 1 and 2, you know that the power of any consequence to alter a behavior is in large part a function of the individual student's MC at that time. For example, you may enjoy eating ice cream every day, but on some days, you crave ice cream much more. You, therefore, eat ice cream twice that day. On the next day, you eat ice cream only once. As a result of the fluctuation in the deprivation level of ice cream throughout the week, its ability to function as a reinforcer would also vary across that same period. That is why I recommend a variety of contrived reinforcers in classroom practice.

The MC condition is a function of the continuum involving deprivation and satiation. Deprivation and satiation are opposite phenomena. An event that is in a deprived state will be more effective as a consequence at that particular time. For example, a parent wants to use computer time as a reinforcer for her child's compliance to designated chores. The parent wants to ensure that computer access would be potent as a reinforcer. She determines the current amount of free access. She determines that she is currently on the computer for one hour per day. To ensure that contingent computer time will function as a reinforcer for doing chores, the parent allows only 30 minutes of free access each day. This restriction of free access places this event in a deprived condition. The remainder of the computer time is a function of her child's completion of three daily chores. Given the level of deprivation imposed, such a contingency will probably exert strongly on this child's behavioral compliance with chores. Conversely, if the parent decided to allow her child one hour of free computer time and then provide for earned time afterward, then the use of computer time as a reinforcer for compliance will be less effective (if at all). The level of free access determines how quickly the state of deprivation sets in.

If you were a psychology, undergraduate major several decades ago as I was, you might have taken a class called learning or animal learning.[3] In that class, I and the other students completed several lab assignments that required us to demonstrate effective application of the basic principles of operant behavior. We were each assigned one adult albino rat. Our assignments involved a variety of behavior change projects. The first major assignment required all the students in the class to teach their rat to retrieve food by depressing the bar in the operant chamber with sufficient downward force. This behavior automatically set off the delivery of a food pellet as a contingency. Can one food pellet as a reinforcer for bar pressing serve as a sufficient reinforcement contingency for bar pressing? We did not engage in any of the methods described in the next chapter on differential reinforcement to identify effective reinforcers such as preference assessments or reinforcer sampling. Dr. Brophy simply instructed us to teach the rat to press the bar with the consequence of such an event being a food pellet.

Prior to any training taking place in the operant chamber, we weighed our rat each day for a one-week period. With a baseline of his

---

3. Thank you Dr. James Brophy for the great and lasting educational experience!

or her current weight, we then reduced the rat's food intake so that the mean body weight fell by 5 percent. This put the rat in a deprived state with respect to food intake. With food being in a deprived condition, the rat would work for those pellets that were used as a contingent event for bar pressing. We simply had to ensure that the learning environment was designed so that the behavior we wanted was progressively shaped and, of course, produced a high rate of reinforcement.

While decreased access to an event leads to deprivation, increased access to an event leads to satiation. Suppose we increased food intake with our rat prior to training. Instead of being 5 percent less body weight, we fattened up the rat to more than 10 percent above his or her original body weight. The result would have been a much slower rate of learning or possibly a failure to learn the target skill! The effect of satiation is to make the reinforcer less powerful and thereby weaken its use as a reinforcer. For example, let us say providing edible reinforcement for correct response during language training will maintain a stable rate of correct responses in a relatively hungry child with severe disabilities and autism. What do you think would happen to food as the reinforcer if such training were done right after the child eats breakfast at school? If a teacher wants to use food as a contingency for correct responses, then it must be in a somewhat deprived condition to function as a reinforcer. Therefore, conducting language training after a noncontingent snack for students with autism and other severe disabilities is usually unproductive.

The implications for behavior change efforts in the classroom regarding the phenomenon of deprivation-satiation are considerable. Too often, teachers may deploy contingencies in which the consequent event is currently in a satiated state. Such an arrangement produces little or no desired effect on behavior. If the teacher becomes aware of a student's satiated level with respect to a given event, he or she can then deprive that event for a period of time (provided it is not food or a civil right of the child) to increase its potency.[4] Then its use in a contingency will be to increase the behavior it follows.

---

4. Classroom personnel should always check with parents, human rights advocates, and administrators regarding the restriction of access to certain events that children are entitled to under law or policy (e.g., lunch or physical education). Such events may not be restricted according to legal statutes and, therefore, require the teacher to utilize other contingencies.

I conducted a study that sought to develop independent feeling skills to a female adult with profound retardation (Cipani, 1981). All attempts to teach independence at mealtime using prompting and fading techniques had proven unsuccessful. I determined that the lack of progress in independent feeding was not due to faulty training procedures. The facility dietary personnel approved a dietary change to help this woman with her bowel movement problems as well as the lack of appetite. Dietary personnel provided her with a nutritiously equal liquid supplement at the dinner meal instead of her usual dinner menu. This change in the diet produced a great change in the client's appetite, and the rate of independent spoonfuls at breakfast and lunch increased dramatically. Once she began to feed herself, the staff no longer had to figure out whether she was still hungry or not. When she was full, she would put her spoon down on the table, and staff would mediate that as a request for not wanting any more to eat. The staff substituted liquid supplements for solid foods during the dinner meal within several sessions of the dietary change, and as a result, independent feeding maintained across time.

How does the magnitude of reinforcement affect response rate? Does one potato chip per correct response produce lower rates of skill acquisition than two potato chips per correct response? Another factor influencing the potency of a reinforcer is the magnitude or amount of the item or event delivered contingently. Magnitude does not have a linear relationship to performance or rate of behavior. The relationship between increasing the amount of the reinforcer per response is curvilinear. A curvilinear relationship denotes that as you increase the number of potato chips for each correct response, the rate of correct responses will increase to a point. However, eventually the rate of correct response hits a plateau, and then the number of correct responses declines with the increased number of potato chips per correct response. Perhaps when the child gets 20 potato chips per correct response, he becomes full of potato chips after two correct responses. Hence, with satiety of that reinforcer, its efficacy for the remainder of the session is abated.

How important is immediacy of delivery of the reinforcer? We often hear that immediacy of delivery is important. What should the interval be between the occurrence of the target behavior and the delivery of the reinforcer? In animal laboratories, when teaching a rat to press the bar, research has shown that half a second or less delay is optimal for acquisition of the bar-press response. As the length of time between the behavior and delivery of the reinforcer increases, acquisition suffers. Given that you cannot communicate to the animal the behavior you wish to reinforce, the longer the interval, the more different behaviors occur in that interval. Therefore, the animal may have performed the bar press five seconds ago, but the animal received the food reinforcer immediately after she sniffed under the bar. Guess what behavior was reinforced in that frame?

What does a teacher or paraeducator need to do with respect to working with students? Is half a second required for delivery of reinforcer? The answer depends on the student's level of disability. With students who have a requisite level of language comprehension, using a point contingency each time they raise their hand and give the correct answer is sufficient to get them to increase that behavior. They will perform that behavior to earn points that they can later trade for a tangible reinforcer or preferred event. One does not need to provide the tangible reinforcer immediately after the correct response.

However, if you are trying to develop various language and pre-academic skills with students who have limited comprehension of language, then a point system may not be suitable. The immediacy of the tangible reinforcer is more relevant until one can establish a conditioned reinforcer. This is particularly true when behaviors other than the target behavior occur within the delay interval (Reynolds, 1975). The example below illustrates what happens when the delay is lengthy for students with severe disabilities.

Teacher 1. As part of a language discrimination task, the teacher wants the child with autism to imitate nonverbal actions. She will reinforce a correct imitation with the delivery of a stuffed animal to play with for five seconds. The presenting instruction is "do this." The teacher says, "Do this," and then she either touches her nose or claps her hands. This teacher proceeds with the training. Her first instruction is for imitation of touching the nose. She says, "Do this" and touches her nose. The student jumps out of his seat, weaves his head in a circle, grabs his foot, and then touches his nose. The teacher goes behind her chair and gets the stuffed animal. In the interim, the student begins spinning his head in a circle and then jumps out of his seat. The teacher finally places the stuffed animal in his possession, and he sits down and begins playing with it. In other words, the delivery of the tangible reinforcer did not occur until a number of behaviors interceded between the correct target response and the delivery of the reinforcer.

Over the next set of trials, the teacher presents the nonverbal imitation trials, but each time the teacher has to retrieve the item from the floor once the behavior occurs. After a ten-minute session, it is apparent that nonverbal imitation is not being acquired, but what seems to be more frequent is jumping out of the chair, which often was incidentally followed by the teacher's handing the student the stuffed animal.

Teacher 2. As part of a language discrimination task, the teacher wants the child with autism to imitate nonverbal actions. She will reinforce a correct imitation with the delivery of a stuffed animal to play with for five seconds. The presenting instruction is "do this." The teacher says, "Do this," and then she either touches her nose or claps her hands. This teacher proceeds with the training. Her first instruction is for imitation of touching the nose. She says, "Do this" and touches her nose. In order to reinforce the correct response immediately, the teacher has to have the stuffed animal in her lap beforehand. Immediately upon the student's imitating the teacher's behavior after displaying several incorrect responses, she puts the stuffed animal in his lap and says, "Great job! You were watching!" She replicates this quick delivery of the toy without letting another behavior occur in the interval before delivery. If another behavior does occur, she does not provide the stuffed animal but instead presents the same instruction again and waits for the correct imitative response to occur. Over the next set of trials, the teacher presents the nonverbal imitation trials and immediately presents the stuffed animal when the imitative behavior occurs. After a ten-minute session, it is apparent that this student is acquiring nonverbal imitation as the number of correct responses increases. Additionally, it is less likely that the student will perform other behaviors once the target response has occurred.

Schedules of reinforcement refer to the response requirements for reinforcer delivery. It is important for a teacher to become familiar with their effects for both developing appropriate behaviors as well as reducing undesirable behaviors. The impact that schedules of reinforcement have on behavior is profound. Teachers need to be aware of these effects as they attempt to build new behaviors in the repertoire of students. It is also important to understand the inherent schedule on which a target problem behavior may be maintained when attempting extinction. Continuous schedules of reinforcement refer to the one-to-one match between behavior and the delivery of the reinforcer. If a teacher gave a point every time a student came into class and said, "Good morning class," that would be a continuous schedule of reinforcement for that greeting. When the schedule is something other than a continuous schedule, we call this an intermittent schedule. Intermittent schedules will receive the majority of attention in this section. There are two broad categories of intermittent schedules: ratio and interval schedules.

Ratio schedules require a certain number of responses to occur. For example, if every third target behavior were to be reinforced, that would be an example of an intermittent ratio schedule. If the number of responses required is a fixed number, it is called a fixed ratio (FR) schedule of reinforcement. We call the delivery of reinforcement for every third response an FR 3, a fixed ratio three. An FR 20 would require delivery of the reinforcer for every 20th response, and we would designate this as an FR20. An FR 1 is a continuous schedule of reinforcement.

Some ratio schedules are not fixed at a certain number but vary around a certain number. We call these variable schedules of reinforcement or VR schedules. In VR schedules, the reinforcer is not fixed at a certain number of responses but rather averages a certain number. For example, if the correct response is reinforced on an average of five responses, it is not the case that the reinforcer would be delivered every fifth response. Maybe the first delivery would occur after three responses, but the next delivery would occur after seven correct responses and so forth. However, the average for the sessions would be five responses per reinforcer delivery. This schedule is a VR 5. When you have a 95 percent average in your statistics class, it would not be the case that every test score was 95 percent. Rather, on some you did worse than the mean; some you did better, but the average (mean) was 95 percent.

Ratio schedules are more common in classroom applications. Interval schedules of reinforcement are uncommon, and will not be covered. You are enjoined to consult a basic learning text for more information.

What schedule should classroom personnel use when she wants the student to acquire a new behavior? A continuous schedule (FR 1) is *essential* when developing a new behavior. It might be useful to think of this requirement in the following fashion: When a behavior is absent (or very low in occurrence), then the teacher must "catch" each instance and provide the reinforcer. Two hypothetical examples can illustrate this requirement for building new behaviors. The first example portrays what happens when the teacher produces an FR 1 schedule for a newly developed behavior. The second example shows what happens when a teacher implements an FR 1 schedule.

Teacher 1. This preschool special education teacher wants her children to come when she calls them to morning circle. She sets a timer for one minute and signals the class that it is time to come to morning circle, where each student will sit on the carpet square. For each student that comes within that time interval, he or she immediately gets a _____ after sitting on the carpet square. For those students who do not make it to the circle, the instructional aides gather them up and bring them to the circle, but they do not receive the _____ after they sit down on the carpet square. Within several days, almost all students are getting on their carpet square before the timer rings.

Teacher 2. This preschool special education teacher wants her children to come when she calls them to morning circle. She sets a timer for one minute, and signals the class that it is time to come to morning circle and sit on the carpet square. On the first day, each student that comes within the designated time immediately gets a cracker when he or she sits on the carpet square. For those students who do not make it to the circle, the instructional aides gather them up and bring them to the circle, but they do not receive a cracker. On the second and third day, the teacher decides to discontinue the contingency for those days. On the fourth day, she reinstates it, but not many students come to the circle. Over the next several weeks, because of the haphazard use of this reinforcer (i.e., an intermittent schedule, not a continuous schedule), the number of students who come to morning circle on time has not improved.

The differential results of the two teachers exemplify what happens in everyday classrooms. Teachers who understand that an FR 1 schedule must be set in the beginning start to see results. Teachers who do not have a continuous schedule for developing new behaviors see sporadic results or no improvement at all. It is essential that teachers understand this basic principle in the everyday use of behavior management strategies.

REINFORCEMENT SCHEDULE FOR MAINTAINING BEHAVIOR. Once a desired behavior is acquired through a continuous schedule, the teacher must set upon the task of maintaining this behavior across time. Intermittent ratio schedules are important when the teacher wants the student to continue performing an acquired behavior. The more frequent the schedule of reinforcement, the greater will be the rate of the behavior within the same session. In other words, if a student performs about 6 target behaviors per day under an FR 1, that will increase in the following week to about 20 target behaviors per day under an FR 4.

Transitioning to a leaner schedule of reinforcement is termed "thinning the schedule of reinforcement" (Reynolds, 1975). The process must be gradual and progressive. For example, a hypothetical teacher wants a child to follow his directives. He begins with an FR 1 and gets a reasonable but not fantastic rate of such behavior for the first two weeks. This teacher decides to thin the schedule every two weeks in the fashion depicted in Table 3.3.

Table 3.3 illustrates what happens when the schedule is thinned to a variable schedule of reinforcement over a period of weeks. Note that the rate of compliance improves dramatically each time the schedule becomes more stringent, requiring more occurrences for the delivery of the reinforcer. Under the VR 4 schedule, the rate of the behavior improves from the first two weeks. The comparison between the first two weeks of an FR 1 (frequencies of 6 and 8) and the two weeks under a VR 6 (55, 61) reveal the drastic change in rate of behavior.

Table 3.3
CONTRASTING RATES UNDER
DIFFERENT SCHEDULES OF REINFORCEMENT

	Week	*Week*
FR1	6 (week 1)	8 (week 2)
FR 4	16 (week 3)	17 (week 4)
FR 6	28 (week 5)	35 (week 6)
VR 6	55 (week 7)	61 (week 8)

The VR 6 schedule produces an increased frequency of the behavior resulting in reinforcement.

In summary, FR schedules produce steady rates of behavior. The VR schedules produce high rates of behavior. If you need additional proof with real life phenomena, just go to the slot machines at Las Vegas and watch people pour money into the slot. Do you think the Vegas casinos know something about schedules of reinforcement?

What is Ratio Strain?

What happens if the schedule of reinforcement is thinned too quickly? Suppose the teacher went from an FR 1 schedule to a VR 80 schedule in one abrupt change. It is very likely that the rate of the behavior would drop off quickly and eventually disappear. This is called *ratio strain* (Reynolds, 1975) and sets up the same effect on behavior as extinction.[5]

Suppose a hypothetical teacher named Mrs. Casey requires a student to finish ten addition and subtraction problems before proceeding to a more preferred activity. She has an FR 10 schedule in effect. After several weeks of success, she decides to give the students between 30–40 problems on the sheet. Over the next several weeks, about half the students are finishing their assignments and proceed to the math game activity with a friend. However, other students are not meeting this requirement and are not finishing their assignments with

---

5. Extinction would be slightly different procedurally in that it programs a complete removal of reinforcement for the behavior.

regularity. For example, one particular student has finished his work only twice out of 15 school days. Mrs. Casey "lost" the behavior of completing the assignment for the students who are failing to finish regularly. Ratio strain is the technical term for this loss of work completion with math problems.

What should Mrs. Casey do? How would you advise her to motivate her students again? It is simple. She should recognize this decrement in some students' performance as ratio strain. The schedule of reinforcement became too lean, too fast! Mrs. Casey should consider reverting to an FR 10 and get her students to finish their assignments with regularity. She would then gradually alter this FR schedule over time, making sure not to lose the behavior again. If she does lose the behavior, she knows that the thinning of the schedule may be the culprit.

Do Intermittent Schedules Make Extinction Difficult?

How difficult is it to implement extinction? The answer is "it depends." If the behavior has recently been acquired and is on a continuous schedule of reinforcement, then it is easier to produce extinction effects (provided the teacher selects an alternate behavior to reinforce). A hypothetical example of behavior maintained by an FR 1 will illustrate the extinction process. This student engages in complaining behavior about the classwork at various times of the day. The teacher records the student's rate of complaining incidents over a four-week period. In this period, the teacher allowed him a preferred assignment whenever he complained about how tough the work was, rendering an FR 1 schedule. Figure 3.2 shows the rate of complaining incidents for the first four weeks and is denoted as FR 1. The teacher begins an extinction program on week five when complaining will no longer result in a preferred instructional activity. Rather, some other designated behavior such as completing a portion of the work without complaining will produce the reinforcer. These data are depicted as the extinction condition in Figure 3.2. Within two weeks, the rate of complaining reached zero levels across the last three weeks of extinction.

Extinction effects are not as rapid or easily achieved on a problem behavior that is maintained by an intermittent reinforcement schedule. Unfortunately, many behavior problems in classrooms currently exist

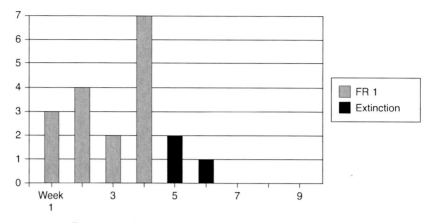

Figure 3.2. Extinction curve given prior FR 1 schedule.

as a result of an intermittent schedule. You will recall that intermittent schedules of reinforcement produce greater rates of behavior than continuous schedules. Such a phenomenon makes extinction of the behavior more difficult as it will take longer to eventually produce a low or zero rate of the behavior. Within the intermittent schedules, variable schedules (e.g., VR and VI) are the most resistant to extinction effects. Variable ratio schedules of reinforcement for a particular problem behavior make life very hard for the teacher! If the student's complaining behavior were under a VR 4 schedule, the following data in Figure 3.3 might be obtained.

Figure 3.3 illustrates that a high rate of complaining persists under the VR 4 schedule, when contrasted with the extinction curve under the FR 1 presented in Figure 3.2. This burst of additional incidents of complaining under extinction requires the teacher to not reinforce such behavior even when it reaches heightened levels of occurrence. The rate of complaining incidents reaches a new high during week six as this student tries fervently to get an alternate activity by complaining (called an extinction burst). It is not until the eighth week that extinction is finally resulting in a lower rate. The lesson learned is the following: The greater the intermittent schedule in effect for the problem behavior, the more resistant to extinction that behavior will be. This translates into the requirement that the teacher has to be even more fervent in not providing the reinforcer in the face of greater levels of the behavior.

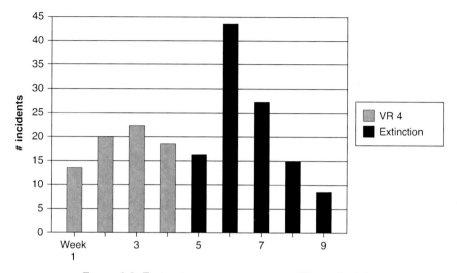

Figure 3.3. Extinction curve given prior VR 4 schedule.

BEHAVIOR-CONSEQUENCE RELATIONS: NEGATIVE REINFORCEMENT

Negative reinforcement is not punishment! Lay people often confuse it with punishment. Negative reinforcement is like positive reinforcement in that the contingency produces an increase in the targeted behavior. Therefore, it is markedly different from punishment (see details of punishment later in this chapter). However, the manner in which it makes a behavior functional is different from the operation of positive reinforcement.

Table 3.5 shows three examples of negative reinforcement. In the first action frame, the child is faced with attending soccer practice on this particular day. Perhaps on this day, she must run many sprints, which makes this practice particularly aversive to her. On the way to soccer practice with her mother, she says she is sick (assume she is not). The result of such a verbal behavior is that the mother checks her out and decides not to allow her to go to practice that day. She turns the car around and heads for home. Such complaining behavior becomes strengthened and more likely in the future when this child faces another unpleasant event when her mom is with her.

The third and fourth rows both deal with behaviors that escape a nonpreferred math assignment. Both the hitting of another child and

Table 3.4
CONTRASTING POSITIVE AND NEGATIVE REINFORCEMENT

Operation	MC	What Does Behavior Do	Effect on Behavior as a Result of Contingency	Behavior More Likely Under Relevant MO (and S-D)
Positive reinforcement	Deprivation state	Produces a desired event, given S-D for behavior	Strengthening future probability	Yes
Negative reinforcement	Aversive state	Terminates an undesired event, given S-D for behavior	Strengthening future probability	Yes

Table 3.5
EXAMPLES OF NEGATIVE REINFORCEMENT

MO	Discriminative Stimulus	Behavior	Consequence: Aversive Event Terminated or Avoided	Probability of Behavior Given MO and Discriminative Stimulus
Advent of unpleasant soccer	Mom with child	Mom, I want to leave. I am feeling sick.	Child avoids impending sprint workout	Strengthened with advent of an aversive practice
Child is presented with nonpreferred math assignment	Teacher	Hits another child	Sent to time-out, thereby removing math assignment for that duration	Strengthened under conditions of nonpreferred math assignment
Child is presented with nonpreferred math assignment	Teacher	Throws material on the floor	Sent to principal's office, thereby terminating involvement with that assignment for the day	Strengthened, same as above

throwing the materials on the floor are successful in terminating the math assignment at that time. As a result of this effect on the environment, such behaviors become more probable under conditions of nonpreferred math assignments. Within school contexts, instructional settings can often be the condition in which negative reinforcement is operable (Cipani, 1995; Iwata, 1987; Weeks & Gaylord-Ross, 1981). The three functions delineated in Chapter 2 under "socially mediated escape" are all examples of negative reinforcement functions.

WHAT IS THE DIFFERENCE BETWEEN ESCAPE AND AVOIDANCE OPERATIONS?

There are two negative reinforcement paradigms: escape and avoidance operations (Iwata & Smith, 2007; Reynolds, 1975). They differ in the manner in which the response terminates or postpones the stimulus. Escape conditioning involves the withdrawal of the aversive stimulus contingent upon the occurrence of the behavior. In escape conditioning the behavior of the student terminates an already present aversive stimulus (Reynolds, 1975). For example, an alarm clock sounds at 6:00 A.M., waking up the sleeping person. The sleeper pushes a button, which terminates the sound. The withdrawal of the aversive noise terminates upon the occurrence of the button-pushing response. If the noise from the alarm clock is of sufficient strength to be aversive to this sleeper, she will become faster at pushing the button to avoid the aversive sound for long durations. Escape conditioning paradigms typically show decreases in the latency of the response from the presentation of the aversive condition across training sessions (Reynolds, 1975).

Avoidance conditioning involves the avoidance or postponement of the presentation of the stimulus contingent upon the occurrence of the behavior. Avoidance conditioning can be an outgrowth of escape conditioning, or it can be developed independently (Reynolds, 1975). In the example used previously, the sleeper begins to wake up ahead of the alarm (discriminative stimulus), pushes the button (avoidance response), and avoids the noise (for at least that morning). Often, a neutral stimulus is presented prior to the onset of the aversive stimulus to serve as an additional discriminative stimulus and facilitate the development of an avoidance behavior. In everyday examples of avoidance conditioning, the verbal stimulus "No!" is usually the neutral stimulus that (we hope) produces the desired avoidance response, thus postponing the onset of the aversive consequence. When "No!" does begin to control avoidance responding, then it has become a conditioned discriminative stimulus (Reynolds, 1975).

Classroom Applications

Research over several decades has shown that many learning environments have maintaining contingencies for problem behavior that involve negative reinforcement operations (Cipani, 1995; Weeks & Gaylord-Ross, 1981; Iwata, 1987; Smith, Iwata, Goh, & Shore, 1995). It often develops as a powerful contingency when appropriate behaviors do not produce escape from instructional tasks. With functional treatment, the manipulation of the negative reinforcement contingency comes when the teacher designates an acceptable social or academic behavior as the criterion for escape from the aversive event. For example, under the conditions of presenting a nonpreferred instructional task to a student in a class for children with behavior disorders, the student throws the material on the floor. Consequently, the task is removed, and the student is sent to talk to the social worker. The escape from such instructional tasks needs to be addressed. The teacher can accomplish this by allowing the student to choose an alternate behavior to escape the specific instructional materials, such as requesting a different but similar task. Further, the teacher would not allow the undesirable behavior to terminate the task. In other words, the teacher must also designate escape extinction for the problem behavior.

What is escape extinction? Escape extinction is slightly different from extinction for SMA behavior problems. You should recall that extinction for a behavior that produces a positive reinforcer involves the withholding of a contingent reinforcer for that specified behavior. Escape extinction involves the continued presentation of the aversive event following the behavior that previously resulted in its termination. In other words, such a behavior does not terminate the undesired activity or event. For example, if screaming previously was successful in having the teacher remove the student from the class (on a VR 3 schedule), then programming escape extinction would result in the student not being removed during any future screaming episodes. In escape extinction, the student stays in the aversive condition. Escape

Table 3.6
ESCAPE EXTINCTION

MO	Discriminative Stimulus	Behavior	Consequence: Aversive Event Terminated or Avoided	Probability of Behavior Given MO and Discriminative Stimulus
Child is presented with nonpreferred math assignment	Teacher	Throws material on the floor	Teacher picks material up and gives back to student	Weakened
		Completes designated smaller amount of assignment	Terminates that task and transitions to a more preferred activity	Strengthened

extinction would be necessary to disable the function of screaming in this case. Certainly, the teacher would want to designate another more acceptable behavior that results in escape.

Table 3.6 illustrates how negative reinforcement contingencies are manipulated using escape extinction. Escape extinction for the target problem behavior appears in the table. Note that the student behavior of throwing the materials to the floor does not result in the termination of the task. The teacher simply hands these back to the student. If the prior response was to remove that task when the instructional materials landed on the floor, the teacher has now rendered that procedure inoperable. Concurrently, the teacher offers the student escape from the task by having him complete a small amount of work. When the student finishes a designated portion of the assignment, the teacher then terminates the task.

BEHAVIOR-CONSEQUENCE RELATIONS: PUNISHMENT CONTINGENCIES

Punishment is not synonymous with negative reinforcement. The behavioral effects produced by each operation (punishment versus negative reinforcement) are different. We define punishment operationally as an environmental event that follows a behavior in a contingent fashion and decreases the level or probability of the target behavior. Events that function as punishers produce the opposite behavioral effect of reinforcers. Table 3.7 depicts a number of examples of punishment and reinforcement operations. Note that the contingency for each behavior is defined as either reinforcement or punishment depending on the behavioral effect observed over time. The

Table 3.7
EXAMPLES OF PUNISHMENT AND REINFORCEMENT OPERATIONS

Behavior	*Consequences (assume a continuous schedule)Behavior*	*Effect on*	*Operation*
Tapping pencil	Teacher says, "Stop that."	Decreases pencil tapping	punishment
Tapping pencil	Teacher says, "Stop that."	Increases frequency of pencil tapping	reinforcement
Tapping pencil	Teacher says, "Stop that."	Rate of pencil tapping stays at high level	reinforcement
Tapping pencil	Teacher says, "Wow! You are talented."	Decreases pencil tapping	punishment
Tapping pencil	Teacher says, "Wow! You are talented."	Increases frequency of pencil tapping	reinforcement
Tapping pencil	Teacher sends child to principal's office.	Decreases pencil tapping to near zero level	punishment
Tapping pencil	Teacher sends child to principal's office.	Increases pencil tapping	reinforcement

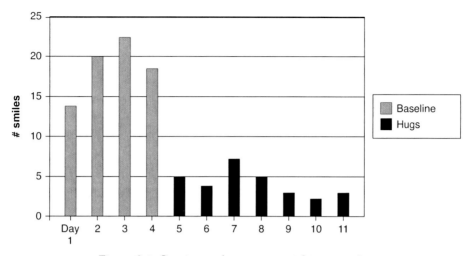

Figure 3.4. Contingent hugs as a punishing stimulus.

form of the consequence does not determine whether punishment is operable. The long-term effect on the child's behavior is the relevant factor.

To reiterate, one cannot judge a punishing stimulus simply by judging the perceived aversive nature of the event or item. For example, giving a hug contingent upon the occurrence of the child's smiling behavior may look like a reinforcement operation. However, if the rate of smiling decreases over time because of this contingency, then, by definition, reinforcement did not occur. Rather, the operation that did occur was punishment, and the consequent even, i.e., a hug, is a punisher. Figure 3.4 shows that the rate of smiling decreases when the contingency of getting a hug for incidents of her smiling is put into effect.[6] As a process, punishment always results in a decrease in behavior. However, some consequences we use that we think will have a punishing effect do not turn out to be punishers.

A preschool special education paraeducator attempts to decrease a particular child's verbal outbursts during storytime. She has read that time-outs always work because children *do not like them.* She decides to put this child in the corner whenever she has a verbal outburst during

6. If you doubt the possibility of this, pick a behavior of your teenage child when s/he is with their friends and without any explanation, give them a hug each time they display that behavior. Tell me what happens!

her reading of the story for three minutes. The teacher implements this contingency consistently. To her surprise, the child's verbal outbursts do not get less frequent but instead increase over time. With this behavioral effect, removal to the corner, i.e., time-out was not a punisher. This contingency produced the opposite behavioral effect which the teacher desired. Removal to the corner served as a negative reinforcer under the classroom conditions in which it was used. Many people believe time-out is a punisher. However, it can often function as a reinforcer when used as a consequence for behavior in a context that is relatively aversive to the student (escape function).

If a teacher or paraeducator is going to use consequences for target student behavior, it is essential that he or she evaluates their efficacy over a period of time. Their effect on the rate of the target behavior needs to be compared against a baseline. Let us say that for a hypothetical student, the teacher decides to use time-out as a contingency for aggressive behavior during all recess and unstructured outside activities. In Figure 3.5, the rate of aggressive behavior in the target student went down as a function of the use of the time-out procedure. Therefore, the teacher deployed an effective consequence in this situation and punishment occurred.

However, in Figure 3.6, the opposite behavioral effect occurred with a different student in the same context. Therefore, time-out was unsuccessful. It did not function as a punisher in this case.

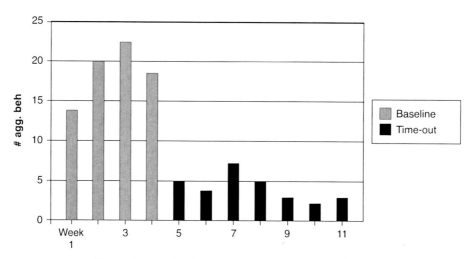

Figure 3.5. Evaluating contingency on target behavior.

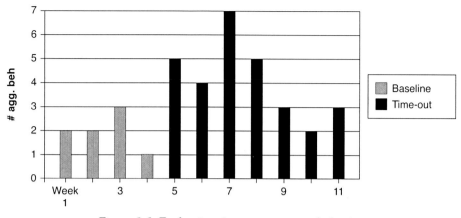

Figure 3.6. Evaluating time-out on target behavior.

There are two types of punishing consequences (Cooper et al., 2007): (a) the application of an aversive event, and the (b) removal of a reinforcing event. An example of the former would involve the occurrence of a behavior followed by the teacher's presentation of some event. Again, if such a contingency resulted in a decrease in the child's behavior, then punishment is operable. In the latter case, the teacher removes an event or object that is contingent upon behavior and is already in the subject's possession. Again, the same requirement regarding the behavioral effect must be observed to define a punishment contingency. Both methods of providing consequences are capable of reducing the future probability of behavior. In school settings, the presentation of an aversive event is often restricted in use. Therefore, the removal of reinforcement is the more preferred method for deploying punishment consequences.

The material in this text focuses heavily on functional interventions to reduce problem behavior. If you feel the need to resort to additional consequences for specific target problem behaviors, you should be aware of some basic principles of punishment. The reading material for these principles and a model for responsible use of contingencies that involve punishment can be found in the free online version of my book, *Punishment on Trial: A Resource Guide for Child Discipline* (Cipani, 2004). In particular, Sections III and IV are of relevance to this content, and you can find them as a free download at www.ecipani.com/PoT.pdf.

CHAPTER 3: SUMMARY TEST

(Answers on CD)

True or False

1. A contingency is a relationship between behavior and the antecedent stimulus.
2. Operant behaviors are controlled by their consequences, and can be either strengthened in probability or weakened.
3. Operant behaviors are a result of an eliciting stimulus.
4. Respondent behaviors occur as a result of stimulus discriminative for positive reinforcement.
5. A stimulus that elicits a response portrays an example of a respondent behavior.
6. The consequences of operant behaviors make these behaviors either increased or decreased in future probability of occurrence.
7. A contingency specifies what happens when a certain behavior occurs.
8. A contingency specifies the relationship between behavior and a consequence.
9. A term for a consequence that produces a high probability of a behavior under a given MC is maintaining contingency.
10. Positive reinforcement is the provision of adult attention for desirable child behavior.
11. If a change in a behaviors consequence increases the probability of the target behavior, positive reinforcement has occurred.
12. The difference between positive reinforcement and punishment is the direction of the behavior change produced under each operation.
13. Negative reinforcement is similar to punishment in that both operations reduce the target behavior.
14. A factor that affects the potency of the reinforcer is the personality of the adult providing the contingency.
15. Magnitude of a reinforcer refers to the amount of the reinforcer given each delivery.
16. Using a high probability behavior to reinforce a lower probability behavior is an example of the Premack principle.

17. When you finish your homework, you can go outside is a Premack contingency.
18. A stereotypic behavior can be used in a Premack contingency to increase task engagement and completion with some students with autism .
19. Increasing the level of deprivation with respect to an item will enhance its potency as a reinforcer.
20. An event is satiated when you deprive a student access to it for a long time.
21. When working with children who have minimal comprehension of language in nonverbal imitation training, the reinforcer should immediately follow the desired imitative behavior.
22. Reinforcing a target behavior every five occurrences is called a fixed ratio five schedule of reinforcement.
23. Reinforcing a target behavior every five occurrences is called a fixed ratio five extinction schedule.
24. Variable schedules of reinforcement will produce higher rates of behavior than fixed ratio schedules.
25. Alternating between an FR 1 schedule and a VR 50 schedule is a good manner of thinning the schedule of reinforcement.

A short, fill-in-the-blanks test can be found in Appendix A.

Chapter 4

SHAPING NEW BEHAVIOR

Perhaps you have been to one of the marine parks where you viewed dolphins jumping out of the water and touching a ball suspended 20 feet above the water. While jumping out of water is a natural behavior for dolphins, touching the ball with their nose is not. You cannot simply hoist the ball 20 feet in the air and wait for the dolphin to touch it and then provide reinforcement, unless you want to wait years before the dolphin is "show ready." The dolphin trainer may first start with developing a whistle as a conditioned reinforcer. Each time the whistle is blown, the dolphin receives fish if she comes within an allotted time period.[1] Once the dolphin is signal trained, the behavior of touching a ball that is 20 feet above water can commence.

The training process might then designate the initial behavior to result in reinforcement as the following: the dolphin getting within five feet of the ball. This criterion would remain in effect until the dolphin is reliably earning fish. It is important to note that the criterion for reinforcement does not change until the reinforcement of the current criterion is producing a sufficient rate of reinforcement. The next approximation might be the following: the dolphin actually touches the ball with her nose. Once this behavior occurs regularly, the criterion for reinforcement should shift. The trainer might hoist the ball one foot above water level with the same requirement of the dolphin's touching it with her nose. When that behavior occurs, the reinforcer is delivered. The approximations to the terminal goal of dolphin's touching the ball that is 20 feet above water level with her nose are pro-

---

1. Would you conduct this training before or after the scheduled lunch meal? Would you give the dolphin an extra helping of fish before training to make sure s/he is full? Why not?

gressively altered until the dolphin is exhibiting the target behavior.

Shaping is the reinforcement of progressive behavioral approximations to the desired criterion behavior. We use *shaping* to develop new behaviors. While the initial utilization of these techniques was honed in laboratory settings, it has widespread application across many teaching environments, both in special and general education. An effective teaching repertoire involves several teaching tools, such as shaping, prompting and fading, and contingent reinforcement.

TOPOGRAPHY SHAPING. Topography shaping involves reinforcement of progressive changes in the form of the behavior to an ultimate criterion form or topography. Many examples of this form of shaping in everyday environments may evade your perception of the shaping processes underway. You see a friend's baby making a number of cooing sounds at five months of age. You visit several months later. To your amazement, this same baby now says distinguishable words such as "mama, dada, baba, and meme." Shaping can be subtle, and in the case of vocal language, a baby's closer and gradual matching of adult speech takes place over a relatively lengthy period. The same child at the age of one now has a vocabulary of 50 words. Again, the social environments, along with the baby's constant production of sounds that come closer and closer to words, are at work.

The development and refinement of many athletic skills are shaped. When I was young, I learned to hit a softball with a bat through continued practice. Each attempt I made when the pitcher threw the ball was an opportunity for my behavior to be shaped by connecting with the ball (or not). The actual form of the swing was shaped over progressive opportunities. When I did connect the bat with the ball, such contact strengthened the prior swing angle and bat speed. The development of T-ball for young children is an excellent example of setting up an initial criterion that allows for a dense schedule of reinforcement as the ball remains stationary on the T. Therefore, greater frequencies of bat-to-ball contact can be achieved, even with very young children.

An adaptive PE teacher wants to teach students with mild mental retardation how to play softball in a game. While the students have learned the rules of the game, some of them still lack the skill to hit a softball with a bat when pitched underhand. They continually miss the ball, often by a considerable distance. While some may contend that these students can never become skilled enough to play softball in a

Table 4.1
SHAPING PROGRAM FOR HITTING A SOFTBALL WITH A BAT

- Define the criterion target behavior (terminal skill): Hitting a softball when thrown underhanded from the pitcher's mound.
- Identify the initial behavior that will produce reinforcement: Hitting a softball when thrown underhanded two feet from the batter.
- Reinforce this behavior whenever it occurs (FR 1 schedule).
- Develop a high rate of this initial behavior: 9/10 consecutive contact incidents of bat with ball.
- Upon reaching a selected rate of this initial skills, change the standard for reinforcement: Hitting a softball when thrown underhanded four feet from the batter.
- Alter the standard for reinforcement to become more stringent by selecting a closer approximation to the desired terminal skill.
- Reinforce only behaviors that meet the new standard.
- Develop a high rate of this closer behavioral approximation: 9/10 consecutive contact incidents of bat will ball.
- Upon reaching a selected rate of this initial skill, change the standard for reinforcement: Hitting a softball when thrown underhanded eight feet from the batter.
- Continue repeating this process until you have reinforced the terminal skill.
- Incorporate these students into games where they get real practice at hitting and running to first base with the rest of their classmates.

game, this adaptive PE teacher has a "can do" approach. She believes that better teaching techniques may prove to be the answer. She decides to shape the behavior of hitting the ball with the bat, much as T-ball does for young children. She provides extended practice swinging the bat with correct posture while the softball sits on a T. Shaping allows the students to develop the desired skill more quickly by reinforcing gradual approximations to that skill. This teacher manipulates the response requirements at various phases of the instructional program to "bring about" the desired behavior. The remainder of the training program appears in Table 4.1.

Children with autism often display poor levels of face-to-face contact with others. Face- to-face contact (or often referred to as eye contact) is important both as a mechanism for learning language and social skills as well as to produce social reinforcement for human interactions. How can you teach a student with autism to make face-to-face contact for a reasonable period of time when someone is talking to him or her? Let us say that eye contact upon request ("Jane, look at me") for duration of at least three seconds is the instructional objective. The training of this skill would begin with eye contact of less than

Table 4.2
STEPS FOR SHAPING PROGRAMS

- Define the criterion target behavior (terminal skill).
- Identify the initial behavior that will produce reinforcement.
- Reinforce this behavior whenever it occurs (FR 1 schedule).
- Develop a high rate of this initial behavior
- Upon reaching a selected rate of this initial skill, change the standard for reinforcement.
- Alter the standard for reinforcement to become more stringent by selecting a closer approximation to the desired terminal skill.
- Reinforce only behaviors that meet the new standard.
- Develop a high rate of this closer behavioral approximation.
- Upon reaching a selected rate of this initial skill, change the standard for reinforcement.
- Continue repeating this process until terminal skill is being reinforced.

the duration of a second as the "reinforceable" event. Once that behavior occurs frequently and in short latency to the teacher command "Look at me" during instructional sessions, a more progressive target can be designated. The teacher may require eye contact of one continuous second as the reinforceable event. Over time, the teacher achieves the long-term instructional objective via a shaping program that started with reinforcing a split second of eye contact. Gradually the terminal requirement for three seconds would be established and met. Once sufficient eye contact is established, the teacher can then develop this skill under natural conditions, such as calling the child's name from across the room.

In reinforcing gradual approximations to a desired goal, a teacher should set a clear behavioral description at each phase. The initial form of the behavior, which results in reinforcement, has to be specified a priori. This allows anyone conducting the shaping and training program to implement it correctly. All personnel would reinforce responses that reach the initial criteria and not reinforce responses that did not meet the stated criteria. Table 4.2 presents the general steps for developing a shaping program.

DIMENSION SHAPING. Another aspect of shaping is to alter progressively one or more dimensions of the criterion form of behavior. For example, a student is currently able to sit and attend to a teacher-presented story for five minutes. Subsequent to that time, he gets up frequently and becomes easily distracted. Unfortunately, the requirement in his class is to sit and attend for 15 minutes. Although these are her requirements, the student gets up a lot, and the teacher has indicated that he is too immature for her class due to his distractibility during her lessons. However, if the teacher would be willing to alter the instructional program, he may be able to acquire such a skill eventually. In this case, dimension shaping would allow for the reinforcement of an initial standard, e.g., seven minutes of engagement required to leave the activity. With this change in the initial criterion, this student becomes successful in achieving that requirement over the next two weeks. The teacher can gradually alter this initial standard for reinforcement over time until the student learns to sit and attend for longer periods.

A study that sought to teach two institutionalized female residents with profound mental retardation to ascend stairs in an appropriate fashion progressively increased the number of correct steps ascended (Cipani, Augustine, Blomgren, 1981). Baseline data indicated that both residents would ascend stairs by using their hands and feet without holding onto the guardrail and often climbing multiple steps in one leap. The therapist modeled the initial correct form, i.e., topography shaping, by physically guiding the residents to perform this behavior when they were placed at the top stairs. In the first phase, the therapist placed the resident two steps from the top of the stairway. The therapist provided prompts for the resident to ascend the stairs by walking up the stairs, one foot at a time and holding onto the guardrail. The therapist provided praise when the resident ascended the last two steps appropriately. When the resident met the criteria for success with this initial phase of program, the therapist placed the resident three steps from the top. The therapist used the same teaching procedure. In this manner, the number of steps ascended correctly (frequency) was progressively increased until the resident was ascending all the steps in the stairway appropriately.

Other dimensions that one can shape are frequency of a behavior, the length of time a behavior occurs, latency of the behavior from a stimulus, and measures of amplitude. Increasing the frequency a behavior is a common requirement for many students' educational plans. If a student infrequently engages in a socially acceptable greeting response with teachers, this rate can be progressively increased via shaping (called a DRH program in the next chapter).

Latency of a behavior that occurs in response to a given discriminative stimulus is particularly important in initiation of a variety of social and behavioral skills. Let us say a student takes two minutes to pick up a bat and go to plate in a baseball game. The desired criterion, i.e., what peers do, is to select their bat and get to home plate within 30 seconds. His lengthy time to get to the plate with the bat could be a significant factor in other peers' wanting to play with him. Failing to teach him how to be quicker in this situation could be deleterious for his continued participation with peers. A teacher could implement a shaping program that brings his behavioral latency down from two minutes to 30 seconds. Perhaps his teacher or coach can invoke a point contingency. If he takes longer than 100 seconds to get to the plate, he loses points. If he loses a certain number of points in a given practice session, he loses the opportunity to bat for the remainder of the session. This standard can be progressively altered, contingent upon success, to more closely approximate a time frame that does not differ substantially from the time frame used by the peers with whom he plays.

Shaping can also be used to develop a different magnitude of the current behavioral form. For example, increasing voice volume was accomplished by developing a shaping program for two students with developmental disabilities (Fleece, Gross, Kistner, O'Brien, Rothblum, & Drabman, 1981). A sound-sensitive apparatus detected small changes in voice volume, making the differential reinforcement of low voice volume speaking possible. When the voice volume hit the initial target decibel level, this illuminated a colorful display. This was progressively altered as the student was able to reliably turn on the display when talking. By using a shaping program, each student's voice volume improved. Table 4.3 presents the general steps for developing a shaping program for a dimension of a behavior.

ABSENCE OF SHAPING. What happens when a teacher does not use shaping to develop a new behavior? In some cases, the result is that the student fails to acquire the skill month after month and year after year! Unfortunately, the student's IEP continues to present the same behavioral and instructional objectives. Perhaps an example from my background can more cogently address the question. As I delineated previously, I took an undergraduate course in learning with a lab requirement. In the lab part of the course, we were required to teach a rat assigned to each of us to press the bar. The other students and I

Table 4.3
SHAPING A DIMENSION OF BEHAVIOR

- Define the criterion target behavior (terminal skill) and the relevant dimension that needs to be improved.
- Identify if the change is desired in the duration it must occur or the frequency of occurrence (higher or lower), latency, or some measure of aplitude.
- Identify the initial level of the dimension that will produce reinforcement.
- Reinforce this behavior whenever it reaches the designated dimension level (FR 1 schedule).
- Develop a high rate of this initial standard.
- Upon reaching a selected rate of this initial criterion, change the reinforcement criterion for this dimension to more closely approximate the desired final criterion.
- Alter the reinforcement standard progressively to become more stringent by selecting a closer approximation to the desired criterion.
- Continue repeating this process to reinforce terminal skill.

realized that we would have to designate gradual approximations to the desired form of bar pressing. Subsequent to our classroom training, we all understood that simply waiting for the rat to press the bar would have a deleterious effect on our grade and the frustrated rat. Do you see the parallel between the *frustrated rat* and students who continually fail to acquire skills in the special and general education classroom?

Most of us designated the initial criterion for reinforcement as the rat being physically in the area around the bar press. A food pellet was delivered any time the rat was physically in the half of the operant chamber containing the bar press. This criterion for reinforcement resulted in the rat spending a lot of time on the side of the chamber where the bar press was. At the same time, it significantly reduced the amount of time the rat spent in the other half of the chamber. With a high rate of reinforcement for this initial behavior, we then changed the criterion. The next criterion for reinforcement might have been for the rat to be within two inches from the bar press. This resulted in the rat spending a significant amount of time very close to the bar press and not in other parts of the chamber. It still did not result in bar pressing; therefore, the bar press response still needed to be shaped. We progressively altered the criterion for reinforcement until all rats had acquired the bar press response at a sufficient level on the continuous schedule of reinforcement. If we had waited for the rats to press the bar to provide reinforcement, most, if not all, the rats used in this class would not have acquired the skill.

HOW DOES A TEACHER DEVELOP COMPLEX BEHAVIORS?

In performing a variety of daily living skills, a number of sequenced steps are involved in the motoric requirements of the skill. To teach a child with moderate or severe disabilities these more complex skills, the teacher needs to task analyze these skills first. Once the task analysis has revealed the smaller units of behavior (or steps) involved in the entire task, the student must learn each step in the correct sequence until he or she is able to perform the entire task. This process is called *behavioral chaining* (Cooper et al., 2007, p. 435) in that these steps are "chained together." Prompting and fading procedures are invaluable in developing such skills.

There are three types of chaining procedures: backward chaining (Cipani, Augustine, & Blomgren, 1981: Spooner, Spooner, & Uliceny, 1986), forward chaining (Smeets, Van Lieshout, Lancioni, & Strict, 1986), and graduated guidance (Azrin & Armstrong, 1973; Tarnowski & Drabman, 1987; Tucker & Berry, 1980). In backward chaining, the students learn the last steps of the sequence first. As the children demonstrate independent behavior in these steps, they learn the steps that occur earlier in the sequence until they are performing the entire sequence independently.

Teaching independent feeding skills is well adapted to backward chaining procedures. The teacher prompts the child to perform all the steps of the behavioral chain, e.g., grasping a spoon, bringing the spoon to the plate, scooping food, lifting the spoon to the mouth, inserting the spoon in his or her mouth, removing the spoon and leaving food in the mouth. As a result of the last step, the child receives the food (reinforcer). The physical prompt is faded on the last step until the child is inserting the food into his mouth independently. When the child is performing this last step without any prompt, the teacher targets the prior step. The teacher fades physical guidance one step before the food is inserted and until both steps are occurring without any prompting. In this manner, the component steps involved in the act of inserting food into one's mouth are chained together in this backward fashion. Training continues until the child performs all the steps of the sequence independently.

Forward chaining involves the reverse order from backward chaining. Forward chaining teaches the initial step of the chain first. When the child masters the first step of the chain, he or she learns to perform independently the first and second step by using prompts on that step and subsequent fading of prompts. This forward process of development continues until the students can perform all steps in the correct sequence. Forward chaining has practical applications in many vocational tasks. For example, a teacher can use a forward chaining method to teach a student with disabilities to collate and staple several printed pages of a mailing advertisement that go in envelopes. The sequence of steps (task analysis) might be the following:

1. Pick up front page from one pile of papers.
2. Pick up second page from other pile.
3. Place second page in back of first page.
4. Staple both pages together with a staple in upper right-hand corner.
5. Fold in thirds.
6. Place in envelope.
7. Seal envelope.
8. Put in the box labeled "finished."

A forward chaining procedure would teach the child to perform steps one, two, and three independently. When these steps reach a mastery level of performance, then the student learns the fourth step in addition to performing the first three steps. Reinforcement would occur when the child completes the third step. After the student learns the first four steps, the teacher can use prompting and fading procedures to chain the fifth step to the previous steps. This process of chaining new steps onto previously learned steps continues until the child performs the entire chain independently.

There are two variations for conducting backward or forward chaining. One method is to go through the entire sequence of steps regardless of which step is targeted in the sequence. This is the whole-task training method. For example, in a forward chaining program teaching 14 hand-washing steps, the child would perform the entire sequence every trial, even when the target step is only the first or second step. The teacher provides physical guidance for the nontarget step(s) of the behavioral chain. If a teacher uses the whole-task method, research has shown that using an effective prompt ahead of the student error on a given step is needed for acquisition (Day, 1987).

Another approach is called the partial-task training method. In this approach, the teacher would present only the part of the task that he or she wishes to target (or that the student has already acquired). For example, a teacher uses a forward chaining procedure for a task that has nine steps. Let us say that the student currently does not perform any of these steps independently. The first step is, therefore, the target step. The command to perform the task is given, e.g., "let's wash our hands." Once the student performs the first step, the teacher stops him or her. The next trial would begin by presenting the command again with the child performing the first step, we hope, with less prompting. Once the child acquires the first step to independence, the target step becomes the second step. The student would perform independently the first step and then be provided an effective prompt so that he performs step number two. When he performs the second step, the task is concluded and a new trial ensues. This process of adding a new target step and providing prompts at that step is continued with only the amount of the task encumbered being performed.

Both methods have been shown to be effective (Cooper, et. al., 2007). My preference is to utilize the partial-task method whenever possible. Some skills do not lend themselves easily to performing part of the skill in isolation and would mitigate the use of the partial-task training method (e.g., independent feeding). However, when feasible, the partial-task method allows the teacher to provide more training trials during the earlier part of the training program on small units of the complex behavior. As the child develops more independence, he or she performs greater lengths of the chain.

Graduated guidance is a third method and involves providing physical guidance wherever needed throughout the entire chain. The teacher always reinforces the child's behavior at the completion of the chain. It is slightly different from forward or backward chaining in that there is no target step. The teacher delivers and fades prompts as needed on all the steps of the chain. The emphasis is on giving minimal amounts of guidance, i.e., as little as necessary for the child to complete the chain. Graduated guidance relies on the delay of the prompts at various parts of the chain to teach the independent performance of the entire chain.

CHAPTER 4: SUMMARY TEST

(Answers on CD)

True or False

1. Reinforcing an approximation to a desired behavioral goal is called shaping.
2. Two dimensions of shaping are topography and volume.
3. Backward chaining involves a procedure where you start from the front of the chain and go backwards.
4. To develop complex behaviors, behavioral chaining methods including graduated guidance are necessary.

Chapter 5

BASELINE ASSESSMENT

Two types of behavioral assessments are applicable for educational settings. Each one serves a different purpose. One type of behavioral assessment delineates the extent of the behavior problem. The question addressed with this type of behavioral assessment is, "How frequent (or infrequent) is the target problem behavior?" This assessment allows the teacher to quantify the level of the target problem behavior **or** appropriate behavior. This type of assessment has been a hallmark of the behavioral model since its inception in school settings. I will term this type of assessment the **baseline (rate) assessment**, which is covered in this chapter in detail.

Another type of behavioral assessment addresses the contextual conditions under which that target behavior **occurs** (Bailey & Pyles, 1989; Cipani & Schock, 2007; Dunlap, Ferro, & DePerczel, 1994; Iwata, Dorsey, Slifer, Bauman, & Richman, 1982; Iwata, Vollmer, & Zarcone, 1990). This type of behavioral assessment answers the question "Why does the problem behavior occur at certain levels?" This form of assessment gathers information on the child's behavior and the contextual classroom variables that relate to the behavior (Dunlap, Kern-Dunlap, Clarke, & Robbins, 1991; Ervin, DuPaul, & Kern, 1998). I will term this type of behavioral assessment the *functional behavioral assessment,* which is extensively covered in the following chapter. The teacher needs information from both types of behavioral assessment to intervene effectively with problem behaviors.

CHARACTERISTICS OF BEHAVIORAL ASSESSMENT

Behavioral assessment constitutes a dramatic departure from traditional assessment approaches and methods. Six general characteristics of a behavioral assessment distinguish it from a traditional approach to assessment. These six characteristics are: (a) primary function of assessment is intervention, (b) focus of assessment is on current context, (c) direct measurement of a problem is paramount, (d) behavior is situational, (e) context variables are relevant, and (f) role of evaluation is to determine treatment effectiveness. These assumptions expand upon previous writings (Ciminero, 1977; Ciminero & Drabman, 1977; Cipani, 1990; Cone & Hawkins, 1977; Goldfried & Kent, 1972).

Primary Function is Intervention

In a behavioral assessment model, assessment and intervention are inextricably intertwined. Assessment activities are directly related to decisions made about the specific form and nature of the behavioral intervention. The data collected in a baseline rate assessment provide evidence of the extent of the problem. The functional behavioral assessment illustrates the environmental function of such a problem behavior. The proposed intervention matches this data by directing the intervention to the solution of the specific behavior problems.

Therefore, the primary result of a complete behavioral assessment (including both types) should be data that lead directly to the generation of a treatment or intervention that is suited for that problem. For example, identifying that a student with special needs engages in a high rate of inappropriate verbal behavior during teacher lessons indicates that this behavior should be targeted. One would not view such data and decide to target his shoe-tying skills. Data from a functional behavioral assessment may reveal that this behavior is effective in recruiting peer attention during teacher lessons. The teacher would then construct a specific intervention to account for such a function. In summary, these findings necessitate a specific, unique intervention.

Therefore, the *differential prescription of an intervention* is based on the obtained assessment data. One simply does not become a time-out expert and use it for all problems. Training someone to use just a hammer and giving him or her job as a carpenter would not lead to a great career choice. Not everything one encounters is a nail. Yet when one does not understand how to assess whether a hammer, screwdriver, or saw **would fix the problem**, a hammer looks like the right answer all the time.

Focus is on Current Context

With the primary function of assessment being the identification of a potential intervention strategy, an analysis of current conditions provides more useful information in performing this function of assessment. Therefore, the focus of a behavioral assessment is on analyzing current environmental variables and their role in the current problem behavior (Bailey & Pyles, 1989; Cipani & Schock, 2007; Cone & Hawkins, 1977). Such data would allow the teacher to favor certain intervention procedures and rule out others. It would be unnecessary to determine what the discipline method was when a child was four years old if he or she is now 14 years old and has been suspended for making disparaging remarks toward the teacher.

Direct Measurement of Problem is Paramount

A direct measurement of behavior is the most preferred method of measurement for a behavioral assessment. A direct measurement of behavior is the *direct observation of the behavior of interest in the setting of interest* (Hersen & Barlow, 1976). Behaviors are operationally defined in discrete, observable, and quantifiable terms to allow for reliable measurement.

Direct measurement requires direct observation of the student(s) engaging in the target behavior in identified target setting(s). Measuring the specific problem behavior in the problem setting(s) qualifies as a valid method of assessment in and of itself. One need not measure a phenomenon that substitutes for the "real life" behavior. For example, if a child exhibits too much out-of-seat behavior during math class, then a behavioral assessment would be concerned with the measurement of out-of-seat behavior during math class. Out-of-seat behavior is referred to as the target behavior, and math class is referred to as the target setting. If out-of-seat behavior is also problematic during reading class, then the measurement of out-of-seat behavior in that context would also be necessary. Any measure other than a direct measurement of out-of-seat behavior in the target setting is an *unsuitable proxy,* particularly when designing an intervention based on such data.

Unobservable traits such as being understanding, respectful, incorrigible, psychotic, ill-mannered, and appreciative are not suitable terms for direct classroom measurement. Such terms require too much inference and subjectivity in the scoring of real-life phenomena. For example, a teacher reports that a student in her class is disrespectful. What would someone see if a child was being respectful? If one does not use specific, concrete observable terms, detection of this phenomenon may not be accurate. The measurement of such an ambiguous term will be flawed from the outset.

Suppose a teacher decides to measure the frequency of disrespectful behavior. She views the student on day one as being disrespectful during four instances based on rude remarks made to her. On day two, she overlooks rude remarks as being instances of disrespect (having been desensitized to their graphic nature the previous day). However, she does count two instances when the child gets up from his seat while she is talking, which she considers disrespectful behavior. You can see the problem. While she forgave the three rude remarks as being disrespectful on day two, she added a new phenomenon to the ever-changing definition of disrespectful behavior. Such variation in what constitutes disrespect would wreak havoc on accurate measurement of the phenomenon. The more subjective the judgment is regarding the occurrence of the problem, the greater the potential measurement flaw. Further, subjective judgments also make effective intervention more difficult (White & Bailey, 1990).

Behavior is Situational

A teacher should not assume that the level of any given target behavior is constant across all conditions. For example, a child may be more aggressive on the playground than during music class. A student may have a greater rate of raising his hand to be recognized with the special education teacher present than when the aide is alone in the classroom. Therefore, the teacher needs to measure the target behavior in all target settings or situations to achieve an understanding of the nature and extent of the problem behavior.

Context is Relevant

In a behavioral assessment, the analysis of the child's behavior is taken in the context of the environmental conditions. Therefore, a behavioral assessment involves not only an assessment of the rate of problematic behavior but also an understanding of the social environment. The rate of target behavior(s) is understood in the context of the ecological conditions under which it occurs. Therefore, the assessment process must occur in the child's natural environment(s) and determine the role of context variables. Therefore, teachers need to be intimately involved in the data collection.

Evaluation is Essential

The process of assessment leads to evaluation. Because the primary function of assessment is to prescribe a potentially successful intervention, the evaluation of the intervention utilizes the same measures to determine the efficacy of the treatment strategy. Evaluation of treatment efficacy is such an important component of a behavioral approach that it directly interfaces with assessment. The target behaviors are measured before, during and after intervention to determine treatment efficacy. Each intervention must "prove itself" with changes in the targeted behavior of the individual student. If an intervention does not produce a desired change in behavior, the teacher makes alterations in the intervention based on the resulting data.

DIRECT MEASUREMENT OF PROBLEM BEHAVIOR

A baseline rate assessment entails a direct measure of the target behavioral problem(s). One can see a child hit someone. One can also see a child fail to comply with a teacher's request. These events are observable and allow the teacher to count the number of times the behavior occurs. A behavioral assessment could accurately quantify and measure such behaviors. In contrast, one cannot measure a child's hyperactivity by counting each instance of the phenomenon. Imagine you are an instructional aide in a hypothetical classroom. A teacher has asked you to make a tally mark every time you see a particular student of hers displaying hyperactivity in the classroom. You do this for the next hour and a half. At the end of the observation period, you report to the teacher that you saw this student become hyperactive twice during the session. She looks at you in amazement! She thought there were at least ten instances of hyperactivity in the first 45 minutes. Your judgment about the phenomenon "hyperactivity" certainly differed from hers. Are you at fault for such inaccurate data? Is the teacher being too critical? The answer is neither of you are to blame. The term *being directly measured* was so ill-defined, it allowed for significant subjective judgments about what real-life events constituted examples of this student's hyperactivity. A direct measure of the phenomenon referred to as hyperactivity requires a behavioral description of the problem.

Delineate Behavioral Description of Problem

To collect direct observational data, you must develop behavioral descriptions that require little inference in measuring the target problem. Therefore, before you collect baseline data on the problem, you must define or **categorize** the problem(s) into specific, observable behaviors. We call these *target behaviors* in that they will be targeted for intervention. For example, observable behaviors such as sitting, standing, crawling, walking, running, hitting, spitting, kicking, getting out of a seat, breaking class rules (if defined in some manner), and completing seatwork allow the teacher to measure a problem behavior accurately. One method of devising behavioral descriptions for problem behaviors is through the research literature.

Here is a good example of defining a complex behavior into observable entities. Zeilberger, Sampen, and Sloane (1968) measured bossing behavior as any occurrence of one student directing another child or adult to do (or not do) something. As you can see, such a definition makes the counting of such a phenomenon possible. If the researchers had just left it to the observer to determine when the child was being "bossy," it would have proved more difficult to measure reliably such a phenomenon.

On-task or attending behavior is often measured as a behavior indicative of student engagement in the instructional process. Walker and Buckley (1968) define attending behavior as the **student's** looking at the assignment pages, working problems or recording problems. Conversely, nonattending would be any behavior that is exclusive of those three observable entities.

In some circumstances, the use of the definitions from research studies may not fit the needs of the particular classroom problem behavior. The teacher would have to develop his or her own behavioral description that represents the problem to be measured. A method that can facilitate this task is the "incident method." The incident method requires the teacher or referral source to generate specific examples or incidents representative of the problem. This can often lead to identifying the observable components of the problem. For example, in a case consultation that attempted to define what the teacher meant by hyperactive, I (the behavioral consultant) asked the teacher to identify specific incidents of a child's hyperactivity. The teacher shared the following four incidents with me.[1]

1. "I'll tell him to finish his work, and he always manages to get distracted by other things and rarely finishes his assigned task" (i.e., behavioral description is the failure to complete task assignments);
2. "I have to repeat myself many times before he desists in an activity I have told him to stop!" (i.e., behavioral description is the failure to desist activity upon the command "stop" being given);
3. "He tears up his papers and materials at times" (i.e., behavioral description is the tearing or destruction of property/materials); and
4. "He occasionally gets angry and frustrated and hits other kids!" (i.e., hitting peers).

Based on this information, the following target behaviors were selected for assessment: (a) completing assigned task, (b) desisting activity upon the command "Stop!" (c) tearing or destroying property/material, and (d) hitting peers. The teacher could then observe the occurrence of each of these four target behaviors and count them objectively.

---

1. Facsimile of actual verbiage reported here.

Method of Measuring Behavior

Once you have devised a behavioral description, you need to designate the method of quantifying such observable entities. Quantifying a behavior refers to how the teacher will score or count the target behavior. There are four methods of measuring behavior: (a) frequency, (b) duration, (c) interval recording, and (d) time sampling methods.

FREQUENCY MEASUREMENT. *Frequency* measurement involves counting the number of occurrences of a target behavior (Bailey & Bostow, 1981; Hersen & Barlow, 1976). Every time the behavior occurs, regardless of the length of time it occurs, it is counted. For example, the frequency of eye contact in children with autism and mental retardation was measured as to its occurrence after the verbal prompt "Look at me!" was given (Foxx, 1977). Using this method of measuring eye contact, if eye contact is made within the time limit, it is scored as an occurrence regardless of its length. One can also use frequency counts to measure completion of assignments. In one study concerned with increasing the low rates of completion of class assignments, the teacher counted the number of completed assignments for each child each day across different assignments (Robinson, Newby, & Ganzell, 1981).

Frequency data are easy to collect if the behavior being measured has a discrete and distinct onset and end. For example, a teacher frequently complains that one of her students gets up from his seat. A baseline rate assessment can determine how often this behavior happens. This teacher can count the number of incidents of out-of-seat behavior. Out-of-seat behavior begins when any part of this student's behind comes off the seat and ends when the student's behind contacts the seat in full. Each time this sequence of events occur, an incident is recorded.

Suppose we are also interested in this student's rate of verbal disruption. We identify the onset of an episode of verbal disruption as any occurrence when the student initiates any rude comment, unauthorized statement in class, or noise that is inappropriate for a classroom setting. The single episode of verbal disruption ends when the student is quiet for at least a five-second period. Following that five seconds, the counting of another episode of verbal disruption would require the same onset and ending phenomenon. If we had more than one student, the criteria for defining and measuring both behaviors would be

Table 5.1
SAMPLE DATA SHEET FOR FOUR STUDENTS

Student's Name	Out-of-seat Occurrences	Verbal Disruption Occurrences
Larry	xxxxxx	xxx
Moe	xx	0
Sarah	0	0
Cassandra	x	0

the same. Table 5.1 provides a sample data sheet measuring the frequency of two hypothetical target behaviors, the number of out-of-seat occurrences, and the number of verbal disruptions (unauthorized talking) during a reading period on 12/7, for four students (initials given).

The data presented in Table 5.1 depicts the rate of target behavior for four students. Each time the teacher observed an instance of the behavior, she recorded it with a tally mark (x) in the correct row (student who exhibited the behavior) and column (which behavior was observed). The teacher used the behavioral descriptions presented and defined an episode with the onset and ending criteria. With that definition, Larry had six instances of out-of-seat behavior in this reading period and three instances of verbal disruption. Sarah did not engage in either target behavior whereas Cassandra had one instance of out-of-seat behavior but no instances of verbal disruption. The rate of out-of-seat behavior ranged from a low of zero to a high of six occurrences (frequency measure) for these four students on this particular day.

Let us say that a hypothetical student has a problem with unauthorized talking to peers during seat assignments. The student's teacher estimates that it occurs a lot, but she cannot be sure if it usually exceeds ten occurrences a day or not. She begins a behavioral assessment by measuring unauthorized talking to peers directly. The teacher defines the target problem behavior as any occurrence of talking to a peer during this time. The episode ends when the student is quiet for five seconds. A new episode would then be recorded if the onset of the behavior was observed subsequently. Over a nine-day period, she observed the following rate of unauthorized talking for each day: 7, 6, 8, 13, 9, 3, 6, 4, and 4.

In research studies, observers learn to score immediately the occurrence of the behavior(s) according to a pre-specified set of criteria (Cipani & McLaughlin, 1983). In classrooms, without the luxury of having observers whose sole function is data collection, the teacher must be the data collector. Therefore, the teacher should develop a measurement instrument that is feasible given his or her instructional duties in the classroom.

DURATION MEASURES. This type of data system involves determining the cumulative length of time a behavior occurred in a defined period of the school day. The length of time a behavior occurs can be a more important and sensitive measure of behavior than frequency counts. Some behaviors may occur infrequently, yet the duration for each episode is extremely lengthy. For example, a child may have, on the average, about one tantrum a day. However, its length of occurrence can be 30–50 minutes in duration. Therefore, simply providing a frequency count of this child's tantrums might not provide an accurate and representative view of the level of the problem. In these circumstances, the teacher might prefer a duration measure over just a frequency count. Table 5.2 provides a sample data sheet measuring the duration of out-of-seat behavior across four hypothetical students.

The data presented in Table 5.3 depicts the duration of out-of-seat behavior for the same four hypothetical students. Each time the teacher observed an instance of out-of-seat behavior, she started a stop watch that recorded the length of time the student remained out of his or her seat. Larry had four instances of out-of-seat behavior, but his cumulative time was only 58 seconds. However, Cassandra, who was out only once, had a lengthy interim of three minutes and 25 seconds. Duration data can sometimes present a picture that is more accurate

Table 5.2
DURATION MEASURE FOR FOUR STUDENTS

Student Name	*Out-of-seat Duration*
Larry	3", 40", 10' 5"
Moe	25", 55"
Sarah	0
Cassandra	3' 25"

regarding the extent of the problem than simple frequency counts.

To be able to use a stopwatch to measure duration of an episode, you must define the behavioral description as to its onset and offset. For example, one can define the onset of a tantrum episode as any of the following behavior(s): crying, flailing on the floor, or banging furniture with hands, feet, or other part of the body while standing up or lying down on the ground. A given tantrum episode terminates when these behaviors cease for at least ten seconds. If one of these behaviors starts after ten seconds has elapsed, it constitutes a new episode, and the duration of the episode is measured for that new event. For example, a paraeducator recorded four episodes of tantrum behavior of the following durations, 3', 4'25", 10'10" and 30" within a 30-minute period. The cumulative time was 18'15".

RESPONSE LATENCY. Response latency measurement is a special form of a duration measure (Cooper et al., 2007). Latency measures quantify how quickly a behavior occurs from some designated start point. The length of time the behavior occurs is not relevant, but the length of time it takes the student to perform the behavior is of importance. Here is a circumstance in which latency measures would be of value. A teacher gives directives to his students to line up **outside** after morning recess. While some students line up right away, others may take too long to follow that directive. One student in this teacher's class has a problem with lining up after morning recess. Upon hearing the command to "line up," he often will kick a soccer ball and then proceeds to chase it. All the other students have to wait until he gets in line to go inside the classroom. Measuring the frequency of his compliance to the directive may not give a true picture of the problem since this student eventually gets in line. However, recording the amount of time that elapses before any student complies with the directive to line up reveals the extent of the problem. Five days of baseline data were collected on this student's latency to comply to this directive. The length of time it took this student to get in line was always greater than five minutes from the time of the directive.

INTERVAL RECORDING. Interval recording involves dividing an observation session into a number of continuous, equally timed intervals. Interval lengths are commonly either 5, 10, or 15 seconds. Therefore, in a 30-minute observation session, there would be 360 intervals using a five-second interval recording method, 180 intervals if the in-

Table 5.3
INTERVAL RECORDING DATA SHEET

Min./Interval	1	2	3	4	5	6
1				o t	t	
2	t			o t	o	
3			t		t	t

terval length is ten seconds, and 90 intervals if the interval length is 15 seconds. Table 5.3 reveals an observation sheet illustrating the first three minutes of a session using ten-second observation lengths measuring two behaviors: out-of-seat behavior (designated by an "o" in the respective box) and talking out (designated by "t" in the respective box).

Table 5.3 illustrates that in minute 1, interval 4, both behaviors occurred within that interval. Interval recording methods generally calculate a percentage of occurrences for each behavior across the entire observational session. One can compute the percentage of occurrence by adding up the total number of intervals in which the behavior occurred and dividing this number by the total number of intervals in the session. Using the data in Table 5.4, the number of intervals in which the teacher recorded talk-outs was six. The total number of intervals in the three-minute session was 18. This presents a ratio of 6/18, or 33 percent occurrence of talking-out behavior. The ratio for out-of-seat instances was 3/18, or 16.6 percent.

There are two methods for scoring behavior in an interval recording system (Powell, Martindale, & Kulp, 1975): (a) whole interval method and (b) partial interval method. The whole interval method scores the occurrence of the behavior only if the behavior occurs for the entire length of the interval. Therefore, if a system designates intervals of ten seconds, the child must exhibit the behavior for the entire ten-second interval in order for it to be scored as occurring. If it does not occur for even a brief period of time within a given interval, the teacher does not score it. The partial interval method scores the occurrence of the behavior if the behavior occurs for any part of the interval. Therefore, if the child exhibits the behavior for only two of the ten seconds of a given interval, it would be scored as occurring in that interval. Using this method, the observer has to determine if the behavior occurred in any part of the interval for it to be recorded in that interval.

The method of scoring that is best suited for any particular classroom observation is a function of interval length. With intervals of longer length (e.g., 30 seconds, 1 minute), the whole interval method will provide an underestimate of the level of behavior (Powell et al., 1975). In the partial interval method, with intervals over 30 seconds, an overestimate will occur (Powell, Martindale, Kulp, Martindale, & Bauman, 1977). The larger the interval, the greater is the discrepancy between these two methods of scoring (whole and partial interval) and the "true duration of behavior." Suffice to say, intervals of five or ten seconds minimize such a discrepancy. Short intervals such as these are advocated when utilizing an interval recording system.

A more feasible interval system for classroom use is *momentary time sampling* (Harop & Daniels, 1986; Powell et al., 1977). It requires the observer to watch the student for only a portion of each interval of the observation session. For example, an observer may watch a student the last five seconds of every five-minute interval of the observation session. Using this format, the observer watches only during a specified part of each interval. The observer then uses a partial interval method of scoring the target behavior. The number of intervals in which an observer scores a behavior over the total number of intervals is the percentage of occurrence. Momentary time sampling recording systems work well because the teacher can temporarily integrate data collection with other instructional duties (McLaughlin, 1984).

Collect Baseline Data

Collecting data on the target problem or appropriate behavior(s) before the teacher uses any formal behavioral intervention or instructional condition is called the baseline condition. We call the data collected *baseline data.* The purposes of baseline data collection are the following: (a) to determine the extent (or level) of the reported problem, (b) to provide valuable information for the initial behavioral standard for reinforcement once intervention is undertaken and (c) to allow for a pre-post intervention comparison to determine the efficacy of the treatment plan.

Data on the same target behavior are collected over time within the baseline condition. This can be in the form of a daily measurement

Table 5.4
FREQUENCY OF OUT-OF-SEAT BEHAVIOR
ACROSS FIVE ADDITIONAL SESSIONS

Session	1	2	3	4	5	6
Frequency	1	6	9	8	14	10

within a certain instructional period. The daily measurement of the student's target behavior continues until he or she achieves a level of stability in the baseline condition. Collecting data on the target behavior repeatedly over a period of time is essential for several reasons. Suppose you want to determine if a student's out-of-seat behavior is at problematic levels. Would it make sense to watch him for just one half-hour session? Suppose on that day of observation he had his best day of the month. He got out of his seat just one time. You might conclude that he is a good student. Table 5.4 depicts what happens when the teacher extends the baseline condition over five more observation sessions. The data show that an inaccurate picture would have been portrayed on this student if just one baseline session were conducted. He gets out of his seat frequently during the additional sessions. As you can see, observing someone for just one session is inadequate. Collecting data over a number of sessions until a stable pattern evolves is critical for a more accurate portrayal of behavior. In contrast, selecting one day of observation can produce deceptive results.

Baseline data are usually graphed in an x, y coordinate system. The y-axis represents the measure of behavior, e.g., frequency, duration, or percentage of occurrence. The x-axis represents time, e.g., sessions, days, weeks, etc. Graphing data, either in line or bar graph form, make it easier to view the level of the behavior over repeated measurements. Figure 5.1 presents ten days of baseline data collection by a hypothetical teacher. Using an interval recording system (partial interval scoring system) across a one-hour language arts period, the teacher collected data on a student's percentage of off-task behavior. The value of each data point is given for viewer convenience. This hypothetical child's off-task rate was between 25 and 60 percent with a mean of 43.8 percent. The extent of his off-task rate during the baseline period is now evident in quantifiable form.

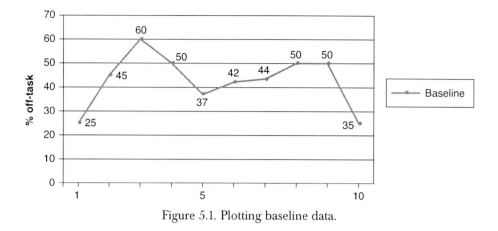

Figure 5.1. Plotting baseline data.

On what types of behavior should the teacher collect data during the baseline condition? Obviously, the teacher should collect quantitative data on identified target behavior problems. In addition to measuring target problem behavior, it is wise to also measure appropriate student behavior as well during baseline conditions. On-task behavior is a measure of how well a student is attending to the teacher presentation or working on the assignment. On-task or attending behavior often correlates (inversely) with problem behavior, so the teacher should measure this during the baseline (and intervention) condition with referrals for problem behavior. When problem behaviors occur frequently during instructional periods, on-task behavior is usually low. Therefore, the intervention for problem behavior should also affect on-task rates (when found low in baseline).

We usually define *on-task behavior* as facial orientation to the work assigned (e.g., reading the book or writing answers on paper) for seatwork assignments. For teacher-presented lectures, we define on-task behavior as face-to-face orientation with teacher (unless directed to read or write during the lecture, then the seatwork definition applies). Any behaviors that do not fall into these designations do not constitute on-task behaviors, but rather off-task behaviors.

A hypothetical example of baseline data for on-task behavior and inappropriate classroom behavior over an eight-day period appears below (Table 5.5). The third-grade teacher uses a momentary time sampling method to determine on-task behavior of one of her students. The teacher uses a frequency count to determine the rate of in-

Table 5.5
BASELINE DATA FOR TWO BEHAVIORS

Baseline Data								
DAY	*1*	*2*	*3*	*4*	*5*	*6*	*7*	*8*
on-task rate %	40	60	30	40	80	20	60	40
# inappropriate behaviors	7	6	7	3	2	12	5	10

appropriate behaviors defined as violating any one of three classroom rules.

The data in Table 5.5 illustrate a range of this student's on-task behavior during baseline from a low of 20 percent (**day six**) to a high of 80 percent (**day five**). Additionally, the range of inappropriate comments is from a low of two occurrences (day five) to a high of 12 occurrences (day 6). These data can also be depicted graphically, if desired.

The teacher can also collect data on the percentage of assignments completed during baseline measurement. Similar to on-task behavior, students who are engaging in problem behavior frequently have a lower percentage of assignments completed than other students. The criteria for judging an assignment as being complete are dictated by the specifics of the assignment given and are usually easy to measure. The teacher uses the number of specific class assignments and their deadlines for completion to derive the percentage of completion (see example below for illustration). The example below in Table 5.6 illustrates the completion rate for four assignments given one morning to be at 33 percent (i.e., 2/6 completed).

Table 5.6
DATA SHEET FOR ASSIGNMENT COMPLETION

	Assignment	*Completed*
1	(20 minutes)	No
2	(10 minutes)	Yes
3	(45 minutes)	Yes
4	(45 minutes)	No
5	(45 minutes)	No
6	(45 minutes)	No

Baseline data also allows one to determine the success of an intervention on target behavior. Too often, a teacher determines student behavioral progress by subjective judgments. All too often, we hear statements such as "he seems to be making progress in his behavior." Collecting baseline data is very important for documenting progress. The teacher can compare the baseline rate of a behavior with the rate obtained during a behavioral intervention to make a quantitative judgment about progress. If an intervention is successful in changing a target behavior, a graph of the baseline and intervention rates of behavior will illustrate that.

In evaluating a change in the rate of a behavior from baseline to intervention, the teacher should observe the following on the graphed or tabled data between the two conditions: First, there should be an evident change in the desired direction (either increase or decrease in rate, percentage, or duration). Second, there should be a significant difference in the mean level between baseline and intervention conditions. Further, there should be little or no overlap with data points between the two conditions.

Self-Monitoring

Self-monitoring, self-recording, and self-observation are terms that refer to the student as the observer of his or her own behavior. Training the student to self-observe and record target behaviors can be extremely useful, especially considering the instructional duties required of the teacher in addition to data collection. Teachers can conduct training in self-monitoring with the student in the following phases: (a) identifying occurrences or nonoccurrences of target behaviors, (b) scoring the occurrence of behavior (i.e., frequency, duration), and (c) actual self-monitoring and data analysis.

Having students self-monitor their on-task behavior is very useful (Gunter, Venn, Patrick, Miller, & Kelly, 2003; McLaughlin, 1983, 1984; Prater, Hogan, & Miller, 1992). A research study illustrates this process. Four children with learning disabilities were taught to self-monitor attention to classroom activities and academic production (Harris, 1986). In teaching the children to monitor their attention to task, a tone from a tape recorder initiated the self-monitoring procedure. Upon hearing the tone, the children would ask themselves, "Was I paying attention?" and then place a check in either the "yes" or "no" column of a piece of paper on their desk used for recording purposes. The teacher gave the children a new piece of paper each day, and the children self-monitored their attention to task five days a week. In addition to self-monitoring of attention to task, these four students also learned to monitor their work production during spelling practice. These children learned to count the number of words written during a practice period in spelling and record this number on a graph in their spelling files.

As portrayed in the above study (Harris, 1986), self-monitoring of on-task behavior in classrooms can occur readily with a brief momentary time-sampling system. This system requires the student to record whether he or she is on task at the point when an audible beep is produced. For example, a teacher constructs a self-monitoring system for a 40-minute instructional reading period. She designs a beeper system that has 30 audible beeps of differing interval lengths for this time period. The students learn to score their behavior as on task at the time of the beep (or not). Once the student records the data, he or she returns to task until the next beep and proceeds in the same manner. Table 5.7 illustrates a ten-beep observation system. The hypothetical student recorded the status of her on-task behavior at ten beeps and determined that she was on task for four of them (designated by a plus). This gives a 40 percent rate of on-task behavior for this observation period. It would be important for the teacher to check the validity of such data by randomly observing the student during select beeps. For more information on using the beeper system classwide, the reader should consult the Cipani (2008) reference.

The teacher can also use self-monitoring with target problem behaviors. An example of this form of self-monitoring involved the targeting of high rate disruptive behaviors in a workshop vocational setting for adults with mild to moderate mental retardation. The behaviors targeted include teasing, swearing, name calling, threatening, and yelling (Gardner, Cole, Berry, & Nowinski, 1983). In a one-day session, the adults learned to record the occurrence of these behaviors by resetting a timer (set originally for a designated duration of time), contingent upon the occurrence of any of those behaviors. If the timer reached the duration specified (e.g., 15 minutes), the clients then accessed reinforcement.

Self-monitoring is obviously less expensive and more convenient

Table 5.7
MOMENTARY TIME SAMPLING
OF ON-TASK BEHAVIOR

Beep	On-Task
1	+
2	–
3	+
4	+
5	–
6	–
7	+
8	–
9	–
10	–
% on-task 4/10 = 40%	

to employ than providing trained observers in the classroom or other environment(s). However, the teacher cannot take for granted the accuracy of self-monitoring. Random spot-checks of reliability on self-monitoring help to produce accurate data (Taplin & Reid, 1973). Having students who self-monitor match an outside observer's data increases the reliability of self-monitoring data (McLaughlin, 1984; McLaughlin, Burgess, & Sackville-West, 1981).

SUMMARY

This chapter presented the requirements for a behavioral assessment that measures the extent of the problem, which is called a baseline-rate assessment. While this chapter delineated the methods for determining if a behavior is in need of intervention, it does not reveal why the problem behavior is occurring. Chapter 6 will provide the methods for determining the function of the problem behavior, i.e., how to decode its purpose or environmental function.

CHAPTER 5: SUMMARY TEST

(Answers on CD)

True or False

1. Rating the level of a behavior does not constitute an objective direct measure of behavior.
2. Because behavior is situational, the student should be observed in the setting of interest.
3. A behavioral assessment can incorporate personality measures via paper and pencil tests.
4. A baseline rate of a student's incorrigibility would be a reliable behavioral measurement.
5. A baseline rate of a student's out-of-seat behavior would constitute a reliable behavioral measurement.
6. The method that requires a teacher to record the length of time a behavior occurs is a duration measure.

A short, fill-in-the-blanks test can be found in Appendix A.

Chapter 6

FUNCTIONAL BEHAVIORAL ASSESSMENT (FBA)

The previous chapter detailed the measurement requirements for determining the extent of the problem behavior(s). With the collection of such data, classroom personnel can make decisions about the necessity for individualized behavioral intervention. While it is essential to know what the current baseline rate of a problem behavior is, such information does not provide any evidence regarding its behavioral function. To know that a child has between four to ten incidents of oppositional behavior each week does not present one with any workable hypothesis about why oppositional behavior is occurring at such a high rate. To gather such information, one must conduct a Functional Behavioral Assessment or FBA.

HISTORICAL OVERVIEW OF FBA

While FBA is a relatively new term for education personnel, its roots extend back to the middle of the twentieth century. The assessment methodologies involved in an FBA are an outgrowth of the field of applied behavior analysis (ABA). The field of ABA has always made experimental analyses demonstrating the effect of certain variables on learner outcome paramount. Research in animal laboratories in the 1940s and 1950s provided the scientific methodology for the experimental analysis of human behavior. These early researchers and clinicians in ABA changed behavior in classrooms, university clinics, hospitals, and institutional settings in the 1960s and 1970s.

These early demonstrations of systematic behavior change primarily involved the manipulation of powerful contingencies for student behavior. As an example, a study demonstrated that the teacher could change the frequency of two target behaviors consisting of student off-task behavior and rule violations by manipulating reinforcement contingencies (Iwata & Bailey, 1974). In one of the reinforcement contingency conditions, the teacher used a response cost procedure. All students received ten points at the beginning of the day. When a student engaged in either of the target behaviors, that student lost a point. A student lost a point for each occurrence of off-task behavior or violation of a classroom rule. A behavioral standard designated the number of lost points that a student could not exceed before losing the daily reinforcer. The rate of both target behaviors dropped significantly under this condition **when** compared to a baseline. Further, such a response cost condition was equally effective when compared to a reinforcement condition.

In the Iwata and Bailey (1974) study, it was not necessary to determine why a student broke a classroom rule, or why he or she was off task at various points of time. Like many research studies of its time, the application of differential consequences for appropriate and/or target problem behavior was sufficient to make substantial changes **in** child behavior. An analysis of the maintaining contingency was not entertained, nor was it apparently necessary (see *Journal of Applied Behavior Analysis,* in particular 1968–1979 for many examples of the powerful effects of manipulating contrived contingencies). While understanding the role of function had been elucidated as a requisite for behavior analysts to derive treatment (Bijou, Peterson, & Ault, 1968), such did not seem necessary with the problems and contexts targeted in the early years of ABA. Behavioral researchers and clinicians produced substantial behavior change by contriving a contingency between the target behavior and a powerful consequence that would override the current functional reinforcer for the problem behavior (Mace, Lalli, & Pinter-Lalli, 1991).

The success of this approach in school settings, called *contingency management,* was substantial in comparison to other intervention approaches of the time. Successful applications of ABA in the 1960s and 1970s could be primarily described as the following: First, identify the target behavior. Next, determine whether one wishes to increase it or decrease it. Following that, contrive a reinforcement contingency if the goal is to increase the behavior. If the target behavior is one in which a decrease is sought, provide a differential reinforcement strategy for that behavior. In some cases, consider providing a punishing consequence for the problem behavior. This approach remained effective as long as the contrived reinforcement and/or punishment contingency far outweighed the functional reinforcer at the time.

The impetus for an analysis of a problem behavior's environmental function would be spawned by several research findings involving the ineffectiveness of contingent time-out (Plummer, Baer, & LeBlanc, 1977; Risley, 1968; Solnick, Rincover, & Peterson, 1977). In the study conducted by Solnick, et al. (1977), a six-year-old child with autism was subjected to time-outs contingent upon tantrum behavior. Such a contingency produced an increase in tantrums, not a decrease! The researchers anecdotally noted that when the teacher placed this girl in time-outs, she would engage in self-stimulatory behavior at will during the time-out. Time-out was not effective when its production resulted in an escape from a less preferred context to a more preferred context.

The role of context in the analysis of problem behavior became more pertinent in the late 1970s and early 1980s in several research studies (Carr, Newsom, & Binkoff, 1976; Carr, Newsom, & Binkoff, 1980; Weeks & Gaylord-Ross, 1981). For example, Carr et al. (1976) conducted a study testing the effects of two contexts on the rate of aggressive behavior. The participants were children with developmental disabilities who displayed unacceptable levels of aggressive behavior. Two test conditions were alternated in the study to determine their role in aggressive behavior. In one test condition, the teacher presented instructional task demands to the child (called the demand condition). In a second test condition, the teacher presented no demands during that period (called the no-demand condition).

The results showed differential rates of aggression between the two test conditions. Presenting task demands resulted in increases in aggressive behavior. The no-demand condition resulted in little or no aggressive behavior for the same two children. Given the material presented in Chapters 1 and 2 of this text, these findings make sense. These researchers examined the behavioral effects of presenting and removing demands. When presenting demands, the teacher altered the child's motivational condition to that of a state of aversion, i.e., an

MC for escape behavior. Concurrently, removing demands in the no-demand condition abated that motivating condition. Therefore, one could not simply explain aggressive behavior in these students as something that just happens or the inevitable result of their disability. They are not driven to aggress against others simply because they have mental retardation! Nor does an explanation of their behavior involving early life experiences (ala psychodynamic theory) seem plausible. The display of aggression had more to do with what the current environment was demanding of them rather than their resolution of the phallic stage. In 1976, this research was groundbreaking in its analysis of the role of context on problematic behavior.

In a subsequent experiment within the Carr et al. (1976) study, these researchers demonstrated empirically that the socially mediated function of aggression could explain why such behavior occurred to task demands. In one test condition, aggression resulted in the removal of the task demand. In the other condition, aggression did not produce escape from tasks. The results should be of no surprise to you in the year 2011 but again were quite remarkable in 1977. When aggression produced escape from the task demand, aggression rates were high in that condition. When aggression did not produce escape, aggression decreased. This demonstrated the role of the social environment in maintaining aggressive behavior.

This line of research brought up a number of questions. Why are task-demands an aversive condition for these children? What can a teacher do if children with severe disabilities find instructional tasks aversive? Could the degree of aversion to instructional tasks be altered by the manner in which teachers' present instruction? In a classic study, Weeks & Gaylord-Ross (1981) first demonstrated a sharp contrast in rates of problem behavior when the student received easy tasks versus difficult tasks. The rate of problem behavior increased in the expected direction—higher rates of problem behavior with difficult tasks. This research extended the findings of previous research in that it identified a very plausible reason for the task aversion of these children in the study. Task demands that involved difficult material, i.e., the students were not adept with solving such problems, was the condition related to high rates of problem behavior.

How can one solve such a problem with difficult material? The nature of the educational system dictates that teachers assign challenging tasks at some point. Teachers have to present new tasks for students in order to have them acquire new skills. Simply having students work on tasks that they are already capable of performing would not result in significant progress in skill acquisition. The solution to this dilemma was found in this same study (Weeks & Gaylord-Ross, 1981). How one teaches a difficult task to children with severe disabilities makes all the difference in the world. Their study compared traditional methods of teaching various discrimination tasks against a methodology termed **errorless-learning**. Researchers measured the rate of student problems across both experimental conditions. Results showed that the use of errorless-learning strategies for teaching the difficult tasks had the effect of reducing problem behavior to low levels. This methodology was effective not only in keeping problem behaviors low (by reducing the aversive aspect of the instructional presentation), but also in enhancing acquisition. In contrast, traditional methods of teaching the difficult tasks resulted in elevated rates of problem behavior.

With these initial studies, there was a growing, compelling argument for understanding behavioral function to solve complex behavioral problems. The scientific apex of an analysis of behavioral function would be a landmark study conducted by Dr. Brian Iwata and his research colleagues at the Johns Hopkins School of Medicine. They developed an ingenious method of determining the possible function of problem behavior (Iwata, Dorsey, Slifer, Bauman & Richman, 1982). They referred to their research methodology as a functional analysis of behavior (FAB), and their research examined the self-injurious behavior of children with disabilities.

Iwata and colleagues designed an experimental testing protocol that mimicked the possible controlling environmental variables of a client's self-injury. They found that they could deliver such a protocol in the clinic setting. The FAB methodology presented four brief test conditions under which the researchers' evaluated self-injury rates: (a) attention, (b) demand, (c) alone, (d) play or enriched environment (Iwata et al., 1982). In the attention condition, contingent upon an incident of self-injury, the therapist would deliver brief physical contact and attention in the form of some statement (e.g., "please don't hit yourself"). The therapist implemented this contingency for each self-injurious incident to mimic the natural environment producing attention for such behavior. If the child's self-injury was currently a function of adult attention in his home or school environments, then such a contingency would occur at some schedule. By providing attention for the child's display of self-injury, the clinic mimicked real-life contingencies when attention was the desired event for the child.

To test a different function for self-injury, the therapist implemented a second test condition termed the demand condition. In the demand condition, the therapist terminated an instructional demand for 30 seconds with an incident of self-injury. The task was re-presented after that time, and the contingency was produced again with each new incident of self-injury. This test condition mimicked what people in the social environment would do if the **child used** self-injury to escape task demands. In other words, self-injury became functional in terminating the instructional tasks. If a given child's self-injury were functioning to escape task demands, then the rate of self-injury would increase whenever the therapist conducted this test condition. A third test condition, called the alone condition, was the test condition for nonsocially mediated functions. Finally, the play-enriched environment was the control condition for socially mediated functions.

If self-injury served a given function, then the rate of it would exacerbate under that condition relative to the other conditions. Iwata et al. (1982) found clear differences in the self-injury rates for the majority of the children in this study. In summary, it was possible to derive a behavioral function in a clinical setting by experimentally testing one condition against others. Since this initial study, there have been many studies using this experimental methodology for determining behavioral function and then designing a functional treatment that produces desired behavioral changes (Carr, Taylor, Wallender, & Reiss, 1996; Derby, Wacker, Sasso, Steege, Northrup, Cigrand, & Amus, 1992; Ervin, DuPaul, & Kern, 1998;. DuPaul & Ervin, 1996; Iwata, Dorsey, Slifer, Bauman, & Richman, 1982; Iwata, Pace, Cowdery, & Miltenberger, 1994; Iwata & Smith, 2007; Iwata, Vollmer, & Zarcone, 1990; Kennedy & Souza, 1995; Mace, Lalli, & Pinter-Lalli, 1991; Zarcone, & Fisher, 1996).

While the research base for FBA and derived functional treatments proliferated through the 1980s and early 1990s, such a methodology did not find a receptive audience in school settings until some unfortunate circumstances in the 1990s in California. As a result of abusive practices occurring in special education settings termed "behavior modification" by some special education teachers deploying such practice, litigation was promulgated against the employing school districts (P. Hunt, personal communication, September 10, 1999). The result was the initial formation of a set of regulations by the state called the Katz bill in the late 1980s. This bill primarily sought to ban "aversives" as a method for changing behavior. This bill did not pass, but a new bill called the "Hughes Bill" emerged, which was more encompassing. This bill required that students with challenging behaviors who qualified for special education services were entitled to a functional analysis assessment. Additionally, the school district was also to develop a positive behavioral intervention plan. This bill did pass the legislature in California and was adopted as the Positive Behavioral Interventions Regulations Statute in 1993. This statute was the precedent for the language that appeared in the 1997 reauthorization of the Individuals with Disabilities Education Act or IDEA. The language involved a functional assessment for children with disabilities who engaged in behavior that could lead to suspension (Bradley, 1999).

FBA METHODS

Collecting evidence regarding the behavioral function of a problem behavior requires an examination of the role of the antecedent and consequent events. One can make conjectures about possible function, which is often the case. For example, someone's pronouncing," I think it is for attention!" looks like an analysis of behavioral function. But what evidence is the proponent of this hypothesis putting forth? Conjecture is one thing, but evidence provides a much stronger argument.

There are several feasible methods for collecting data on the relationship between behavior and its context (i.e., the action frame). The first two methods are nonexperimental methods. They are commonly referred to as descriptive methods. Descriptive methods involve observing and measuring behavior and its current context (O'Neill, Horner, Albin, Storey, & Sprague, 1990). For example, a teacher observes that a designated problem behavior of a primary elementary SDC student occurs frequently under instructional conditions that involve seatwork during language arts. The rate of problem behaviors is less often during storytime. This observation leads to some possible hypotheses. Could it be that writing tasks are aversive for this student and create the context for escape behavior? Perhaps the length of the independent seatwork is the variable. Descriptive data merely depict relations between behavior and its context. The user makes the interpretation of what that means, in terms of function.

Experimental methods involve active manipulation of the context factors to determine if those are responsible for the heightened rates of behavior (Ervin, DuPaul, & Kern, 1998; Fisher, Adelinis, Thompson, Worsdell & Zarcone, 1998; Iwata, et al., 1982; Repp, Felce, & Barton, 1988). For example, if one systematically manipulates the amount of independent seatwork given each day, this experimental analysis may yield the culprit in the generation of the behavior problem. On some days the teacher designates the amount of the independent seatwork to be one- third of the usual amount. This condition is identified as short assignments. Over a two-week period, half the days constitute short assignments, while the other days provide the usual amount. This is an experimental testing of the length of the assignment as a causal variable in the rate of problem behavior. The teacher studies what the effect of short versus normal length seat assignments are on problem behavior. If different rates of problem behavior arise out of the different test conditions (i.e., short versus usual), then this experimental evidence points to this variable.

Interview approaches serve as an indirect method of data collection. Material on FBA methods commonly present interview approaches to collecting FBA information. This belies the fact that very often someone other than the teacher or paraeducator who is in the room is conducting the FBA. I believe that developing skills in the direct line personnel is the most efficient manner of assessing the function of problem behavior. If you do find yourself in a position in which you are consulting on a case, you can examine Cipani and Schock (2007) for potential interview questions. However, you should then supplement such information with some other methods delineated below for additional verification.

The first two methods presented below are descriptive analysis methods. The last method, in-classroom hypothesis tests, is an experimental method.

Safe/Risk Problem Behavior Assessment

Many educators and parents feel that the display of problem behaviors by some students occurs for no apparent reason. How often have you overheard someone say, "He just does it. There is no reason for him doing it." When asked if there are times when he is more likely to do it, their response is "No, it just happens. You never know when he is going to do it. His behavior is unpredictable!" While this type of response is appealing in its simplicity, it often is not the case!

Suppose incidents of a student's target behavior often occur under certain antecedent conditions, but not others? Would that not point to behavior as more predictable? For example, a student displays frequent tantrums during PE class. After observing him for several days, it becomes clear that there are antecedent conditions that are more likely to evidence the screaming episodes. The individual yells at peers more often when playing a competitive game during PE than when exercising. We would say that playing competitive games is a risk condition for the individual's screaming episodes. A *risk condition* denotes a higher probability of the target behavior, i.e., stimulus control. Exercises during PE would be a safe condition for that same behavior.

This type of an analysis (i.e., examining the rate of behavior as a function of antecedent conditions) has been referred to as a *safe/risk analysis* (Azrin, McMahon, Besalel, Donahue, Aciemo, & Kogan, 1994). From these data, one can possibly glean antecedent events that are likely to occasion problem behavior at heightened levels termed risk conditions. Additionally, one can also uncover antecedent events that are not likely to occasion problem behavior at heightened levels, termed *safe conditions.*

EXAMPLES OF SAFE/RISK ANALYSIS. By collecting frequency data as a function of time of day, the teacher may be able to zero in on the antecedent conditions (both discriminative stimuli and MO) for problem behavior. Such data may reveal that there are times or activities when problem behavior is much more likely, i.e., predictable, than others. A hypothetical student named John gets out of his seat frequently during math seat assignments. In contrast, during arts and crafts time, he almost never gets out of his seat. He is just fascinated with cutting and pasting. If you were asked if John is likely to get out of his seat in the next ten minutes, you would inquire as to whether

John is doing a math assignment or engaged in arts and crafts. If John were engaged in arts and crafts, you would bet on him not getting out of his seat in the next ten minutes. In contrast, you would bet that he is certainly likely to get out of his seat at least once in the next ten minutes if he is doing math problems.

SCATTER PLOT DATA. The collection of data needed to conduct a safe/risk analysis of problem behavior is an observation method called *scatter plot* data. The *scatter plot* (Touchette, Langer & MacDonald, 1985) allows the user to determine if certain times and events seem to occasion higher levels of problem behavior across time.

In the original study, (Touchette et al., 1985) a scatter plot was used to gain information on the antecedent conditions for three clients of the facility. For example, Joan, a fourteen-year-old adolescent with autism, had a history of aggressive behavior toward adults and other peers dating back to the age of four. When her behavior became uncontrollable at home, her parents placed her in a residential program. The staff recorded the occurrence of Joan's assaultive behavior in 30-minute intervals. They constructed a grid with three codes. If a 30-minute block of time had only one assault, the teacher placed an open circle on the grid for that time period. More than one assault during a 30-minute block of time required the teacher to place a filled-in circle on the new grid. Blocks of time in which no assaults occurred had no circle. It was now easier to view which times during the day and associated activities correlated with high rates of behavior. These data allowed these researchers (Touchette et al., 1985) to determine if there were blocks of time in which the assaultive behavior was prevalent across a number of days. Concurrently, they determined which times of the day and associated activities correlated with low or zero rates of behavior.

The range of aggressive behaviors across three weeks was between 53–82 occurrences. However, by collecting frequency of aggressive behavior as a function of time, the context for aggressive behavior was revealed. The highest rates of aggressive behavior occurred Monday through Friday between the hours of 1–4 P.M. This period correlated with group activities. The data collected also revealed that low rates of aggressive behavior occurred during the morning period. The instructional delivery in the morning was more of a one-to-one tutorial approach. This information helped researchers to design a program

Table 6.1
SCATTER PLOT DATA

Occurrence of Refusal to Comply with Teacher/Staff Instruction

Time of Day (activity in parentheses)	M	T	W	TH	F
8:30–8:30 A.M. (good morning routine)		x		x	
8:30–9:00 A.M. (math seatwork problems)	xxx	xx	xxx	xx	xxx
9:00–9:30 A.M. (math lecture instruction)	x			x	
9:30–9:50 A.M. (break/recess)	x				
9:50–10:30 A.M. (reading literature)	xxxxx	xxxxxx	xxxxx	xx	
10:30–10:45 A.M. (clean-up)		x			x
11:00–11:30 A.M. (reading instruction)	x	x			

that engineered a social environment that immediately changed the display of this behavior. They increased the presence of those events and activities not associated with aggression (i.e., safe conditions) and decreased or eliminated the risk conditions for aggressive behavior, i.e., group activities.

ILLUSTRATION OF SCATTER PLOT DATA WITH VERBAL REFUSAL. The following hypothetical data on an elementary student with learning disabilities and behavior disorders illustrate the utility of a scatter plot data set. The target problem behavior is verbal refusal to comply with teacher instruction. The student will often say, "No, I don't feel like it," and other similar verbal behaviors indicating refusal to comply with a directive or request. In Table 6.1, each x denotes an occurrence of the target problem behavior. Note that the teacher has recorded each occurrence of refusal behavior as a function of the time of day and activity present across all five days of the week.

In examining the rates of refusal behavior depicted above, the teacher notes times when the behavior is highly likely as well as times when the behavior is very unlikely. For example, during the 9:50 to 10:30 instructional period (i.e., silent reading at desk) on Monday, the child refuses to comply with a teacher request five times. Refusal behavior is highly likely during this instructional period as evident by the data for the remainder of the week. In examining the data, two instructional periods account for the overwhelming majority of refusal behavior: 8:30 to 9:00 A.M. and 10:00 to 10:30 A.M. These are both instructional conditions that require independent seatwork. It is also important to note that there are certain times when refusal behavior is unlikely to occur. Having these data broken down in half-hour time segments allows one to identify what activities occur at times when the child exhibits the higher rates of refusal behavior. One can then begin to examine more closely the antecedent conditions in which the likelihood of high rates of problem behavior exist. The teacher can possibly determine the person(s) discriminative for such behavior as well as the motivating conditions by trying to assess function.

In the above example, the data plotted reveal the following: The safe antecedent conditions were good morning routine, break, math lecture, clean-up time, and oral reading instruction. During safe conditions on a given day, the refusal behavior either occurred once or twice or not at all. This contrasts with the high rates exhibited during the risk conditions (e.g., Math seatwork).

The teacher or paraeducator can collect data on several students with a scatter plot. Again, she would plot the occurrence of the individual student's target behavior(s) as a function of time. Each student being observed should have a different data sheet to allow for easy examination of data. If there are multiple behaviors being tracked for a given student, code each target behavior with a different letter for easy examination of data.

USING SCATTER PLOT DATA ACROSS A CLASS PERIOD. Scatter plot analysis might also identify a pattern of disruptive behavior within a class period that coincides with a specific activity occurring at that time (e.g., change from teacher lecture to independent seatwork). An example of this type of classwide scatter plot analysis appears in Table 6.2. Disruptive behavior, consisting of making inappropriate noises, bothering other students during reading time, and making inappropri-

Table 6.2
SCATTER PLOT DATA ACROSS AN ENTIRE CLASS

	Monday	*Tuesday*	*Wednesday*	*Thursday*	*Friday*
0–5 min	X				
6–10				X	
11–15		X			
16–20			X	X	
21–25	XX	X	XXX	XXXX	
25–30	XXX	XX	XX	XXXXX	X
31–35	X	XXX	XX	XXXXX	
36–40	XX	*	XXXX	XXX	X
41–45	XXX		XX		
Total	12	7	14	19	2

ate gestures, is plotted each five minutes as a function of successive five-minute segments. The reading period is 45 minutes long.

The scatter plot notes disruptive incidents as a function of five-minute time segments during the reading period. The rate of occurrence for the entire period ranges from a low of two to a high of 19 across this one-week baseline. However, the pattern of behavior within the 45-minute reading period provides useful information. Note that the students in the class rarely display disruptive behavior for about the first 15 minutes of the period (one on Monday, one on Tuesday, and one on Thursday). However, contrast this low frequency pattern with the cluster of incidents that occur as the reading lengthens in time. For the last four five-minute intervals, disruptive behavior is the rule. This scatter plot presents clear evidence that this class has greater difficulty the longer the students must sit in their seats and read a book. If the period only lasted 15 minutes, the display of disruptive behavior might be under good control. Perhaps breaking this lengthy period up into mini-periods with different activities interspersed between silent reading periods might be a wise decision.

To determine if certain activities are safe or risk conditions across an entire class, you should record the specific instructional tasks present during specific time periods. For example, you could code seatwork as SW, lecture as L, and reading groups as RG. You should also keep in mind the following questions when examining scatter plot data:

- Are there times when the behavior is highly likely?
- What activities or events are typically associated with these times (risk situations)?
- Are there times when the behavior is highly unlikely?
- What activities or events are typically associated with these times (safe situations)?

USING SCATTER PLOT DATA IN INTERVENTION. A safe-risk analysis can lead to an intervention that produces a change in the rate of the target behavior rather quickly. In examining the scatter plot data and identifying the antecedent contexts to problem and appropriate behavior, the teacher may be able to arrange the presence or absence of these contexts. For example, if a certain context predicts a high rate of problem behavior, then reducing the presence of such a context would immediately affect the potential for problem behavior occurring. This intervention removes the MO for the problem behavior, making it unnecessary to engage in such a behavior. Concurrently, increasing the length of time a safe condition is in effect or the frequency of such conditions makes problem behavior less likely. We often refer to this technique as **antecedent stimulus control procedures**. It changes the exhibition of behavior by removing the MO. It is particularly suited for students who exhibit problem behaviors under very specific stimulus or setting conditions and do not exhibit these behaviors at other times.

Bonnie, a fictitious student with autism engages in self-abuse, hitting herself in the head multiple times. Such behavior causes her teachers and parents great concern, and they often discontinue the activity she is engaged in when the self-abuse becomes severe in form. A scatter plot of Bonnie's self-abusive incidents reveals that she has high rates of the behavior during adaptive PE, particularly when the teacher asks her to run on the track. Other PE activities, such as basic exercises and games, are less likely to result in self-abuse rates. The behavioral specialist sets up a program that initially avoids asking her to run on the track, which of course brings the rate of self-abuse to zero levels during this time period. Bonnie engages in the activities involving safe conditions for self-abuse during PE time. The behavioral specialist then develops a hierarchy of activities and length of time she will run, beginning with just walking to the track and back. Further, the behavioral specialist wisely designates a contingent reinforcer for engaging in this approximation to the desired goal of running around the track. When this condition does not generate any additional hitting to the head, she then walks to the track and halfway around. The teacher employs this gradual progression of the requirement, successfully increasing Bonnie's tolerance to walking around the track. The general steps for using scatter plot data as an intervention are:

1. Identify target behavior(s).
2. Identify through scatter plot data the antecedent conditions that occasion high rates of behavior, i.e., risk conditions.
3. Identify the antecedent stimulus conditions that occasion higher rates of appropriate behavior, i.e., safe conditions.
4. Increase the frequency and duration of the events or stimuli identified in #3 as safe conditions.
5. Eliminate (if possible) or greatly reduce the presentation or length of time of the events, stimuli (#2) as risk conditions.
6. Contingent upon significant reductions in problem behavior, the teacher gradually introduces the antecedent conditions for problem behavior back into the client's environment, both in duration and in frequency (called stimulus fading).

Descriptive Analysis

The teacher can also collect information on a problem behavior's function by observing and recording the student's behavior and its context in real time. The literature often refers to this method as an A-B-C descriptive analysis chart (Bijou, Peterson & Ault, 1968: Mace, Lalli, & Pinter-Lalli, 1991; Lalli, Browder, Mace & Brown, 1993). The data collector writes down the description of each incident in three columns (antecedent, behavior, consequence) immediately after the incident has occurred, as it is still fresh in their memory. The action frame presented in Chapter 1 can serve as the model for data entry within the descriptive analysis chart. The chart would be made up of many entries depicting the action frames of context and the target behavior. First, we will cover a descriptive analysis for socially mediated access problem behaviors.

SOCIALLY MEDIATED ACCESS. One fills out a descriptive analysis chart by entering information in the four columns depicting an action frame (see Table 6.3). Under the antecedent conditions (A), the user would fill out two sets of information. The motivating conditions are the particular item or event that is in a relatively deprived state for SMA behaviors. A relative deprivation state must be existent for an SMA behavior to function as an effective means for accessing the desired item or activity. For attention to be in a deprived condition, the student must be without adult attention at the time preceding the behavior. Therefore, the MO would indicate withdrawal or absence of attention. Similarly, the absence of peer attention at the point when the behavior occurs would be the scenario. The teacher would record this absence of peer attention in the relevant column in the action frame. Absence of the tangible reinforcer would be the antecedent context if the delivery of the tangible reinforcer maintained the behavior problem. Second, under discriminative stimuli, the user would identify the person(s) who delivered the consequent event maintaining the target behavior.

In the next column marked "behavior," the teacher would fill out the behavior observed. The target behavior, as well as other behaviors that may occur subsequent to the antecedent conditions would be delineated. The user then fills in whether the student received attention for each behavior described. In the action frame, the consequent event relates to the MC recorded in column A.

Table 6.3
ACTION FRAME FOR SMA FUNCTIONS

Antecedent Conditions (A)		Behavior (B)	Consequent Conditions (C)
Motivating conditions	Discriminative stimuli	Behavior	Consequent events

Table 6.4
AN ACTION FRAME FOR COMPLAINING BEHAVIOR

Antecedent Conditions		Behavior	Consequent Conditions
Motivating conditions	Discriminative stimuli	Behavior	Consequent events
Morning math period: Deprived of attention (no (adult in vicinity when assignment is given)	Instructional aide	Complains ("I can't do this. I quit.")	Aide encourages her to try harder
		Complains more vociferously	Aide continues working with other student
		Complains and slams book on desk	Aide provides small amount of help on assignment and praise for subsequent work

Table 6.4 shows three entries made by the teacher during the morning math period. In the morning math period, the instructional aide working in the classroom did not provide attention for two incidents of minor complaining. However, with an additional behavior of slamming the desk, the student receives attention from the aide at that point. Subsequently, she stops complaining and gets back to her work once the aide has provided a little help along with praise for continuing her work. The teacher collecting this descriptive data delineates the MC as the absence of attention. This inference is made on seeing two things: (1) adult attention was in relative deprivation and not being provided prior to the behavior occurring and (2) the complaining and mildly disruptive behavior stops once the last attempt to get attention is successful, i.e., when she complains and slams her book closed. If the teacher provides attention, and the complaining continues, the function of such behavior is not teacher attention.

In watching students and determining what function the problem behavior serves, it is important to observe what happens to the problem behavior once the positive reinforcer is accessed to a sufficient degree. The teacher should observe the student desisting or disengaging in the problem behavior shortly thereafter. There would be no need for the behavior to continue! Here is an example. Let us say that getting a desired item is hypothesized to be the function for a pre-

Table 6.5
DESCRIPTIVE ANALYSIS CHART REGARDING DEPRIVATION OF ATTENTION

Antecendent Conditions (A)		Behavior (B)	Consequent Conditions (C)
Motivating conditions	Discriminative stimuli	Behavior	Consequent events
Morning math period: Deprived of attention (no adult in vicinity when assignment is given)	Instructional aide or teacher	9:02 A.M. Raises hand	Aide says, "Wait a minute, I have to help Bobby."
		9:05 A.M. Raises hand and pleads for help verbally	"Hold on. I will be right there."
		9:10 A.M. Complains and rants, I don't want to do this. It is stupid work.	Teacher comes over to him and says, "Okay, if you can calm down, I will help you."

school special education student's crying. If the teacher gives the child the toy, and the child continues to cry, does it make sense that she cried to get that toy? One would venture that crying had a different function at that time. Perhaps this young child wanted a different toy? Perhaps she wanted to leave the area.

DISCERNING FUNCTION FROM A DESCRIPTIVE ANALYSIS. In examining the descriptive analysis chart, you look for patterns between behavior and reliably occurring consequences in the presence of identified people and deprivation conditions. You need to determine if a reliable contingency exists between the problem behavior and the hypothesized maintaining contingency. If such a function exists, the target behavior should be more efficient and effective at getting the desired event than other behaviors. Recording action frames for alternate behaviors provides such evidence. Collecting this type of information on a chart would look like this (Table 6.5).

Note that two behaviors occurred several minutes before the complaining behavior. Unfortunately, these two forms, occurring at 9:02 and 9:04, resulted in the **student** not getting help. This log record demonstrates the inefficiency of these two prior incidents to get help. It, therefore, bolsters an inference by the teacher that this student's

Table 6.6
DESCRIPTIVE ANALYSIS CHART

Antecedent Conditions (A)		Behavior (B)	Consequent Conditions (C)
Motivating conditions	Discriminative stimuli	Behavior	Consequent events
Morning math period: Given drill sheet with 100 problems at 10:00 A.M.	Instructional aide	10:05 A.M. Complains ("I can't do this. I quit.")	Teacher asks student to try, that it is a challenge he should take on.
		10:16 A.M. Does eight problems and then asks if he can do something else.	Teacher, "Well you have done eight. Great job. I know you can do these. You just have 92 more to do."
		10:19 A.M. Throws books on the floor and stands up at desk and screams, "I know my rights!"	Teacher allows student to choose another activity if he will stop complaining.

complaining and ranting behaviors serve an SMA adult attention function.

SOCIALLY MEDIATED ESCAPE. The teacher can also use the descriptive analysis chart to analyze problem behaviors maintained via socially mediated escape from relatively aversive events. Table 6.6 shows several entries that the teacher made during the morning math period. The MC was the presentation of the math drill sheet (aversive event) at 10 A.M.

Note that several behaviors occur prior to the target behavior, including throwing materials or loud boisterous complaining. However, such behavior did not result in the teacher's or the aide's removal of the drill sheet in favor of an alternate more preferred activity. Only the target behavior results in a change in assignments. If the teacher observes this pattern during other times when the MC is presented, there is an increased possibility that such problem behavior will serve an escape function. It is particularly important to observe that other less disruptive behaviors are ineffective at escape.

EXAMPLE OF A DESCRIPTIVE ANALYSIS CHART. Jack is a hypothetical seven-year-old student in Mrs. Sythe's class at Willow Elementary. He exhibits verbal complaining and whining during instructional periods, particularly those involving independent seatwork in math. Jack has a history of difficulty in educational settings since attending special education preschool programs at the age of four. He qualified under communicative disorders at that time, as his language scores were appreciably below age level equivalents on tests of expressive language. Classroom staff reported that he engaged in mild tantrums during his preschool program, but data was not collected. Only anecdotal reports of his behavior on individualized education plans (IEP) were available. Following his preschool experience, he went to a special day class for children with developmental disabilities. His transition IEP also included a one-hour period in kindergarten. The general education teacher considered his behavior problems to be deleterious to his learning environment as well as the other kindergarten students. While attending the mainstream setting, he engaged in frequent tantrum and oppositional behavior, running out of the classroom and back to the SDC room. During three of these tantrums, in addition to vociferously complaining about his work, he kicked his desk with sufficient force that the desk toppled over. The parents and the other members of his IEP team felt that he may not have been "ready" for the inclusion program, and they wrote a new IEP, sans kindergarten. Since that time, where he no longer attends the mainstream setting, severe behavioral incidents have not occurred. He still engages in verbal complaining and whining about the assignment in the SDC.

Jack has been receiving individual therapy since he left the kindergarten mainstream site. Some members of the IEP team felt he had "emotional issues." Unfortunately, the teacher has not observed any results in the class from the therapy he is receiving from the school counselor. Classroom management strategies used include notes home to his parents when he has a "really bad day," visits to the principal, and setting him in front of the teacher's desk. Only anecdotal data suggest that such efforts of unknown consistency do not appear to have solved the problem behavior.

Jack's complaining behavior seems to occur when the teacher's attention to this student is nonexistent during independent seatwork. Brief observation of the student indicates that at some point during or

Table 6.7
JACK'S COMPLAINING BEHAVIOR

Antecendent Conditions (A)		Behavior (B)	Consequent Conditions (C)
Motivating conditions	Discriminative stimuli	Behavior	Consequent events
1:15 P.M. Teacher with small group not with target student)	Teacher	1:22 P.M. Jack calls out teacher's name improperly and complains about the amout of work.	Teacher stops groups after a while and asks, "What is the problem?" and provides help to student.
Same	Teacher	1:26 P.M. Jack raises hand and asks for help, saying it is too difficult.	Teacher says, "That is the way to ask for help, Jack. I will be with you soon."
1:27 P.M. Teacher is still at her desk talking to another student.	Same	1:27 P.M. Jack moans aloud about the assignment.	Teacher says, "Please keep your voice down. I will get to you soon."
Same	Same	1:30 P.M. Jack becomes louder, saying that he never gets help. "You only help Bobby!" he says and threatens to kick the desk.	Teacher says, "If you can ask nicely, in one minute I will be with you." Teacher goes over to student after one minute. Verbal complaining stops once teacher is with student, and she tells him he has to do less than half of the assignment, but he needs to finish that amount. He proceeds with the assignment.

after the problem behavior, Mrs. Sythe provides him with attention in some form. Below are a few sample entries (Table 6.7).

Note that the teacher is working with other students at 1:15 P.M. Therefore, Jack does not have her attention. In the past, he knows that he has to get her to come to his desk if he has any hope of a reduction in the class assignment. Several attempts to get the teacher to his desk fail. It is only when he "ups the ante" at 1:31 that shortly thereafter, the teacher provides him with a restructured assignment (i.e., less than half of what he is supposed to do). Now there is a negotiation strategy for you! This scenario is interesting in that teacher attention is not the driving force for his behavior, but rather it is what the teacher does when she attends to him. The reduction in amount of work is the desired event; hence the task becomes less aversive.

IN-CLASSROOM HYPOTHESIS TESTING FOR SMA FUNCTIONS

The two previous FBA methods involve a description of the events that are temporally related. The teacher or paraeducator then tries to identify a problem behavior's function by interpreting the observations and data. While such a technique works well for classroom use, the reliability and subsequent validity of the interpretation is a function of the individual interpretation. It does not provide experimental evidence that the selected hypothesis is correct. A third FBA method, the in-classroom hypothesis test (Repp & Karsh, 1994), involves an experimental manipulation of classroom antecedent or consequent conditions. This method of assessment provides valuable and substantive evidence for one's hypothesis about a problem behavior's function.

An in-classroom hypothesis test has two dimensions (Cipani & Schock, 2007, 2011): (1) it is conducted in the setting of interest and (2) a functional treatment (based on the entertained hypothesis) is alternated with a baseline condition. The baseline condition (test condition A) consists of the contingencies that are existent at the time the target behavior becomes problematic. In other words, the teacher has already collected or will collect baseline data on the rate of the problem behavior (see previous chapter on baseline rate assessment) within this method. The test condition labeled B involves the implementation of a functional treatment that would be indicated if the behavior problem served a particular function. Test condition B involves the reinforcement of an alternate behavior along with extinction programmed for the target behavior. If the target behavior's function is access to positive reinforcement, the alternate replacement behavior would serve to produce the desired positive reinforcer. Concurrently, extinction would also be in effect for the target problem behavior. Extinction would

Table 6.8
SEQUENCE OF TEST CONDITIONS

Date	12/1	12/3	12/3	12/4	12/5	12/8	12/9	12/10
Test condition	A	B	A	B	A	B	A	B

involve the lack of the desired event when the target behavior occurs.

This methodology allows for a comparison between the rates of problem behavior during the functional treatment condition versus the rates of problem behavior during the baseline condition (i.e., treatment not implemented). The teacher can also compare the rates of the alternate behavior selected for reinforcement between these two test conditions (see Table 6.8).

The conduct of the in-classroom hypothesis test is in a short instructional (or noninstructional) period. This allows for an experimental test of the hypothesis with a greater possibility of accurate data collection within the shorter period. The teacher designates one class period as the time for such an experimental test. For example, a prior safe/risk analysis might have identified the 10:00–10:45 A.M. instructional math period as a context of more frequent target behavior exhibited by the select student. The teacher could then use this period to alternate the two test conditions on subsequent days. The following material addresses the in-classroom hypothesis test for each socially mediated category and function. The following material presents a discussion of the conduct of the in-classroom hypothesis test for the various hypotheses about the function of the problem behavior.

The in-classroom hypothesis tests for the three SMA functions appear in Table 6.9. In the second column, the test condition A for each test would be a baseline. The Test condition B for each hypothesis appears briefly in column 3.

Table 6.9
TEST CONDITIONS FOR SMA FUNCTIONS

Function	*Test Condition A*	*Test Condition B: Functional Treatment*
SMA attention	Baseline	Contingent adult attention for replacement behavior, removal of attention for target behavior
SMA peer attention	Baseline	Group contingency
SMA tangible reinforcers	Baseline	Contingent provision of identified tangible reinforcer for alternate behavior, withholding of tangible reinforcer for occurrence of target behavior

ADULT ATTENTION CLASSROOM HYPOTHESIS TEST. The teacher alternates a baseline condition for the selected hypothesis with an intervention that matches the treatment function. If teacher attention is maintaining the target problem behavior, then a functional treatment as a test condition B would involve two components: First, the teacher provides attention contingent upon an alternate (replacement) behavior. Second, the teacher would not provide attention for the target behavior. The baseline condition (test condition A) would just involve the conditions currently in effect. If the rate of target behavior is substantially different between the two test conditions, then the teacher had confirmed the attention hypothesis. If there is little or no difference, then the teacher should entertain an alternate hypothesis regarding the function.

A hypothetical special education teacher sets up an experimental test to ascertain if adult attention is why a particular student frequently makes tangential off-track comments during language arts period. During the test condition A, she does not change anything except that she is now recording the frequency of these comments. During the sessions of test condition B, she provides positive comments for behaviors other than tangential comments. She decides to praise the student on an FR 2 schedule when he speaks about the story at hand. In other words, this alternate behavior will produce her attention in this test condition. In addition, during test condition B, when this student makes a tangential comment about the current story, she will not acknowl-

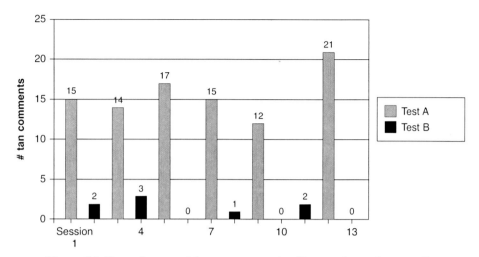

Figure 6.1. Rate of tangential comments under Test condition A versus B.

edge it. She will ignore it and call on another student in the group. The teacher continues to collect data on the rate of tangential comments but also collects data on the rate of on-topic comments (i.e., the reinforced behavior in test condition B). She implements these two test conditions (A versus B) in 13 sessions during the language arts period over the next three-week period. Figure 6.1 depicts the rate of tangential comments as well as the rate of on-topic comments in parentheses.

Figure 6.1 illustrates how the teacher obtained data in 13 brief sessions. It is important to note that a switch in test conditions brings about a change in the rate of the target behavior (see frequency of target behavior in test condition A compared to test condition B rate of target behavior. What is also of interest is that the rate of the alternate behavior changed as a function of test conditions. In summary, when test condition A was in effect, the rate was low to zero per session (Figure 6.2). When the teacher provided attention on an FR 2 schedule during test condition B, the rate rose substantially, with a range of 10-22 on-topic comments. These data indicate that attention is a "driving force" with this student's verbal behavior in language arts class. When the child receives attention for on-topic comments, comments increase while tangential comments drop to zero or near zero levels. This teacher successfully decoded the child's behavior problem.

PEER ATTENTION CLASSROOM HYPOTHESIS TEST. For a **peer-attention** hypothesis, the baseline is the current set of contingencies

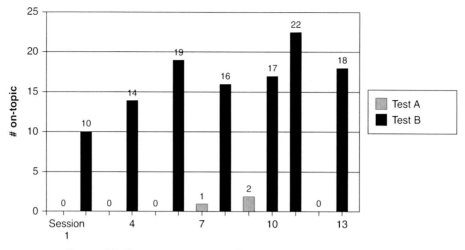

Figure 6.2. On-topic comments during test conditions A and B.

that are existent in the class. This would constitute test condition A. Test condition B would be a group contingency[1] that targets the class level of the target behaviors performed for peer attention. For example, a senior high SDC teacher suspects that peer laughter is maintaining a student's inappropriate behaviors, which include making inappropriate noises, gestures, or comments. She has noticed he tries hard to come up with comments that make the students around him giggle. She defines this class of behaviors as the target behavior. She will measure their frequency across both test conditions. She alternates the current condition (baseline) with an intervention condition for peer maintained behavior. In this test condition, she imposes a group contingency. All incidents of this behavior are counted across all class members. If the total number of such incidents is three or less for the class for the history period, everyone gets eight minutes at the end of the class to talk with one another. If they exceed this limit as a group, then the teacher withholds conversation time, and they have to finish a short assignment in that same period. If the peer-reinforced function is correct, test condition B should show markedly lower rates of such behaviors than in text condition A, in which peer reinforcement is probably still available for this behavior.

---

1. Group contingencies will be covered in the functional treatment chapter.

Table 6.10
IN-CLASSROOM HYPOTHESIS TEST

Session	*1*	*2*	*3*	*4*	*5*	*6*	*7*	*8*	*9*	*10*	*11*
Test condition A	11	16	17	11						14	9
Test condition B					2	2	1	3	1		

The teacher collects these data for eleven sessions across a three-week period. Table 6.10 depicts how the rate of such comments changes as a function of the different test condition in effect. In test condition B, when peer attention is probably removed for the inappropriate target comments, the rate is down (2, 2, 1, 3 for days 5–9 respectively). When the teacher removes the group contingency for the class's inappropriate comments during the baseline, the rate of this behavior dramatically increases. This student contributes the majority of the instances during these days, and peers often egg him on.

TANGIBLE REINFORCER CLASSROOM TEST HYPOTHESIS. For testing this hypothesis, the teacher would implement a baseline for test condition A against a test condition B that provides a tangible reinforcer (or points toward such) for an alternate behavior. For example, a teacher hypothesizes that one of her student's tantrum behavior results in his access to computer time. She realizes that in some small percentage of times, she eventually gives in to the tantrum and lets him go to the computer if he is quiet for one minute. Due to the immediate result of terminating the tantrum and keeping him quiet while she is on the computer, she has fallen fell into this trap! Unfortunately, its long-term effect is that he appears to be having more tantrums than ever. It is very possible that the result–getting on the computer–is maintaining such a sequence of events.

The teacher has collected baseline data for five days on the cumulative duration of tantrums, the results of which appear in Table 6.11. Given that she already has data for test condition A, she now implements test condition B. First, tantrums will now only postpone the advent of computer access. Second, the teacher selects an alternate behavior as a means for him to earn computer time. This student can earn ten points for every five minutes she does not have a tantrum. If she earns 30 points in a 45-minute period, she can get computer time

Table 6.11
BASELINE AND INTERVENTION TEST CONDITIONS

Session	1	2	3	4	5	6	7	8	9	10
Test condition A	5'45"	12'45"	7'50"	20'	12'45"					
Test condition B						3'20"	1'	0'	0	45"

for 20 minutes. The data in Table 6.11 illustrate that when tantrums no longer function to get computer time, as is the case in Test condition B, their duration decreases markedly. Access to computer time was the driving force for this behavior problem. The teacher now knows what behavioral intervention will be effective for solving tantrums during other instructional time periods.

IN-CLASSROOM HYPOTHESIS TESTING FOR SME FUNCTIONS

The in-classroom hypothesis test for SME behaviors follows a similar methodology as the test for SMA behaviors. The teacher uses two test conditions. In both test conditions, the teacher presents the MC, whether it is an unpleasant social situation, lengthy instructional task or assignment, or difficult material (see Table 6.12). Therefore, the teacher would present the hypothesized aversive condition in test condition A and test condition B. For example, in the escape from unpleasant social situations, the teacher would have to arrange for the designated unpleasant social situation to occur. In test condition A, the existing target behavior would probably produce escape for a designated short period. If the teacher suspects an SME function, then the test condition B would involve the programming of escape from the aversive condition when the designated alternate behavior occurs. Concurrently, the teacher would designate extinction for the SME target behavior, which would disable its ability to facilitate escape of the existent conditions. To confirm the SME diagnosis, there should be disparities of the target behavior frequency across the two test conditions. The data should reveal that whatever behavior produces escape

Table 6.12
SME BASELINE AND TEST CONDITIONS

Function	*Test Condition A*	*Test Condition B: Functional Treatment*
SME: Unpleasant social situations	Presence of unpleasant social situation.	Contingent on replacement behavior, unpleasant condition is terminated (FR1).
SME: Relatively lengthy tasks or assignments	Presence of relatively lengthy task or assignment.	Contingent on replacement behavior, lengthy task or assignment is terminated.
SME: Relatively difficult tasks or assignments	Presence of relatively difficult task or assignment.	Contingent on replacement behavior, difficult task or assignment is terminated.

becomes more probable.

A hypothetical teacher has a student with traumatic brain injury who hits himself on the leg when the teacher places him next to same aged peers. This teacher does not believe that her attention is the maintaining contingency. She believes that he does not like to be next to those students for some reason. She observed that her attention to him when he did not hit his leg had no effect on this behavior. He would continue hitting himself on the leg until the teacher removed him from the others. When the teacher removed him, he would stop the behavior. This sequence of events seemed to point to the self-injury serving an escape from the social situation mediated by the teaching staff.

She decides to confirm her suspicion but also would like for him to have a better means of escaping this situation. She conducts the following test: Each day of assessment, the hypothesized unpleasant social situation occurs at three different times. A yes indicates that he hit his leg three times (FR 3) and the teacher delivered escape. Therefore, a yes denotes three occurrence of the target behavior. In session one, the teacher composed three presentations of the unpleasant social situation that day. All three presentations resulted in the occurrence of the target behavior three times (denoted by yes), resulting in termination of the event by the teacher. On day two, the teacher again instituted three presentations, except the teacher prompted the student to request dismissal from the interaction, which the teacher immediately

Table 6.13
IN-CLASSROOM HYPOTHESIS TEST

Session	1	2	3	4	5	6	7	8	9
Test condition A	yes, yes, yes		yes, yes, yes			yes, yes, yes		yes, yes, yes	
Test condition B		yes, no, no		no, no, no	yes, no, no		no, no, no		no, no, no

honored (FR 1 schedule). A yes indicates that the target behavior occurred at that opportunity, whereas a no indicates that the alternate behavior occurred during that opportunity (i.e., no hit). Table 6.13 shows how frequently the target behavior occurs when the student finds himself in an unpleasant social situation. The data indicate that whatever behavior produces escape is the more probable. In test condition A, it is self-injury, and such a behavior occurred at the scheduled rate quickly. During test condition B, the verbal request to leave became more probable while self-injury underwent extinction.

The teacher would use a similar methodology for the two escape functions involving instructional conditions. The two categories are the following: (1) escape from relatively lengthy task assignments or lessons and (2) escape from relatively difficult tasks. Again, it is important to select one instructional period to conduct this brief test. If the teacher has conducted a safe/risk analysis, the teacher can use the instructional period in which the problem behavior is more prevalent. This high frequency context would provide a great test of the hypothesis.

To determine what effect the length of the task or assignment is having on problem behavior, the two test conditions should try to equate the difficulty of the materials presented. Preferably, the material should be relatively easy so that difficulty can be ruled out. The baseline condition would involve the usual length of the instructional assignment or task within the period. Further, the normal procedure for handling the target behavior would be in effect.

Following this baseline condition with data collection on the target behavior, the teacher would shorten the instructional period by 50–70 percent, announcing that if the student(s) finishes the short assignment, he or she can have access to a preferred activity. For example, in the shorter instructional session, the teacher would announce to the student, "When you finish this amount, we will go to a more preferred task." If escape due to lengthy tasks or assignments is relevant to the individual student, than the data should show that when the length is shortened, and a contingency for completing is in effect, the student exhibits fewer behavior problems. If the teacher were interested in fully ascertaining if the short assignment condition was the causal factor, the teacher would institute a brief return to test condition A after several sessions of this short assignment condition.

In testing the SME function of a relatively difficult task or assignment, the teacher should hold the length of time constant between test conditions A and B. Test condition A would entail a baseline with the usual task or assignment, possibly in a briefer instructional period than usual. For example, the teacher could shorten the usual period of 40 minutes to 25 to remove the length of the assignment as a possible explanation. The length of test condition B would also be 25 minutes. The difference would be that test condition B involves relatively easy content or material. Instead of the fourth grade level material from which the teacher would normally give the child assignments, she would select easier material. For example, the teacher could select assignments that match the student's standardized test scores. In the relatively difficult condition, the current instructional materials would suffice. In test condition A, the teacher would deploy the fixed ratio 3 schedule for reinforcement of the target behavior. In test condition B, the teacher will reinforce only the protest behavior (Can I stop now?). Contingent upon a protest, the teacher would provide easier materials for a period of time.

FUNCTIONAL ANALYSIS OF BEHAVIOR

Functional analysis of behavior or FAB (also known as analogue assessment) is a more labor-intensive method. Conducting a FAB allows you to "test" potential hypotheses in a simulated setting (Iwata, et al., 1982; Iwata, et al., 1990). Since teachers have access to the students in their natural setting, they may find the classroom hypothesis test more suitable to collect experimental analysis data. But a FAB is well-suited for personnel who do not have classroom access to the students, such as itinerant personnel. It answers the question of why the problem behavior is occurring in terms of the probable maintaining contingency. Since teachers and para-educators have the student readily available, an analogue assessment may be cumbersome since it requires a pull-out. Rather, the in-classroom hypothesis tests would be more suited for in-situ assessment. For more information on how to conduct an FAB, the reader should review Chapter 2 of Cipani and Schock (2011).

SUMMARY

An FBA goes beyond the information derived from a baseline rate assessment2. It provides the teacher with varying degrees of valid evidence about a problem behavior's particular function. To conduct functional treatment, it is imperative to have data from an FBA that provides a reasonable hypothesis about the function of the behavior available. The FAB experimental method is useful for itinerant personnel to use in collecting data through a pullout model, such as the case in the original Iwata et al (1982) study. However, since a teacher has the student in his or her class, and a pull-out for one student may not be feasible. Three methods of determining function are plausible methods for the classroom teacher. Two methods do not actively manipulate any variable and are more descriptive in nature. They are safe/risk analysis involving scatter plot data and a descriptive analysis method using a action frame log entry. The last method, an in-classroom hypothesis test, is an experimental method.

CHAPTER 6: SUMMARY TEST

(Answers on CD)

True or False

1. The Iwata et al., 1982 study used interview information to determine the function of each child's self-injury.
2. In the Iwata study, the enriched environment provided items and toys for the child to play with.
3. In the demand condition, an occurrence of self-injury resulted in the task demand being removed for a short period of time.
4. In the Gaylord-Ross and Weeks (1981) study, the presentation of difficult tasks resulted in an increase in problem behaviors when contrasted with the rate of problem behavior under the easy tasks condition.
5. A risk condition is an antecedent condition where the problem behavior is likely.
6. A scatter plot method of data collection is used to reveal how often a replacement behavior occurs.
7. A scatter plot records the frequency of the target problem behavior as a function of time.
8. A descriptive analysis is an experimental manipulation of potential functions.
9. A descriptive analysis should record the presence of the hypothesized aversive events in considering problem behaviors that serve SME functions.
10. An in-situ hypothesis test determines function by mimicking the hypothesized reinforcer for the problem behavior.

A short, fill-in-the-blanks test can be found in Appendix A.

Chapter 7

FUNCTIONAL INTERVENTION STRATEGIES

A major component of functional treatment is the designation of the replacement behavior. The concept of a replacement behavior is often misunderstood. It is not a matter of simply specifying that some selected behavior should replace the target behavior. A replacement behavior refers to the designated function of a selected behavior; not its topography or form. The replacement behavior should subsume the current identified environmental function of the target problem behavior. Therefore, a currently functional target problem behavior becomes nonfunctional with respect to the identified contingent reinforce. Secondly, a currently nonfunctional appropriate behavior becomes functional.

Let us say a male resident of a group home for persons with disabilities is aggressive toward other residents. One of the program managers arbitrarily decides that the replacement behavior should be to have this client put his hands in his pockets. That plan certainly sounds good. Having him put his hands in his pockets is physically incompatible with hitting people. However, it offers little in the way of understanding why (i.e., maintaining contingency) the hitting behavior occurs. Suppose the hitting occurs frequently when he is sitting on the couch watching TV. He hits other residents during this time when they talk aloud, probably making it difficult for him to hear the TV program. The hitting often results in that person leaving the area. Hence, its function is to terminate an unpleasant social situation. Is it reasonable to expect this client to keep his hands in his pockets the next time someone talks during his TV program? I believe the hands will come out of the pocket and deliver the shot that produces cessation of talking from his neighbor. Then the hands will probably go back into the pockets.

Table 7.1
ESSENCE OF FUNCTIONAL TREATMENT

Target behavior	Eliminate or disable current function
Replacement behavior	Enable and enhance desired environmental function

The designation of a replacement behavior requires the teacher to make two changes in the student's environment (see Table 7.1). These entail the disabling of the target behavior's function and enabling the replacement (appropriate) behavior's function.

How does one disable a target behavior's socially mediated function? Removing the functional reinforcer would make such a behavior nonfunctional. Hence, this part of functional treatment involves producing extinction for the target behavior. Extinction involves withholding the functional reinforcer when the target behavior occurs. Functional treatment would require the teacher to eliminate the maintaining reinforcer for the target problem, or at least weaken it (i.e., disabled). The weakening of the relationship between problem behavior and reinforcer can be based on the contingency being markedly less reliable than the one that exists for the replacement behavior.

How does one *enable* an alternate more acceptable behavior? Providing the functional reinforcer contingent upon the occurrence of the designated alternate behavior makes such a behavior functional under the relevant MO. Hence, it is essential to have differential reinforcement of the alternate behavior (which implies an extinction process for other behaviors). The designated alternate replacement behavior is often termed a replacement behavior.

A replacement behavior serves the same environmental function as a problem behavior. The newly designated behavior replaces the target behavior's function. Therefore, a teacher *cannot* designate a replacement behavior without an understanding of the target behavior's function(s) under specific antecedent contexts. The selected replacement behavior must be capable of producing the same reinforcer(s) as the problem behavior given the MO and other antecedent setting conditions. Table 7.2 presents the steps to use in identifying a functional replacement behavior.

Table 7.2
THE STEPS TO IDENTIFYING REPLACEMENT BEHAVIORS

- Identify the function and specific reinforcer of problem behavior by assigning it to one of the socially mediated categories involving access or escape.
- Designate an alternate appropriate behavior(s) that **will** produce the same function as the problem behavior in identified antecedent social contexts under the relevant MO, whether naturally or contrived.
- If the problem behavior serves more than one function, identify the different functions for each antecedent context (MO and discriminative stimuli) and repeat above steps for each unique source of stimulus control.

What types of options are there for designating a replacement behavior? There are three major categories: (a) designating a specific alternate behavior, (b) designating the completion of some small task or assignment, and (c) designating the absence of target behavior for some period of time (or lower rate). This chapter will discuss functional treatment for SMA problem behaviors first.

FUNCTIONAL TREATMENT: SMA CATEGORIES

In order for a replacement behavior to *replace* the target behavior's socially mediated access function, it is critical to ensure that the target behavior no longer results in the delivery of the socially mediated reinforcer. In cases of SMA problem behaviors, extinction is necessary. Given that the behavior of others maintains problem behaviors in this category, one can achieve extinction if adults behave differently when the target behavior occurs! Adults must now *tolerate* the occurrence of the target behavior by withholding the desired event (Iwata, 2006).

An action frame illustrates how a SMA target behavior becomes functional. Table 7.3 illustrates how the replacement behavior can become more likely under states of deprivation (see second row) by producing the reinforcer. The last row illustrates how to render the target behavior ineffective in producing the desired reinforcer. Hence, problem behavior undergoes extinction while the newly established function becomes strengthened. *It is important to realize that the teacher may initially have to prompt the replacement behavior in order to get the student to exhibit it (in favor of the time-honored target behavior).* Once the student has performed the replacement behavior ahead of the prompt, the

Table 7.3
ANALYSIS OF REPLACEMENT AND TARGET BEHAVIORS

MO	*Behavior (engaged in)*	*Environmental Result*	*Maintaining Contingency*
Deprivation state (relative)	Replacement behavior occurs	Someone delivers the event or item addressing deprivation	Socially mediated positive reinforcement
Deprivation state (relative)	Target behavior occurs	Deprivation state or condition remains	Extinction; Appropriate behavior not functional in producing desired item or event

teacher can probably discontinue the prompting strategy as the reinforcer delivery influences the behavior to be performed under the MO.

Adult Attention

Treating a problem behavior maintained by adult attention involves two basic changes in the manner in which the social environment responds. The following two changes are necessary: (1) disable the target behavior's socially mediated function and (2) enable the replacement behavior's function. Functional treatment involves a switching of contingencies. Table 7.4 depicts this switch in functional treatment.

When the MC for attention is high, the probability of a given behavior is a function of its effectiveness and efficiency to produce

Table 7.4
FUNCTIONAL TREATMENT CONTINGENCIES

MC for Attention	*Efficiency to Produce Attention: Replacement Behavior*	*Efficiency to Produce Attention: Problem Behavior*	*Probability of Replacement Behavior*
high	high	low	high

attention. Functional treatment requires the teacher to enable the replacement behavior by making it more effective at producing adult attention. Concurrently, the teacher disables the target problem behavior by making it inefficient and less likely to produce the reinforcer.

HITTING GETS YOUR ATTENTION. This hypothetical case from Chapter 2 depicts a parent who reinforces her son's hitting behavior via attention. Robert's hitting his siblings occurred when he wanted to be picked up, i.e., gets his mother's attention. The action frame illustrated that minor forms of whining were ineffective **at** producing attention, i.e., being picked up. As a result, he hits his baby brother and after a short admonishment, he is picked up.

Treating this behavior problem requires two sets of contingencies. The extinction component for the act of hitting is obvious. Hitting behavior should not result in Robert's mother picking him up. However, the designation of a replacement behavior has to take into account the condition that exists, i.e., several young children want Mom's attention. Given that Mom cannot grow more arms; the plan has to consider that only one child can be picked up at a time. Therefore the most reasonable approach is to impose a turn-taking system, where the child learns how to wait his turn. It is imperative to use an oven timer to demarcate time when using this program. If Mom tells Robert to wait two minutes to be picked up, two sets of contingencies are arranged.

When Robert waits his turn, he is picked up once the oven timer elapses. If he engages in a target behavior, Mom admonishes him and resets the timer for the full two-minute length. This rearrangement of contingencies invokes a shift in what behavior gets enabled (waiting) with attention and what behavior delays attention by another two minutes (hitting). Mom can progressively increase the length of time once Robert demonstrates success at waiting for two minutes.

BLURTING OUT ANSWERS. How many times do you see children blurt out answers when told previously that they should raise their hands? You may wonder why they persist in such behavior when it seems clear that the teacher does not provide attention to them. The answer is "You did not watch long enough." It takes attending to their response once every several occurrences to maintain such a behavior. But why do they not raise their hands? The answer is "Blurting out answers is more efficient in getting attention than raising their hands." As you now know, a functional response will be more probable over a less efficient response. Perhaps these students have learned that when they really want attention, blurting out is more probable in getting attention than raising one's hand and waiting after five to ten opportunities to be called upon.

The solution to this problem is simple, yet elegant. Based on the baseline level of blurting out, a behavioral standard is designated. Staying below a low level of blurt outs in a designated length of time could result in teacher attention during a special social conversation time period. Going above the designated level of blurting out would not produce this special attention reinforcer. Also, the teacher would ignore the student's inappropriate attempt to get attention. The teacher can progressively alter the behavioral standard once the student achieves the standard reliably over time. In this manner of shaping a lowered level of the blurting out behavior, the teacher can eventually alter the goal to a targeted low or zero level of disruptive behavior.

Peer Attention

Treating a problem behavior maintained by peer attention requires two basic changes: (1) the target problem behavior's socially mediated function no longer produces peer attention and (2) the replacement behavior now functions to produce peer attention. When the MC for attention is high, the probability of a given behavior is a function of its effectiveness and efficiency to produce peer attention. Functional treatment requires the *planned contingencies* enable the replacement behavior by making it more effective at producing peer attention. Concurrently, planned contingencies make the problem behavior less likely to produce the peer attention. The $64,000 question is "How does a teacher get classmates to withdraw attention for the misbehavior while attending to an appropriate behavior or the absence of problem behavior?" The answer: **Group contingencies**.

There are many types of group contingencies (Speltz, Wenters-Shimamaura, & McReynolds, 1982). One type targets the behavior of the few offenders by designating a differential reinforcement contingency for just their behavior. Such a practice may have some policy and legal issues that make it impractical for classroom use because it requires singling out specific students. The other type requires that the standard for behavior or performance be across the entire group. If the performance of the entire group achieves the behavioral standard, then everyone earns the designated reinforcer. If the group fails to achieve the standard, no one earns. The standard for performance or behavior is based on the group cumulative frequency of behavior (or some other measure of group performance). Therefore, no one student is singled out. This form of group contingency is advocated for removing peer reinforcement for problem behavior in classroom settings.

As an example, school staff employed a group-oriented contingency for specific misbehaviors that occurred on an elementary school ground before school and during recesses (Holland & McLaughlin, 1982). If a given class had no students who engaged in any of the identified misbehaviors, then that class got ten points for that particular period. If one student engaged in a target behavior, his or her class lost one of the ten points. Classes that obtained 45 points for the week became winners and received certificates.

In order to implement a group contingency of this type, the teacher must do the following:

- Collect baseline data (8–10 days) on the specific target behaviors across the entire group for the defined period.
- Determine the group average rate of target behavior across the baseline period.
- Generate a reasonable behavioral standard for the group by examining the average rate and the range of target behaviors.
- Identify the group reinforcers to be earned when the group achieves the goal by not exceeding the behavioral standard.
- Evaluate plan and progressively alter the behavioral standard to the desired target level.

CLASSROOM EXAMPLE OF AN EFFECTIVE CONTINGENCY. Mr. Jenksen, a hypothetical senior elementary grade teacher, decides to implement a systematic plan for three of his students: Juan, Serena, and John. They frequently engage in behaviors he addresses as inappropriate when they are working in a small group. These behaviors generally involve inappropriate verbal comments to one another. The peer attention these behaviors evoke maintains these comments. Most of the other small groups at this time do not have a significant problem with this instructional format but do occasionally indulge in the same behavior patterns as the target group. He considered splitting these three students up but was afraid that their behavior might disturb the other students who were currently doing well. Given that there are five small groups at this time, he decides to set up a program for each small group. Each group would have their own behavioral standard based on baseline data.

The plan offers each group of students a reinforcer for staying below a predetermined level of target behavior across an entire school day. Prior to implementing the behavioral intervention, Mr. Jenksen collected seven days of baseline data on each group's rate of inappropriate comments. On the first day of baseline, Mr. Jenksen informed all the groups of the need for appropriate conduct when they are in the small-group format. He told them that he would be observing them for designated inappropriate comments and recording them on a tally sheet. During baseline, he scored each incident of an inappropriate comment, informing the particular student of the infraction and requesting that he or she refrain from making such comments. This often produced giggling on the part of the other students. Mr. Jenksen informed each group of the number of total times their group made an inappropriate comment at the end of each day.

Subsequent to this baseline phase, Mr. Jenksen believes it is time to initiate the plan. The initial goal for the three groups was selected by taking into account the level of behavior exhibited during the baseline period. This makes the selection of the initial standard or behavioral goal reasonable and **doable** from the standpoint of the particular group. For Juan's group, the behavioral goal was nine or fewer inappropriate comments. Other groups had different behavioral standards. Any group that stayed below the target level received six points that day. If the group was at 50 percent or less of their target for a given day, this constituted a great day. Such performance earned students in that group ten points each. The groups accrue points across the entire week. They can trade in their points for Friday "fun period," with the following exchanges:

25–35 points–Friday Fun period from 2:00–2:30
36–45 points–Friday Fun period from 1:45–2:30

Table 7.5
INAPPROPRIATE COMMENTS DURING BASELINE

Day	*1*	*2*	*3*	*4*	*5*	*6*	*7*	*8*	*Average*
# of Occurrences	8	7	9	9	15	9	11	7	9.4

46–60 points–Friday Fun period from 1:30–2:30 and treat from surprise box

EVERYONE LOVES THE CLOWN (EXCEPT THE TEACHER). In Chapter 2, a hypothetical high school SDC student, Geraldo, made frequent jokes and comments during the teacher lecture. The students laughed at him and he became popular. After reflecting on the disruption such comments engender, the teacher determines that such behavior is maintained by the peer attention it garners. She decides to set up a program as a group contingency. She measures the entire class' rate of inappropriate comments during her lectures and comes up with the following rate across the eight days of baseline (Table 7.5). The range of comments is between 7 and 15, with the average being 9.4.

The teacher decides to use the following group contingency, focusing on the target inappropriate comments: When the class stays below nine inappropriate comments on a given day, all the students get ten minutes of social time at the end of the day. If they exceed that level, they have to do an extra assignment during that time and it becomes homework if not completed. The first eight days of this group contingency resulted in the following rates of target behavior: 5, 8, 13, 6, 15, 4, 4, and six. This data indicates that the students were able to achieve the social time reinforcer six of the eight days. The average rate dropped almost two occurrences per day with a mean of 7.6 occurrences. She will gradually lower the number of inappropriate comments by progressively changing the behavioral goal as a function of success in achieving the current goal.

How does this program alter the existing functional contingencies for inappropriate comments? As the class gets closer to the behavioral standard, peers will be less likely to provide attention, given the power of the ten-minute social period. Thus, tying everyone's fate to the desired reinforcer translates to a natural removal of peer attention for the behavior that will lose the reinforcer.

VERBAL ARGUMENTS WITH THE TEACHER. This example from Chapter 2 involved several students in the class who were arguing with teacher directives. Unfortunately, simply setting up an individual contingency for one or several of the offenders would be ineffective. It would be overpowered by peer reinforcement. However, a group-oriented contingency could work for this problem. Similar to the situation above, the teacher would need a baseline of the rate of verbal arguments with the teacher. Verbal arguments would include any verbal statement made that defies or questions a teacher directive regarding a request for some behavior on the part of the students. Examples could include "Why do we have to do something so lame?" Or "I would not give this assignment to my dog."

To produce peer withdrawal of attention, the teacher would set a behavioral standard for the entire class based on the baseline data. The group contingency requires that the teacher base the standard on the group's level of this behavior. The reinforcer is available for the group if they do not exceed the standard (e.g., eight or less) or withdrawn for the students if they do exceed the standard.

In this particular hypothetical example, the range of arguments with teacher directives in the baseline ranged from 6 per day to 15, with a mean of 11. If the teacher sets the behavioral standard at 11 for a given day, any rate at or below that level would entail the entire class's getting an extra five minutes of lunch recess. Failure to achieve such would require that the class come in at the usual time.

Tangible Reinforcers

Treating a problem behavior maintained by social mediation of a tangible reinforcer involves two basic changes: (a) the teacher disables the target behavior's socially mediated function and (b) the replace-

Table 7.6
FUNCTIONAL TREATMENT FOR SMA OF TANGIBLE REINFORCERS

MO for Desired Item or Activity	*Efficiency to Produce Desired Item or Activity: Replacement Behavior*	*Efficiency to Produce Desired Item or Activity: Problem Behavior*	*Probability of Replacement Behavior*
high	high	low	high

ment behavior's function is now enabled. Functional treatment involves a switching of contingencies as depicted in Table 7.6.

IT'S COMPUTER TIME. It might be easy to see how a teacher can reinforce such disruptive behavior with access to a preferred event. A student is creating a disruption in the class and at some point in the episode, the teacher places him on the computer. Such a change does quell the student's disruption at that time (a relief for the teacher). Unfortunately, the long-term result of failing to decode the function of this problem behavior is to ensure its existence for the foreseeable future. Solving this problem involves a rearrangement of contingencies. Currently, this hypothetical teacher interprets this display of inappropriate behavior to mean that he needs a change in activity. Disruptive behavior should not produce computer time. Rather, an alternate appropriate behavior should replace it.

There are many possibilities for strengthening a particular replacement behavior in this case. For example, contingent upon a designated request (appropriate replacement behavior), the student receives access to the computer for a short time. Of course, one would withhold computer for a specified amount of time if this student engaged in target problem behavior. However, such a program has significant shortcomings. While disruptive behavior would decrease so too might work performance. It may be possible to put a limit on the number of breaks that a student could request.

A better strategy would be the following; designating the completion of some number of task(s) as the behavioral standard for accessing the computer. For example, in the beginning, the teacher might require this student to do two and a half pages of class work as the requirement for earning ten minutes on the computer. Of course, the teacher could progressively increase this with success. Disruptive behavior should not lead to computer access. Rather disruptive behavior serves to delay access.

I AM HUNGRY NOW. How does one develop an alternate behavior for the student reported in Chapter 2 who engaged in self-injury? Self-injury was instrumental in accessing food. If the child is incapable of producing vocal requests, the child needs to develop alternate forms of communicating desire for food. The treatment plan would involve reinforcement of signing behavior with food and the removal of food when he engages in self-injury. Table 7.7 delineates the specifics of this program.

Table 7.7
BEHAVIORAL INTERVENTION PLAN

Target Behavior: self-injury, hits to face and head area.

Rationale for Plan: The continued presence of this client's target problem behavior warrants health and welfare concerns. Such behavior also interferes with instruction since his desire to eat can occur during an instructional period.

Target Behavior's Function: SMA tangible reinforcer, food.

Functional Behavioral Assessment Data: Observation of client revealed that self-injury at various levels and intensities usually results in getting food. This was particularly true after a lengthy episode in which staff would give him crackers which, of course, would put a halt to his self-injurious behavior while he consumed his snack (and shortly after that).

Additionally, the teacher or staff member implemented two test conditions across seven days to verify experimentally the hypothesis regarding the function of self-injury. In one test condition, self-injury was reinforced on a fixed ratio 3 schedule (test condition A). In the second test condition (B), staff prompted and reinforced the sign for "eat," which resulted in getting food. The rate of pinching as a function of test condition A or B appears below.

Test Condition	A (first) day)	B (2nd day)	B	B	A (5th day)	B	B
Rate of pinching	14	5	2	0	26	0	0

The comparison of the A versus B condition indicates that when self-injury is the only venue for getting food, such behavior occurs frequently. When an alternate behavior is prompted and reinforced, self-injury was lower for all five days (see test condition B). Further, once the student acquired the request without needing a prompt, self-injury became nonexistent (see last three data days under test condition B). Access to tangible reinforcer is the hypothesized function of self-injury.

Alternate Behavior: Raising hand to produce staff attention.

Contingency for Target Behavior: When the student engages in self-injury, the teaching staff will not provide food for at least 30 seconds after the last hit, facing away from the student. Following such behavior and its subsiding, the staff will provide effective prompts for the alternate replacement behavior.

Contingency for Alternate Behavior: When student manually signs "eat," the teacher will provide crackers or preferred food items in small bites so as to allow many opportunities to earn food via manual sign. If requests for food begin to occur too often or in contexts where food is normally not given, the teacher should consider an additional component to the program. For example, the teacher can add on a DRH to the DRA program. To reduce continued access to food just for signing, the teacher could impose a task requirement as an additional requirement. For example, when the client desires food and the student signs for food, the additional requirement is for the client to complete a short task before the teacher will honor the sign.

Table 7.7 continued

Behavioral Plan to Strengthen Alternate Behavior: Currently, the student needs to be physically prompted to perform the manual sign. Two sessions of structured training will occur each day until the manual sign for "eat" is occurring without any prompt other than a general prompt like "What do you want?"

Instructional Modifications: Not applicable since behavior is serving an attention function.

FUNCTIONAL TREATMENT: SME CATEGORIES

In functional treatment of SME behaviors, the action frame can be used to explain how to make an alternate acceptable behavior functional while making the current target behavior less functional (or non-functional). Table 7.8 illustrates how the replacement behavior can become more likely under states of aversive presentation. This function develops or occurs as a result of the replacement behavior's being made effective by the social environment at terminating the undesired event. The last row illustrates how to render the target behavior ineffective in terminating the aversive condition. Hence, such problem behavior undergoes extinction in favor of the designated replacement behavior's newly established function.

Unpleasant Social Situations

Treating a problem behavior maintained by escape from unpleasant social situations involves two basic changes: (1) disable the target

Table 7.8
FUNCTIONAL TREATMENT OF SME FUNCTIONS

MO	*Behavior (engaged in)*	*Environmental Result*	*Maintaining Contingency*
Aversive state (relative)	Replacement behavior occurs	Someone terminates the aversive condition	Socially mediated negative reinforcement
Aversive state (relative)	Target behavior occurs	Someone does not terminate the aversive condition	Extinction

Table 7.9
REDUCED REQUIREMENT

Presence of Aversive Condition (relative)	Behavior	Effect in Terminating the Aversive Event	Future Probability of Behavior Under MO
Time for PE, 100 jumping jacks	Does 25	Completes her participation in that activity	More likely to get 25 jumping jacks as her portion of the activity

behavior's socially mediated function via escape extinction, and (2) enable the replacement behavior's function by terminating the aversive condition (or postponing its advent). Functional treatment requires the social environment to enable the replacement behavior by making it more effective at escaping such an event. Concurrently, the target problem behavior is disabled by making it inefficient and less likely to terminate such a condition. Because of this switch in contingencies, the probabilities of the two behaviors change under the MO. The probability of the student's exhibiting the problem behavior becomes low while the likelihood of the replacement behavior is high.

I DON'T LIKE PE! What is a replacement strategy for children who dread PE? Perhaps requiring a small amount of participation and then allowing them to leave the activity. A plan that requires that the student perform a fraction of the expected amount of activity to get out of the remainder of the performance requirement can be effective (see Table 7.9). Requiring less can do the trick.

As a side note, one reason for this hypothetical student's dislike of the activity may be her lack of skill or performance. Of course, letting her out of PE does not aid skill acquisition. One cannot acquire skill at a given exercise if one is successful at not engaging in it. Practice does make better. Setting up a contingency that requires some practice in the physical activity as an effective manner of terminating the event may also begin to change this student's participation in another manner. As she becomes more engaged in exercise because of this contingency, her skill level becomes more pronounced. If she still has difficulty in the exercises, perhaps a little more attention to the instructional technique being used is in order.

ANOTHER EXAMPLE. What would be the functional intervention strategy for a hypothetical eleven-year-old student with learning disabilities who engages in disruptive and aggressive behaviors during assemblies? Perhaps moving him to an area where he is away from other students when he is disruptive will solve the problem of bothering the other students in the assembly while still requiring him to sit there until he demonstrates the escape behavior, i.e., sits for two minutes without disruption. The teacher could enhance this procedure with an additional consequence when removal to an area away from other children becomes necessary, such as loss of recess time.

Progressively increasing the requirement could shape greater levels of tolerance to sitting in assemblies. The teacher could set the initial start point at two minutes. With success in achieving such, the teacher could increase the length to four minutes following two successful assemblies. Possibly, at the end of the year, this student may be able to sit for 15-20 minutes, the average range of assemblies in this school. The written plan appears in Table 7.10.

Relatively Lengthy Tasks or Assignments

For some children, having to work for long periods in independent seatwork produces that same state of aversion. For some children, math periods that last 50 minutes are 40 minutes too long. If the period lasted for only ten minutes, there would be no problems. However, a 50-minute period produces behaviors that occur under conditions requiring escape. Therefore, the functional treatment strategy allows an alternate behavior, e.g., finishing one's work for a shorter assignment, as the venue for terminating the task. Given that length of the instructional condition is the parameter, shortening it is necessary. Note that this intervention changes behavior initially by altering the aversive nature of the instruction (duration or length) thus affecting the student's motivating condition. Of course, as the student succeeds in performing the shortened task, the teacher can progressively alter the task length until it matches the criterion level needed for that grade level or program.

Treating a problem behavior maintained by escape from lengthy tasks or assignments involves two basic changes in the manner in which the social environment responds. The two changes necessary are the following: (1) the teacher disables the target behavior's socially medi-

Table 7.10
BEHAVIORAL INTERVENTION PLAN DURING ASSEMBLIES

Target Behavior: disruptive behavior during assemblies.

Rationale for Plan: The continued presence of this client's target problem behavior makes him less open to large peer-group activities and can lead to more severe forms of escape. Developing an effective plan will allow him to remain with his peers when in large groups.

Target Behavior's Function: SME; unpleasant social situations.

Data on Functional Analysis: Observation of this student reveals that disruptive behavior is of increased frequency with longer assemblies. The teacher used two assemblies for this observation. The data on the target behavior for each assembly are delineated in five-minute increments (scatter plot below).

	Assembly 10/10	*Assembly 10/20*
0–5	X	
6–10	X	X
11–15	XX	
16–20	XXXX	XXXX
21–25	XXXXXX	XXXXXX
25–30	XXX	XX *
Total	15	15 (did not attend full)

* Sent to principal's office for becoming unmanageable

Alternate Behavior: Sitting without engaging in disruptive behavior for defined time period.

Contingency for Target Behavior: Contingent upon disruptive behavior, teacher moves student to an area away from other students and resets the timer for the full DRO interval.

Contingency for Alternate Behavior: Sitting for two minutes without disruptive behavior leads to escape from assemblies.

Behavioral Plan to Strengthen Alternate Behavior: Shaping of the dimension of time sitting appropriately in assemblies, i.e., sitting without engaging in disruptive behavior.

Instructional modifications: Not applicable, since behavior is serving an escape function during a social situation, not an instructional situation.

Table 7.11
FUNCTIONAL TREATMENT FOR LENGTHY INSTRUCTIONAL PERIODS

Presence of Aversive Condition (relative)	Behavior	Effect in Terminating the Aversive Event	Future Probability of Behavior Under MO
Lengthy instructional period (language arts	Breaks contingent on sustained work	Effective	More likely
	Disruptive behavior	Not effective	Less likely

ated function via escape extinction, and (2) the social environment now enables the replacement behavior's function by terminating the aversive condition (or postponing its advent). Functional treatment requires the teacher to enable the replacement behavior by making it more effective at escaping lengthy tasks or instructional periods. Concurrently, the teacher disables the target problem behavior by making it inefficient and less likely to terminate such a condition. Because of this switch in contingencies, the probabilities of the two behaviors change (see Table 7.11). Escape extinction is often procedurally different from extinction procedures for SMA behaviors. With escape extinction, one does not allow the target behavior to escape the instructional condition; instead the alternate behavior is allowed to accomplish that.

If escape from the task (a break from the existing instructional material) is contingent upon completing a smaller amount of the total task, then such behavior will become functional. Concurrently, escape from the task should not occur or not be as lengthy as the break for disruptive behavior. The teacher can accomplish this by a priori designating how much work the student needs to complete before the student can switch to an alternate more preferred activity, thus temporarily escaping the existing instructional materials and lesson. Of course, after the break, the same contingencies go into effect.

The rearranged contingencies for a hypothetical student might be the following. If the student works for ten minutes on the assigned task without disruptive behavior, he or she can get a break for four minutes as timed by an oven timer. If he engages in disruptive behavior prior to the ten minutes elapsing, the teacher resets the timer for an additional three minutes on top of what existed. As this student becomes adept at achieving a change in activities with this new contingency arrangement, the teacher can progressively impose a more stringent requirement for task engagement time. The teacher can progressively alter the standard for reinforcement as a function of performance. With this gradual alteration of task engagement, the student can eventually reach levels of task engagement with no disruptive behavior for a desired length of time. This plan enables appropriate behavior and disables the function of disruptive behavior.

WORK UP TO IT. If you were just starting to initiate an exercise program, do you think that one that lasts two hours each day would be suitable for you? Suppose the exercise period is shortened initially to 15 minutes of sustained exercise, would that be less aversive for a beginner? If the length of such an activity is lessened, avoidance of the activity becomes less likely.

One must realize that tolerance of lengthy instruction needs to be progressively developed. Shortening the specific activity in the mainstream class to a more reasonable length would be "clinically indicated." The teacher might accomplish this by shortening the actual time spent in the mainstream setting (see Table 7.12). If the student is successful in completing the work, he or she would get a tangible reinforcer and return to the resource room or classroom. If unsuccessful in completing the short assignment (that is relevant to the instruction being delivered), the student would just return to the special education setting without obtaining the tangible reinforcer. Providing a tangible reinforcer helps to increase the student's motivational state to perform adequately on the task.

Table 7.12
BEHAVIORAL INTERVENTION PLAN FOR MAINSTREAMED STUDENT

Target Behavior: mild disruptive behavior and verbal complaints about work in mainstream setting.

Rationale for Plan: The continued presence of this target problem behavior and the concurrent lack of performance on the instructional materials in the mainstream setting make future integration efforts less likely.

Target Behavior's Function: SME; lengthy tasks or assignments.

Functional Behavioral Assessment Data: Observation of student reveals that as length of time spent in mainstream setting gets longer, problem behavior increases in

Table 7.12 continued

frequency, and concurrently, on-task behavior drops to very low levels, requiring numerous prompts from aide to get back to work.

Additionally, the teacher implemented two test conditions on alternate half hour days. In one test condition, the teacher cut the length of time spent in the mainstream setting from one hour to 20 minutes (test condition A). In the second test condition (B), the length of time spent in the mainstream setting was the usual one hour. The data on the target behavior under the B condition are for the hour-long instructional session. The data for the test condition A are for the 20-minute session. In parentheses is the average interval of nonoccurrence for the session.

Test Condition	B	A	B	A	B	A	B
Rate of problem behavior	6 (every 10')	0	10 (every 6')	1 (every 20')	6 (every 10')	0	10 (every 6')

The comparison of the A versus B condition indicates that when the length of the mainstream participation is lengthy (one hour), problem behaviors occur at elevated levels (see test condition B). When the student receives a brief assignment as in test condition A, its rate goes to zero or near zero levels. Escape from lengthy instructional sessions is the hypothesized function.

Alternate Behavior: sustained on-task behavior and assignment completion in mainstream setting.

Contingency for Target Behavior: Contingent upon target problem behavior such as complaining about assignment or mild disruptive behavior, the instructional assistant adds an extra two minutes to the DRO interval length that exists at the time. The initial DRO interval length is set at six minutes.

Contingency for Alternate Behavior: Contingent upon completing the assignment with no target behaviors occurring for a six-minute DRO interval, the student receives ten points to be traded in for free time in the special setting with friends at the end of the day. She must earn at least 20 points to earn 8 minutes, 30 points earns her 12 minutes. Failure to earn requisite number of points results in withdrawal of special activity time.

Behavioral Plan to Strengthen Alternate Behavior: Since the student is capable of performing the work, the teacher uses nothing more than simple reinforcement contingencies for the alternate behavior which were nonexistent previously. Additionally, producing extinction for the escape behaviors will alter the contingencies even more.

Instructional Modifications: None needed since the student is capable of doing the assignment. The teacher and the IEP team will alter the length of time in mainstream setting initially. With success the teacher will progressively increase the length of time in the mainstream setting.

I'LL HIT MYSELF. For students with severe disabilities that engage in severe self-injury, the teacher must drastically alter the amount of the work requirement when such behavior is functional in terminating lengthy tasks. It is also important to establish that the required performance is in the repertoire of the child or that effective prompting is provided before the self-injury initiates. In some cases, the teacher may program escape from the instructional setting for completing just one simple task, such as putting two items in a cup upon command.

DEVELOPING CONTINUOUS ATTENTION. The Good Listening Game.[1] Many young children have difficulty in preschool and early elementary grades attending in a continuous fashion to an adult's reading of stories or presenting content material. They engage in a number of interfering behaviors (I.B.s) which divert their attention from the story. These I.B.s can range from turning one's head away from the adult reader and getting up from the seated area to many other types of I.B.s and sometimes disrupting peers from attending in the process. Whatever the form, I.B.s result in the break of the child's sustained attention from the material the teacher is presenting.

Continuous attention needs to be gradually shaped. For example, a child may be able to sit on a carpet square for about a minute, listening to the teacher read a story before the first occurrence of interfering behaviors. Unfortunately, 95 percent of the reading periods are in excess of five minutes. A discrepancy exists between the child's current level of sustained attention and the level of attention that is required. The interfering behaviors become more frequent and pronounced as the story progresses in duration. Consequently, the child may never acquire the skill to attend continuously when the lengths of the stories far exceed his or her current level.

To solve this dilemma, the teacher can use a shaping program that progressively increases the time requirement. The Good Listening Game[1] develops an initial level of *continuous* attention (without interfering behaviors) to adult oral presentations, such as reading a story or text material, while the child remains in a seated position. The Good Listening Game can often be conducted in nonschool environments. For school environments, pull-out programs could deliver this game. It is best performed with one child at a time. However, the teacher can

---

1. I developed this as part of a training program called the Sustained Performance Curriculum.

use the principles of shaping across a school year to increase progressively children's attention to adult presentations.

A child's motivation to comply with the game requirements may not be sufficient for each session. It is, therefore, imperative with most children (there are exceptions) that a highly preferred activity follow the successful playing of the game in the manner of the Premack Principle. For example, if the child is successful in completing the requirements of the game, he or she then goes to a preferred activity. For home use, parents can set up the Good Listening Game right before afternoon cartoons, allowing an effective Premack contingency.

It is important to define for yourself and the child what are the specific interfering behaviors that will result in the contingency delineated below. Children vary with respect to those behaviors that break sustained attention. For some children, such behaviors are blatantly obvious. The child may turn away from the adult to look at something or someone. For others, it can be a variety of fidgety behaviors. It is important to define individually and list these at the outset so that the game can proceed in a manner that will decrease such behaviors. This game focuses on sustained attention; therefore, the single occurrence of interfering behaviors breaks sustained attention. Each occurrence of an I.B. should produce an immediate specific consequence. It is, therefore, important for you to have a clear definition of I.B.s for a child so that you can enact the consequence immediately. When in doubt, any behavior that looks like nonattending should qualify.

Set the game up by getting the area ready for story time. The teacher or parent should designate length of time the child must continuously attend to the story (without asking questions). For example, "I will be reading the Christmas story for two minutes." Set an oven timer for that value. Explain the structure of the Good Listening Game, including how long the story will last, what are the behaviors that result in a consequence, and what activity follows the successful completion of the game.

Begin to read the story or content material. Do not interrupt the flow of the story by asking questions during the reading (only for the beginning phase of the Good Listening Game to ensure child's continuous listening). If an I.B. occurs, stop reading immediately, reset the oven timer for an additional amount and begin again (this is the consequence for I.B.s used in this game). Play the game until the child has

Table 7.13
DATA DURING STORY TIME

Name of Child: J.D.

Time: 7:40 p.m.

Story Read: three minutes

Interfering Behaviors (I.B.s): asking questions, making comments, turning around, getting up, playing with shoes or socks

Rate of I.B.s in consecutive 30-second intervals (three minutes = six intervals)

30 sec. int	Frequency of I.B.s
1	0
2	0
3	X
4	XXX
5	XX
6	XXXXX

reached the designated time criterion for completion, i.e., oven timer goes off and no I.B.s have occurred for that time.

Determining the initial length of the story or presentation is very important. Setting a lengthy time for the escape criterion would doom the game to failure. You should conduct a brief baseline assessment to determine the initial length of the story time. For the first three or four sessions in playing the game, read a story for about a five-minute period (use oven timer). Tell the child to do his or her best to listen to the story. As you read the story, note the time during the story when each I.B. occurs in 30-second blocks of time. An example of this type of data is given in Table 7.13. The data are presented in successive 30-second intervals.

The first I.B. occurred sometime during the first 30 seconds of the second minute of the story (denoted by X in interval three). Subsequent to that, you can see the frequency of the I.B.s rise dramatically (e.g., 3 I.B.s in interval four, etc.). The time between breaks in continuous performance, therefore, gets shorter (which is not good). If the other sessions' data mimic what appears above, a good initial start point for this student might be a one-minute story, but probably no longer than one and a half minutes. A bad (i.e., unreasonable) value to select would be three minutes, since it is highly unlikely that this child will be able to perform at this level right off the bat. Set up for success!

The escape contingency is conditional upon the student's not engaging in a single I.B for the length of the story. If an I.B. does occur, the teacher adds on an additional amount of story time to the oven timer. For example, if a student engages in an I.B. within the story time designated at one and a half minutes, an additional 30 seconds is added to the oven timer at its current value.

Once the child has been successful with the initial length of the story time, e.g., not performing an I.B. in four to five sessions, the teacher can gradually increase the length of the story. For example, if you started with a three-minute requirement, and you had success for five of six sessions, then you might adjust the value to four minutes. If you started with an initial value of one minute, you might adjust to 1.5 minutes. This process of increasing slightly the length of the game is contingent upon success with the prior time requirement. Success means completing the story for the designated length of time without having to reset the timer. If you have to add additional time for a session, that session the teacher would not designate **this** as a success. *If the number of times the child is unsuccessful becomes frequent, this is a hint to reduce the storytime length.*

As mentioned earlier, in the beginning of the Good Listening Game, do not interrupt the flow of reading of the material by asking questions assessing the child's comprehension. This is to develop the length of sustained listening to a reasonable level for the school program. Once the child has developed an adequate level of sustained attention and listening, you can then intersperse questions about the material that the child can answer (start with only one story interruption for comprehension questions in the beginning). When you want to begin reading the story again, provide a clear signal, e.g., "O.K., let's get back to the story." Any I.B.s that occur subsequent to this signal should result in the immediate cessation of story reading and adding an additional amount to the timer. It may take the child some time to learn to sustain attention to the reader once questions are interspersed within the story.

Relatively Difficult Task or Assignment

This category is different from all the other SMA and SME functions. To address this function adequately, the teacher must alter the difficulty of the task. The teacher can accomplish this by using three different methods: easy interspersed tasks, teaching prerequisites, and guided practice on specified target skills.

IMPLEMENTING INTERSPERSED EASY TASKS. An instructional mismatch occurs when a teacher asks someone to perform instructional tasks that are beyond his or her current capability (Cipani & Belfiore, 1999). When students repeatedly face such a daily condition, they can become disruptive. Fortunately, there is a technique that teachers can use to increase the student's task engagement when facing challenging reading material–interspersed easy tasks. This technique alters the aversive nature of the material as do the other two methods used to intervene with behavior problems in this category.

The use of easy interspersed tasks involves designating a ratio of easy to difficult items. Roberts and Shapiro (1996) demonstrated that the best results for reading assignments are when the ratio of training words to review words is 0.50 (i.e., 50% known words and 50% new training words). If possible, try to intersperse known words within the context of new words on training exercises. For example, if you were to present ten new words to read in a reading assignment, you might consider reducing the new words to five and adding five known words to the list, coming up with ten words.

The use of easy interspersed material may require some front-end modifications of the material on the part of the teacher (Koegel & Koegel, 1986). The teacher may accomplish the interspersing of easy material by breaking up a student's assignment into several mini-assignments. The student may read half a page of the target reading material followed by a practice list of known and unknown words from the text (would probably constitute an easier task). The teacher would then repeat this process for the remainder of the assignment. Additionally, you will want to reduce the amount of independent seat assignments with grade level texts since the student is not competent on the material to rehearse alone. The response cards technique would be most suitable with these students (see Chapter 10).

The diagnostic steps to conduct prior to utilizing the interspersed easy task technique are the following:

- Collect information on the student's current rate of on-task behavior and level of problem behavior during assignments (termed baseline data).
- If rates of on-task behavior are low and rates of problem behavior are high, consult any testing data that may give an indication as to the student's achievement level in reading and other relevant content area (including comprehension levels).
- If standardized testing is unavailable, conduct an informal assessment by having the student read passages in the currently used text and then read passages from a text of lower grade reading level.
- If the student performs significantly better on material of a lower reading level, then it is quite probable that an "instructional mismatch" exists. Present the student with a few assignments from the text with the lower reading level over the next couple of days.
- Compare the rates of problem behavior and on-task behavior during these assignments with the rates of problem behavior and on-task behavior obtained during the baseline (see #1 above).
- If rates of behavior dramatically differ, this student would benefit from interspersed easy tasks.

The following behavioral intervention plan indicates how the teacher would deploy interspersed easy tasks with an additional contingency for a hypothetical student (see Table 7.14).

TEACHING AND DEVELOPING PREREQUISITE SKILLS. It is often the case that students who are several grade levels below their counterparts in academic content areas engage in problem behavior. Such behaviors function to avoid or terminate class assignments or tasks. While easy interspersed tasks are an intervention that can be brought to bear quickly, it is not a long-term solution. The skill deficits that exist still require remediation, and the teacher may need a revision in the curriculum (Dunlap, Kern-Dunlap, Clarke, & Robbins, 1991).

How likely is it for a student to be successful in adding two, three digit numbers with carry to tens and hundreds places if she is incapable of adding two, two-digit numbers without carrying? Very often, class assignments become aversive because the student cannot per-

Table 7.14
WRITTEN BEHAVIORAL PLAN–INTERSPERSED EASY TASKS

Target Problem Behavior(s): (1) High rates of disruptive behavior and (2) low rates of on-task behavior during reading periods

(1) Disruptive behavior is any behavior that disrupts the learning environment for the teacher or the class. The following specific observable behaviors constitute examples of disruptive behavior (identify what class rules when violated would be incidents of disruptive behavior):

- unauthorized out-of-seat incidents during seatwork or lecture
- inappropriate noises
- teasing comments
- refusal (can be either verbal or physical) to comply with teacher instruction
- profanity or loud verbally abusive behavior

(2) On-task behavior is defined as the student engaged in the reading material (face-to-book orientation) or attending to the teacher's presentation (facing toward teacher). Any behavior that does not fall into this class of behaviors is off task. Attending to the book or teacher while engaged in some other activity, e.g., playing with a string, talking to someone, is off-task behavior. On-task behavior will be monitored via the beeper system and will be summed as a percentage of time on-task, e.g., ten on-task recordings on beep against 20 total beeps equals a 50% on-task rate.

Baseline Data:
- Using the above definition of disruptive behavior, the teacher recorded the following rates of disruptive behavior during reading assignments over an eight-day period: 3, 4, 2, 6, 1, 2, 3, 2.
- Using the above definition of on-task behavior, the teacher recorded the following percentages of on-task behavior during reading assignments over an eight-day period: 30, 44, 20, 46, 15, 25, 40, and 40.

Results from FBA: Student is reading two grade levels below curriculum materials being used in the class during reading periods. Two separate tests conducted by the teacher on oral reading accuracy and fluency with random selections from the text revealed a significant number of errors and a nonfluent oral reading of words, taking about three times as long to get through the two paragraphs as other students would take. Additionally, during one period when she was given a reading assignment from a text that is two grade levels below her standardized reading level, the student's disruptive behavior decreased 70% from baseline mean and on-task behavior improved dramatically during that one test period.

Target Objective: The student will reduce her level of disruptive behavior to an acceptable level (averaging no more than one occurrence per week).

- Short Term Goal): Two or fewer occurrences
- Three-month goal: One or no occurrences

Table 7.14 continued

> • Long-term Objective: averaging no more than one occurrence per week
>
> **Initial Plan:**
> The technique of interspersed easy items or tasks will serve to facilitate the student's ability to stay engaged in the reading assignment. This technique will present her with mini-tasks, which involve an assignment in the reading text interspersed with an easier task (known words from a reading list).
>
> In addition to the use of interspersed easy tasks, the teacher will also implement the beeper system with self-monitoring. The teacher will use this additional component to enhance the student's motivation to stay engaged in the task. During the reading assignment, 15 unpredictable beeps will occur. When the beep goes off, the student records on the self-management form whether she was attending to the in-seat assignment (i.e., she was either reading or writing) or was off task. If the student was attending (i.e., on-task), she records a fixed number of points (e.g., five points) for that beep signal. If she was off task, she records no points for that beep signal. The timing of the beep is unpredictable so that the student never knows when she will be monitored.. The student has to earn a certain number of points (e.g., 60 out of a 75 maximum total) in order to complete the assignment successfully. When she achieves this designated number, the teacher allows her to conclude the seat assignment for the remainder of the reading period. The student is then able to select an alternate preferred activity as a reward. This selected activity can be an in-seat activity such as reading a preferred magazine, a coloring activity, doodling, drawing, computer time, small individual games, etc.). The student is allowed to remain in the preferred activity as long as she does not violate the rules established for this activity.

form the beginning prerequisites of the task. Of course, one way to reduce the aversion to the target skill is to develop the prerequisite skills to a competent level before presenting the student with the target task.

Particularly in math, the acquisition of target skills relies heavily on the child's adeptness at prerequisite skills. A hierarchical approach that requires child mastery of prerequisite skills before targeting more advanced skills is essential. Children who lack prerequisite skills have a difficult, if not impossible, time attempting to keep up with their class. It is hard to teach a child to multiply two numbers with several digits with carry to all places when she is incapable of multiplying a two-digit number by a one-digit number without carrying. It is like putting the apple cart before the horse. A hierarchical approach also allows you to provide targeted instruction on the prerequisite skill. You directly teach the skill of interest. The student does not have to discover how to do something (thus leaving many children in the dust). It is our job, as teachers, to identify what the child needs to learn and target that skill.

PROVIDING GUIDED PRACTICE. Let's say you are interested in learning a new computer skill. You attend a class in which the instructor explains all the various functions of the software and demonstrates each function once. The presentation was about an hour in length. You go through your day, wanting to get home and try out the new software but do not get an opportunity to get on your computer until 8 P.M. You load the software and get ready to use it. Unfortunately, you forgot how to perform some of the initial functions and after trying like crazy to get it to work, you give up. You state, "I am just not good with this computer stuff!"

What is unfortunate is that the training did not provide any (let alone sufficient) supervised rehearsal of each skill by the participants. It is highly likely that many of the participants could not work with the new software once they got home. The instructional program is to blame! If this happens to adults, you can imagine what transpires with students in math, science, and other content areas when a teacher presents new concepts with insufficient guided practice during class time. Particularly for students with special needs, frequent opportunities to respond under supervision are essential to learner progress. This aspect of teaching is so important that I have dedicated an entire separate chapter in this text to cover an instructional method that accounts for repeated opportunities: response boards.

SUMMARY

Functional treatment requires a switch in the existing classroom contingencies. The teacher needs to disable the target problem behavior's current function and concurrently enable the replacement behavior's function. One cannot implement a functional treatment if a functional behavioral assessment has not revealed a potential or probable behavioral function for the target behavior. This chapter presented potential differential reinforcement plans that would provide an alteration of the existing contingencies for both problem behavior and the designated replacement behavior.

CHAPTER 7: SUMMARY TEST

(Answers on CD)

True or False

1. A replacement behavior for aggressive behavior is usually asking someone nicely for a desired item.
2. A problem behavior maintained by escape from an aversive event would be targeted for extinction if a replacement behavior is made to produce escape from that situation.
3. A replacement behavior replaces a behavioral function.
4. If a target behavior serves an escape function (from relatively lengthy tasks or assignments), a replacement behavior could involve the reinforcement of assignment completion with contingent praise.
5. If a behavior serves an access to tangible reinforcers function, than a teacher could treat that behavior functionally by providing such access contingent upon a small amount of work completed.
6. In functional treatment, the use of the functional reinforcer for the replacement behavior is essential.

A short, fill-in-the-blanks test can be found in Appendix A.

Chapter 8

NONSOCIALLY MEDIATED FUNCTIONS OF PROBLEM BEHAVIOR

While the overwhelming majority of behavior problems in classrooms involve socially mediated contingencies, not all behavior is a function of what people do after the behavior (Cipani, 1990; Cipani & Schock, 2007; Kennedy, Meyer, Knowles, & Shulka, 2000; Vaughn & Michael, 1982; Vollmer, 2006). For example, if you drove your car today, how did you get the engine to start? Putting the key in the car and turning it with a certain amount of force produces the desired result (car starting) directly. If starting the car is the desired event, it occurred by the chain of behaviors you performed, independent of anyone's mediation. Here is another example. If you were hungry this morning and wanted an apple out of the refrigerator, you probably just got one on your own. Getting an apple was a function of a chain of behaviors that you displayed in a sequence, which led to ingestion of the apple. How did you get in your home after a day of classes? When you got home after class, you put the house key in the lock of the door and opened the door. It is important to note that all these examples involve a chain of behaviors that produce the reinforcer immediately and directly. Another person does not have to mediate the behavior by producing the reinforcer. Alternately, if you want to cool off after being in the sun too long on a hot day, you jump in the pool or take a shower. The change in outer body temperature is immediate and occurs without someone else doing something.

Additionally, certain behaviors are maintained because they directly terminate aversive conditions that exists. Similar to the above nonsocially mediated positive reinforcement contingencies, people do not mediate the termination of the aversive event. If you want to cool off after being in the sun too long on a hot day, you jump in the pool or take a shower. The change in outer body temperature is immediate and occurs without someone else doing something. If you are dead tired, lying down on your bed produces the reinforcer directly (termination of motoric activity). You walk into a noisy room to study for the midterm exam and find the level of noise aversive and subsequently walk out. The aversive situation was directly terminated when you left the room. A socially mediated behavior that would produce the same result would be if you had said, "Can we have some quiet here," and everyone obeyed your request.

Here is an example that many college students are intimately familiar with on a personal level. Let us say you have to study for an exam coming up. Also let us assume you are a student who wants to do well in college, because grades affect what happens after college. The advent of the exam exerts some level of motivation for engaging in study. You begin studying in earnest. After one hour of continuous reading and study, you get "tired." At that point, you put down your textbook, get up, and take a break. This chain of behaviors produces escape from the study materials directly, without another person's mediation of such behaviors. Once you had a sufficient amount of time away from the materials, you return to them for additional study. You can take a break from study when you deem it necessary. Unfortunately, students in K–12 grade levels cannot decide when to take their breaks. A high school student cannot simply get up and take a break, without the teacher doing something. Therefore, other behaviors must "fill the void," when the state of aversion reaches an uncomfortable level. Hence, many problem behaviors are socially mediated in classrooms due to the inability of students to choose when to take a break.

This chapter covers behaviors that produce the desired consequence directly, hence nonsocially mediated behavior problems. Some problematic behaviors are functional because their occurrence directly produces the desired event (in the case of positive reinforcement). Some problematic behaviors directly terminate an aversive condition, which makes them functional under those conditions. I will detail both of these direct functions with relevant examples in the rest of the chapter.

NONSOCIALLY MEDIATED FUNCTIONS:
POSITIVE REINFORCEMENT

Teaching personnel should not always assume that the problem be-havior is socially mediated. Assessing for potential nonsocially mediat-ed functions of problem behavior is particularly relevant when work-ing with students with severe disabilities who have limited communi-cative capability. These students' inability to exhibit behaviors that rel-iably result in other people delivering desired items or activities makes such direct attempts the primary venue for meetings their needs. There are two categories involving behaviors that produce the positive reinforcer directly: (a) Producing tangible reinforcers directly and (b) producing sensory events and stimuli that function as positive rein-forcers.

NONSOCIALLY MEDIATED ACCESS
TO TANGIBLE REINFORCERS

This category of function involves a behavior that produces de-sired items or events directly. Grabbing or taking some item, without asking, is an example. Most of the classroom behavior problems that fall into this category are phenomena that occur with students with severe disabilities. Such students, due to their communication deficits, can resort to such a behavior because alternate behaviors are not in their current repertoire. If the student has a reinforcement history of such behavior being successful in getting desired items, such a pattern of behavior will become a primary method of accessing certain rein-forcers. In these cases, the child needs to be taught the appropriate manner of accessing desired reinforcers.

INAPPROPRIATE GRABBING OF DESIRED ITEMS. Some young chil-dren will grab items or objects without asking. Such behavioral inci-dents can often be corrected easily with nondisabled children. Parents and teachers present mild disapproval with a corrective action to in-hibit such nonsocially mediated attempts in the future. Simply telling the child, "we ask before we grab something," is often successful in teaching the appropriate behavior to young children.

However, for students with severe disabilities, changing such be-haviors may require more effort to intervene effectively. If the student is unable to vocally request a desired item, such a deficit makes grabbing the desired item the most efficient means of access. Grabbing items becomes more probable when two antecedent conditions are in effect: (a) the MC for the specific item is relatively strong and (b) there is no reliable socially mediated alternate (more preferred) behavior. In the latter case, the social environment is unable to determine when such desire is prevalent and hence unable to reinforce some non-vocal request response.

For example, a student with profound mental retardation wants to play with a piece of shoelace string. She wiggles the shoelace in front of her face, being engrossed with such a phenomenon for long periods of time (stereotypic behavior). When the morning instructional period starts, the teacher takes the piece of string from her, to deny her access to it. Let us say that she is not used to abstaining from playing with the string for longer than 30 minutes. If the morning instructional period is lengthy, and she cannot have her string until noon, you can see the problem. Access to the string becomes a progressively more deprived state. This deprivation state sets the stage for a behavior that has resulted in string access in the past. As a result, she runs and grabs the string. As she runs to get the string, she knocks over some papers and books on the teacher's table. The teacher deems her obsession with the shoelace to be interfering with her instructional program.

Any designed behavioral intervention must take into account that obtaining the shoelace string is the driving force behind such disruptive behaviors. Therefore, interventions that manipulate other consequences will prove ineffective. An intervention that has classroom personnel ignore these "breaks" for the string will prove ineffective. Using a contrived reinforcer for not engaging in the disruptive behavior will also not yield desired outcomes. Making string access contingent on an alternate behavior is the key to solving this problem.

A functional intervention for this problem in a classroom setting would be twofold. First, the teacher would designate the completion of some amount of work as the behavioral criterion to gain string access for a designated period of time (see Premack contingency in Chapter 3). This teacher could also require the student to perform a non-vocal request for the string access once the student has earned the shoelace because of completing the work (see Table 8.1). Second, the teacher should prevent unauthorized access to the item. Access should only

Table 8.1
FUNCTIONAL TREATMENT FOR GRABBING PROBLEM

MC for Playing with Shoe Lace	*Efficiency to Access String: Completing Three Tasks Followed by Signed Request*	*Efficiency to Access String: Unauthorized Grabbing*	*Probability of Replacement Behavior*
high	high	low	high

occur when the student has performed the work requirement and requested the shoelace from the teacher. If the teaching personnel develop and reinforce such a sequence of behaviors, task completion and non-vocal requesting will increase. This intervention will also affect the disruptive behaviors.

Developing a task performance contingency for this item, would have two behavioral results. First, work performance would increase because of the strengthening of the contingencies for doing class work. Therefore, work completion (currently a low probability event or behavior) would be greatly improved. Second, this functional plan disables the problem behavior's current function. Leaving the seat without permission and grabbing the string would not result in playing with the shoelace. As a result, dashing out of one's seat to get the string will undergo extinction.

JUMPING OUT OF ONE'S WHEELCHAIR. A nationally recognized behavior analyst (Dr. Jon Bailey) was called to consult with a facility on a case involving a 29-year-old man with profound mental retardation (Bailey & Pyles, 1989). The problem behavior involved jumping out of his wheelchair unaided. In one unfortunate incident, he leaped from the wheelchair and landed on the floor headfirst. This incident produced severe contusions and abrasions on his head, with significant blood loss. He was rushed to the hospital's emergency room.

Why would someone do such a dangerous stunt? The staff reported that their attention followed such incidents involving jumping out of the wheelchair. Many staff people thereby surmised that their attention must have been reinforcing the behavior of jumping from the wheelchair. In fact, some staff persons felt that he *liked* the medical attention he received when he bled profusely! I must say, that is one heck of a price to pay for bandages! While there certainly was probably a reliable relation between jumping out of the wheelchair onto the floor and getting staff attention, was attention the maintaining event for such behavior? Could it be that staff attention is tangential to the "real purpose" of this dangerous form of leaving the wheelchair? Particularly with individuals with severe disabilities, some behaviors occur because they are the most direct route to the desired reinforcer or most efficient manner of escape from the aversive condition.

Upon further query of staff and observation, the consultant identified another consequence of the behavior. First, the consultant identified that this person spent an overwhelming part of his waking hours every day in a wheelchair. Given his size, it was difficult for staff to take him out of the wheelchair with some level of frequency and regularity. What was directly produced when this person flung himself from the wheelchair was access to the floor and concurrently escape from his wheelchair. This client had devised his own manner of getting floor time. He became a jumper! He jumped out of his wheelchair and then he had access to the floor. Unfortunately, in this case described above, what did not seem to be existent was a more desirable and less dangerous socially mediated behavior (e.g., waving his hand to get out of wheelchair). Setting up a schedule of removing him from the wheelchair several times a day would be a step in the right direction.

Again, it is often that people will ascribe adult attention as the function to many student behavior problems. Particularly with individuals with severe disabilities, some behaviors occur because they are the most direct route to the desired reinforcer or most efficient manner of escape from the aversive condition. Unfortunately, in the case described above, what did not seem to be existent was a more desirable and less dangerous socially mediated behavior (e.g., waving his hand to get out of wheelchair).

HYPOTHETICAL EXAMPLE: REQUESTING HELP. Mr. Turin, a high school special education teacher has a class of students who are learning independent skills for daily living. Mr. Turin wants to teach one of his students, Mary, how to request her communication board when she needs help with some task. Currently, she sometimes gets hurt or makes a mess trying to do something she cannot do and could use help. For example, she could not open the juice box when she was eating her lunch the other day. She took a butter knife and tried to poke a hole in it and cut herself slightly on the wrist. The use of the butter knife is maintained because of its non-socially mediated function, i.e., cutting bread. It would be wise to develop an alternate socially mediated behavior for accessing help. The request for help when she wants something but cannot safely or effectively perform the requisite behaviors that produce it need to be shaped and reinforced.

To provide direct training on asking for help with her communication board, Mr. Turin presents her with the following situation. He asks Mary when she comes in to "Go hang up your coat on the coat rack." To make it a circumstance requiring help, he has placed the coat rack high enough so Mary cannot reach it. When this circumstance presents itself, Mary should get her communication board, and request help by pointing to the symbol on the communication board asking for "help." The teacher would then proceed to help her hang her coat on the rack. The teacher uses this strategy for many other items. Eventually, this generalizes to times when Mary needs help with other items or activities. The training procedures used by this teacher are the following:

1. Develop child's ability to use the communication board.
2. Present child with a request.
3. Present child with situation where s/he needs communication board to ask for help because compliance to the request is hindered.
4. If child does not get her communication board out, prompt that behavior, "Do you need your communication board?"
5. Prompt if necessary the child pointing to the symbol for "help."
6. Reinforce a request for help made via the communication board. Do not mediate situation unless communication is made through the board.

Immediate Sensory Effects

These behaviors have often been termed stereotypic or self-stimulatory behaviors. Stereotypic behavior involves a pattern of a behavior that occurs repetitively in bursts of time. For example, some students rock back and forth repeatedly, hundreds of times throughout the day, every day. For other students, licking a certain window constitutes their preferred and frequent ritual.

Children with autism and severe disabilities, who engage in repetitive behaviors for lengthy periods, often do so to produce an immediate sensory result. These children, who often do not find social interactions with other children and adults desirable, find immediate environmental effects desirable (Hanley, Iwata, Thompson, & Lindberg, 2000). Watching water hit a plate in the sink produces a sound and a visual event. Spinning a plastic plate on a tile or linoleum floor produces a sound and a unique visual event. The immediate sensory events produced by these repetitive behaviors are the culprit in the maintenance of such behaviors. Such a NONSOCIALLY mediated function makes effective treatment of such ritualistic behavior more difficult to procure.

TIME-OUT MEANS TIME TO "SELF-STIM." A landmark study provided evidence that repetitive stereotypic behavior can produce directly its own sensory reinforcer (Solnick, Rincover, & Peterson, 1977). A six-year-old girl with autism who engaged in tantrum behavior received time-out when she engaged in tantrum behavior. Unfortunately, time-out did not produce the desired decrease in tantrum behavior. Why did contingent time-out fail to reduce tantrum behavior? These researchers spent time watching the girl when she was placed in time-out. While she was in time-out, she repetitively engaged in stereotypic behavior, in the form of weaving her fingers in a pattern. Being in time-out produced a "safe" condition for her to engage in such behavior unregulated by anyone. Concurrently, the teacher would prevent stereotypic behavior during instructional contexts. Sending her to time-out contingent upon tantrum behavior, where she has ad lib access to engage in finger weaving was obviously a flawed plan.

This study has important implications for the use of a time-out procedure with students with disabilities and/or autism. If the student can entertain him/herself via stereotypic behavior, then a time-out procedure may have disastrous consequences for the target behavior under that contingency. A functional behavioral assessment would indicate that such a contingency is enabling the target problem behavior, not disabling it.

DISCERNING FUNCTION. In some cases, stereotypic behaviors might serve an escape function. For example, Durand and Carr (1987) found that children engaged in self-stimulatory behaviors such as body rock-

Table 8.2
PERCENTAGE OF STEREOTYPIC BEHAVIOR
UNDER TWO TEST CONDITIONS

Baseline	30%	60%	40%	50%	60%				
Ignore						50%	50%	60%	40%

ing and hand flapping, when task difficulty increased. When difficult material was presented, engaging in stereotypic behavior would certainly allow for the temporary halt to engaging in the task. To address the need for helping the student with difficult material, the experimenters developed an instructional intervention. They taught the student to say or communicate the phrase, "Help me," following an incorrect response. Once the student communicated the need for help, the teacher would then provide help to the student on the task. As a function of the development of this skill, the student's self-stimulatory behavior was markedly reduced during task demands.

It would be important to discern if stereotypic behaviors are a function of the immediate sensory event they produce. Setting up a test condition that would be predicated on it being socially mediated, by ignoring it when it occurs may present data that would rule out an SMA function (see functional behavioral assessment chapter for details). You would then compare this condition with a baseline condition where attention is provided on the usual schedule. If the rate of stereotypic behavior does not drop during the ignore condition, one can conclude that a sensory reinforcer is probably maintaining the particular form of behavior. Table 8.2 presents hypothetical data that shows the rate of stereotypic behavior about the same between the baseline and ignore conditions. This would be indicative of a hypothesis of sensory reinforcer for such behavior.

Suppose the rate of stereotypic behavior goes down when attention is removed for such behavior? Table 8.3 depicts such a behavioral effect. The removal of teacher attention as well as any potential access to tangible reinforcers, produced an extinction condition. The decrease in this behavior (see second row) if replicable would point to a socially mediated function for stereotypic behavior.

Pica: Putting Inedible Items in Your Mouth. Another behavior possibly maintained by producing a direct path to the desired

Table 8.3
EVIDENCE OF SOCIALLY MEDIATED FUNCTION

Baseline	30%	40%	40%	50%	40%				
Ignore						10%	10%	0%	5%

event is pica. Pica is the term for the act of putting inedible objects in one's mouth. For example, a hypothetical child with autism sticks inedible plastic things in his mouth and gnaws on them. We might consider the act of grinding and gnawing on such items (like chewing gum or hard candy) as a pleasurable event for this student. This form of behavior can be maintained by the phenomenon that is directly produced by the behavior. While social attention in the form of a reprimand may also follow the behavior, it is irrelevant to the actual function of the behavior. If removing attention for this behavior does not result in an amelioration of such behavior, "negative" attention was not the desired consequence for this student's pica behavior.

Determining the specific reinforcer for pica is important. Suppose a student engages in pica because he is hungry and occasionally, the item he puts in his mouth can be eaten. He may not be very discerning in terms of which items are edible, hence sometimes items that are not edible, and are on the floor, end up in his mouth. The treatment for such a function would be to teach him to nonvocally request food from a staff person by going up to them, getting their attention and then signing, "Eat." To set up the teaching environment for this skill, his teacher asks the aides in the classroom to set up a mid-morning snack time. In order to teach him to request food, contingent upon the student signing, "eat," he is given a small bite of the snack food. This allows the staff to provide 12–20 opportunities each snack period to sign "eat." Once the student is independently signing eat when the aide has face-to-face contact with him, the instructional staff now want to teach him how to get someone's attention. The teacher begins a program to teach him how to come and get one of them to make his request for food. The teaching procedures for developing appropriate attention-getting behavior in students with severe disabilities are:

1. Develop sign for eat using discrete trial format and small amounts of food as the reinforcer for manual sign.

2. During snack time, instead of facing the child, the teacher will face away from the child, but sitting next to him.

3. Gesture him to tap you on the arm.

4. Contingent upon the child tapping your arm (each time), you will turn and face the child. Ask "What do you want?".

5. Reinforce the child's signed request, "eat" by providing a small amount of snack item, thus setting up another opportunity to repeat the process when the child finishes the small amount.

6. Repeat the above procedure each day until arm tapping is occurring consistently.

7. Move one to two feet away, then gesture for the child to tap your arm.

8. Reinforce the child's chain of behaviors involving walking towards you and tapping you on the arm by saying "What do you want?" Repeat steps 5–6.

9. Alter the distance you are from the child on consecutive sessions so that eventually the child can walk up to you, wherever you are in the classroom area, or other room, and exhibit appropriate attention-getting behavior.

10. Use the same process with a few other situations where the child desires an activity or item, until the attention-getting behavior generalizes to multiple conditions.

NONSOCIALLY MEDIATED FUNCTIONS: NEGATIVE REINFORCEMENT

This category of function involves problem behavior that directly terminates the involvement of the student in aversive activities or interactions. The same categories of aversive events would be relevant under nonsocially mediated functions. However, the difference is that that the target behavior directly terminates, for some period of time, the student's presence in the aversive event. Passive off-task behavior is probably the best example of a nonsocially mediated escape problem behavior. When you get tired of studying, you stop and look out the window. If that is somewhat of a relatively short in duration and infrequent event, it causes no problem. Unfortunately, when it is of lengthy duration, a teacher in school will admonish the student to get back to work. To deal with high rates of passive off-task behavior

Table 8.4
NONSOCIALLY MEDIATED ESCAPE BEHAVIOR

Motivating Conditions	Discriminative Stimuli	Behavior	Consequent Events
Aversive task	Lack of proximity of adults, or adult who will not stop behavior	Runs out of class	Terminates seatwork condition for some period of time

across an entire class or group, a response cards format that is interspersed with seatwork would greatly help (see Chapter 10).

RUNNING OUT OF CLASSROOM. A student with mild disabilities and behavior disorders runs out of the classroom several times a week. The teacher and school psychologist feel that the teacher's attention to such incidents is the function. Based on that hypothesis, they agree that the teacher should ignore such him when he runs out of the classroom. The teacher agreed to stop running after him when he bolts out the door. They will just make sure that he does not run off campus or into another classroom. Unfortunately, after several weeks of ignoring these incidents, they have not seen a decrease in such episodes. Rather, the student is more frequently leaving the classroom unauthorized.

It seems that the attention hypothesis was wrong. It has become more clear the instructional conditions that prevail when the student leaves the classroom. Such incidents never seem to happen around language arts activities, but seem more probable in math period, particularly when there is a seat assignment. If the MC is the particular task assignment, and not the absence of attention, then leaving the classroom functions to terminate the assignment, not gain teacher attention (see Table 8.4).

SUMMARY

Not all problem behaviors are socially mediated. Particularly if you are a teacher of students with severe disabilities and autism, you need to consider that some problem behaviors are maintained because of their direct result on the environment. This chapter highlighted some of the nonsocially mediated functions problem behaviors can have. In the case of behaviors that produce a positive reinforcer directly, there are two categories: (a) nonsocially mediated access to tangible items and (b) immediate sensory events. Nonsocially mediated functions can also occur for behaviors that directly terminate an aversive context or event. It is imperative for the teacher of students with severe disabilities to understand this type of function and be able to prescribe a behavioral intervention that functionally addresses the reason for its occurrence.

CHAPTER 8: SUMMARY TEST

(Answers on CD)

True or False

1. Nonsocially mediated functions would entail both positive and negative reinforcement operations.
2. Sticking something inedible in one's mouth would probably be nonsocially mediated if the behavior occurs across many social contexts.
3. A problem behavior that is maintained by socially mediated access to tangible reinforcers is a good example of a nonsocially mediated function.
4. Stereotypic behaviors produce sensory events that will always function as a reinforcer.
5. Stereotypic behaviors produce sensory events that can function as a reinforcer.
6. Running out of the classroom is a behavior that always occurs for the attention it receives.
7. What a teacher does after a behavior serves to maintain behaviors that have a nonsocially mediated function.

A short, fill-in-the-blanks test can be found in Appendix A.

Appendix A

TEST ITEMS WITHIN CHAPTERS

This text is intended to target and develop performance skills that are overtly demonstrated in a classroom. The following performance tasks for the chapters provide an assessment of the skill via a scenario where the display of the knowledge of how to perform the skill is inherent in the essay response. While test items at the end of each chapter for measuring specific aspects of knowledge is essential, it is not completely sufficient for practice. Ultimately, the terminal skill would be the display of competence on the performance tasks delineated below.

If you are an in-service instructor, you can devise essay questions that measure the performance tasks for the given chapter by following the format for the questions offered below.

Fill-in-the-Blanks Test
(Answers found on CD)

Chapter 1

1. A behavioral frame consists of an analysis of these three conditions (A-B-C), _____.
2. The two variables in the antecedent condition are _____.
3. A deprivation state or _____ can be an antecedent condition for a student's behavior.
4. When a behavior does not result in a reinforcer, what happens to the motivating condition?
5. If a deprivation condition for any individual is _____, then going 4 hours without playing outside may or may not produce an MC for that event.
6. The deprivation condition makes a behavior that is effective _____ it more likely.

7. What is the MC for SMA behaviors? _____ What is the MC for SME behaviors? _____

8. A socially mediated behavior is one in which the reinforcer is _____.

9. People are _____ for certain behaviors under certain MCs.

Chapter 2

1. When the target problem behavior is functional in producing a reinforcer; what is the relative effectiveness of appropriate behaviors under that particular MC? _____

2. Deprivation of a particular event is _____ an absolute state across all humans.

3. If attention from an adult is in a relatively deprived state, what makes a behavior functional?

4. The three SMA categories are: _____

5. The three SME categories are: _____

6. Teacher attention is a _____ function.

7. If aggression is more effective in terminating an unpleasant social situation than another behavior, it will be _____ under that aversive condition.

8. SME functions occur to _____ conditions as an antecedent to behavior.

9. A relatively lengthy instructional task sets up a _____ condition for a behavior that serves an SME function.

10. An undesirable behavior such as aggression can be functional under antecedent conditions of relative deprivation of tangible items by _____.

11. A behavior that is multi-functional can be highly probable under _____ motivating conditions.

Chapter 3

1. A contingency is a relationship between _____.

2. Operant behaviors are controlled by their _____, and can be either strengthened in probability or weakened.

3. The consequences of operant behaviors make these behaviors either _____ in future probability of occurrence.

4. If a change in a behavior's consequence increases the probability of the target behavior, _____ has occurred.

5. The difference between positive reinforcement and punishment is the _____.

6. Negative reinforcement is similar to positive reinforcement in that both operations _____.

7. Using a high probability behavior to reinforce a lower probability behavior is an example of the _____.
8. When you finish your homework, you can go outside is an example of the _____.
9. A stereotypic behavior of a child with autism could be used in a Premack contingency to increase task engagement by making authorized access to such behavior contingent on _____.
10. What can be done to enhance the potency of an event to function as a positive reinforcer?
11. An event is satiated when you _____ a student with free access to it for a long time.
12. Reinforcing a target behavior every nine occurrences is called a _____ schedule of reinforcement.
13. Reinforcing a target behavior about every five occurrences is called a _____ schedule of reinforcement.
14. Progressively altering the schedule of reinforcement from an FR 1 schedule to a VR 5 schedule is called _____ the schedule of reinforcement.

Chapter 5

1. Because behavior is situational, the student should be observed in the _____ of interest.
2. A behavioral assessment _____ incorporate personality measures via paper and pencil tests.
3. A baseline rate of a student's incorrigibility would _____ be a reliable behavioral measurement.
4. A baseline rate of a student's out-of-seat behavior would involve a _____ count of each occurrence of that behavior.
5. The method that requires a teacher to record the length of time a behavior occurs is a _____.
6. Interval recording determines the _____ of a behavior within a given interval.
7. Response _____ is the duration of time a behavior occurs from a designated stimulus.
8. On-task behavior is best measured by an _____ system.
9. The method that observes the student at select points in time and records the occurrence or nonoccurrence of the behavior is a _____.

Chapter 6

1. The Iwata et al. 1982 study used _____ to determine the function of each child's self-injury.

2. In the Iwata study, the demand condition _____.
3. In the Gaylord-Ross and Weeks (1981) study, the presentation of difficult tasks resulted in _____ in problem behaviors when contrasted with the rate of problem behavior under the easy tasks condition.
4. A risk condition is an antecedent condition where the problem behavior is _____.
5. A scatter plot method of data collection is used to reveal how often and _____ a target problem behavior occurs.
6. A scatter plot records the frequency of the target problem behavior as a function of _____.
7. An in-situ hypothesis test determines function by _____.

Chapter 7

1. A problem behavior maintained by escape from an aversive event would be targeted for _____ if a replacement behavior is made to produce escape from that situation.
2. A replacement behavior replaces a _____.
3. If a target behavior serves an escape function (from relatively lengthy tasks or assignments), a replacement behavior could involve the reinforcement of assignment completion with _____.
4. If a behavior serves an access to tangible reinforcers function, than a teacher could treat that behavior functionally by providing such access _____ a small amount of work completed.
5. In functional treatment, differential reinforcement entails the use of the _____ for the replacement behavior.

Chapter 8

1. Sticking something inedible in one's mouth would probably be _____ if the behavior occurs in the absence of people.
2. A problem behavior that is maintained by a child grabbing the item without permission is probably a good example of a _____.
3. Stereotypic behaviors produce sensory events that can function as a _____.
4. Running out of the classroom is a behavior that may occur to _____ escaping the classroom context.
5. What a teacher does after a behavior serves to maintain behaviors that have a _____.

Appendix B

PERFORMANCE TASKS

Chapter 1

Chapter 1: None

Chapter 2

Chapter 2 Performance Task: Able to determine socially mediated function of problem behavior.

As Measured By (AMB): Able to generate a scenario that depicts either an SMA function or SME function, by describing the existing MC, the maintaining contingency, the relative efficacy of the target behavior to produce the function versus other behaviors, and the effect the reinforcer has on the MC. The following assessment identifies the requirements of this Task.

Sample test item:

Target behavior: Refuses to do work.

Hypothesized behavioral function: Escape from lengthy task assignment.

Provide a scenario that supports the escape function (given lengthy task assignment) for this target behavior by:

- Describe existing MC.
- Describe contingency.
- Describe how target behavior is MCre efficient & effective in producing specific reinforcer, by presenting a behavioral frame of target behavior and other behaviors in terms of function.
- Describe how delivery of reinforcer affects the MC.

- Draw a behavioral frame depicting the function of the target behavior and other behaviors, i.e., a graphic depiction of above information.

Chapter 3

Chapter 3: None

Chapter 4

Chapter 4 Performance Task: Able to contrive a reinforcement plan using shaping, by delineating the initial standard as well as the progressive alterations as a function of student progress. for problem behavior, using a potential reinforcer(s) identified via one of several methods.

Chapter 5

Chapter 5 Performance Task: Collects a direct measurement of the target problem behavior (and alternate behaviors), by using a concrete behavioral description and objective method of quantification.

AMB: Able to collect baseline data on a direct measurement of a target behavior and plot such data on a graph, using an observational measurement system or a criterion-referenced test in the case of a learning objective.

Test item:

Target behavior: Verbal refusal to engage in assignment.

Provide a direct measurement system for the target behavior that delineates the following:

- Behavioral description of the target behavior with Test items.
- Observational system using a method of measuring the behavior that is congruent with behavioral description.
- Hypothetical baseline data graphed.

Chapter 5 Performance Task: Collects a direct measurement of the target problem behavior (and alternate behaviors), by using a concrete behavioral description and objective method of quantification.

AMB: Able to construct a measurement method for a given target behavior problem along with the presentation of hypothetical baseline data.

Test item: Directly measuring aggressive behavior towards adults.

- Explain how you would develop a frequency measure of aggressive behavior. What would be the hypothetical definition of aggressive behavior for this case, including concrete examples. Present a hypothetical baseline condition with al least seven sessions of data for this behavior. Then explain how you would determine if this level of out-of-seat behavior is in need of intervention.
- Explain how you would develop a duration measure of aggressive behavior. What would be the hypothetical definition of aggressive behavior for this case, given the duration measurement, including concrete examples. Present a hypothetical baseline condition with al least seven sessions of data for this behavior. Then explain how you would determine if this level of out-of-seat behavior is in need of intervention.
- Explain how you would develop an interval recording system for aggressive behavior, with the length of the interval specified and the method of scoring the behavior. What would be the hypothetical definition of aggressive behavior for this case, including concrete examples. Present a hypothetical baseline condition with al least seven sessions of data for this behavior. Then explain how you would determine if this level of out-of-seat behavior is in need of intervention.

Chapter 6

Chapter 6 Performance Task: Collects data that can identify context of problem behavior, including antecedent and consequent variables.

AMB: Able to collect data regarding possible function of a problem behavior with either a descriptive analysis assessment, in-classroom hypothesis test, or a safe/risk analysis from scatter plot data.

Test item:

Target behavior: Getting out of seat.

Hypothesized behavioral function: Adult attention.

- Provide a descriptive analysis, using a behavioral frame for several frames that illustrate how the target behavior obtains adult attention whereas other behaviors were ineffective.
- Provide scatter plot data that identifies periods when the problem

behavior is highly likely and when it is very unlikely.

- Provide an in-classroom hypothesis test that presents data indicative of an attention function for out of seat instances, include a delineation of specifics of the two test conditions and data on the rate of out of seat across a number of alternated sessions of test condition A and test condition B.

Chapter 7

Chapter 7 Performance Task: Uses hypothesis regarding function of problem behavior to derive a functional treatment program involving differential reinforcement.

AMB: Able to apply one of several functional treatment plans involving differential reinforcement (with use of the functional reinforcer) to a target behavior problem with an identified functional SMA or SME category.

SMA Functions

Test item:

- Target behavior: A student's out-of-seat behavior.
- Instructional target: Decrease rate of out-of-seat occurrences for this student.
- Function: Peer attention.

Using a DRL procedure, identify how you would do the following:

- Collect baseline data on the group.
- Determine the behavioral standard for the group.
- Specify the exact contingency, involving the behavioral standard and reinforcer delivery for the group.
- Specify what happens when out-of-seat behavior occurs with anyone in the group.

SME Functions

Test item:

- Target behavior: A student's disruptive behavior.
- Instructional target: Decrease rate of designated disruptive behaviors

for this student.
- Function: Removal from instructional setting.

Using a differential reinforcement procedure for task completion, identify how you would do the following:

- Collect baseline data.
- Determine the behavioral standard for the DRH.
- Specify the exact functional treatment contingency, involving the behavioral standard for escape from instruction.
- Specify what happens when the student does not reach the behavioral standard.

Test item: Manipulating the antecedent condition.

- Target behavior: An SDC student's tantrum behavior when he wants to get out of a language task involving identifying comMCn objects.
- Instructional target: Decrease rate of tantrum.
- Function: Immediate release from instructional condition.

Using a strategy of ameliorating the MC, identify how you would do the following:

- Collect baseline data.
- Determine how the MC for escape from language tasks will be identified.
- What would be done to lessen the MC at this time if it is task difficulty.
- What would be done to lessen the MC at this time if it is task duration.
- If a contingency will be used in addition, specify the exact contingency, involving the behavioral standard and escape from language session.
- Specify what happens when tantrum behavior occurs.

REFERENCES

Azrin, N. H., & Armstrong, P. M. (1973). The "Mini-Meal"–a method for teaching eating skills to the profoundly retarded. *Mental Retardation, 2,* 9–13.

Azrin, N. H., McMahon, P., Besalel, V. A., Donahue, B. C., Aciemo, R., & Kogan, E. S. (1994). Behavior therapy for drug abuse: A controlled outcome study. *Behavior Research and Therapy, 32,* 857–866.

Bailey, J. S., & Bostow, D. E. (1981). *Research methods and applied behavior analysis.* Tallahassee, FL: no Copy Grafix.

Bailey, J. S., & Pyles, D. A. M. (1989). Behavioral diagnostics. In E. Cipani (Ed.), *The treatment of severe behavior disorders: Behavior analysis approach* (pp. 85–107). Washington, DC: American Association on Mental Retardation.

Bijou, S. W., Peterson, R. F., & Ault, M. H. (1968). A method to integrate descriptive and experimental field studies at the level of data and empirical concepts. *Journal of Applied Behavior Analysis, 1,* 175–191.

Blair, K. C., Umbreit, J., & Boss, C. S. (1999). Using functional analysis and children's preferences to improve the behavior of a child with behavior disorders. *Behavior Disorders, 24,* 151–166.

Bradley, R. (1999, September). *Functional assessment and the Federal IDEA mandate.* Paper presented at the Florida Association for Behavior Analysis Convention, Tampa, FL.

Carr, E. G., Newsom, C. D., & Binkoff, J. A. (1976). Stimulus control of self-destructiuve behavior in a psychotic child. *Journal of Abnormal Child Psychology, 4,* 139–153.

Carr, E. G., Newsom, C. D., & Binkoff, J. A. (1980). Escape as a factor in the aggression of two retarded children. *Journal of Applied Behavior Analysis, 13,* 101–117.

Carr, J. E., Taylor, C. C., Wallender, R., & Reiss, M. (1996). A functional analytic approach to the diagnosis of a transient tic disorder. *Journal of Behavior Therapy and Experimental Psychiatry, 21,* 291–297.

Charlop, M. H., Kurtz, P. F., & Casey, F. G. (1990). Using aberrant behaviors as reinforcers for autistic children. *Journal of Applied Behavior Analysis, 23,* 163–181.

Ciminero, A. R. (1977). Behavioral assessment: An overview. In A. R. Ciminero, R. S. Calhoun, & H. E. Adams (Eds.), *Handbook of behavioral assessment* (pp. 3–13). New York: John Wiley & Sons.

Ciminero, A. R., & Drabman, R. S. (1977). Current developments in the behavioral assessment of children. In B. B. Lahey & A. E. Kazdin (Eds.), *Advances in clinical child psychology* (Vol. I). New York: Plenum.

Cipani, E. (1981). Contingency and ecological components in training a profoundly retarded adult to self-feed. *Behavioral Engineering, 7,* 23–26.

Cipani, E. (1990). The communicative function hypothesis: An operant behavior perspective. *The Journal of Behavior Therapy and Experimental Psychiatry, 21,* 239–247.

Cipani, E. (1994). Treating children's severe behavior disorders: A behavioral diagnostic system. *Journal of Behavior Therapy and Experimental Psychiatry, 25,* 293–300.

Cipani, E. (1995). Be aware of negative reinforcement. *Teaching Exceptional Children, 27,* 36–40.

Cipani, E. (2004). *Punishment on trial.* Reno, NV: Context Press. (www.ecipani.com /PoT.pdf)

Cipani, E. (2008). *Classroom management for all teachers: Plans for evidence-based practice* (3rd ed.). Columbus, OH: Prentice Hall.

Cipani, E., Augustine, A., & Blomgren, E. (1981). Teaching severely and profoundly retarded residents to open doors: Assessment and teaching methods. *Journal of Special Education Technology, 3,* 42–46.

Cipani, E., & Belfiore, P. J. (1999). Presenting instruction: Easy (to hard) does it. *Proven Practice, 2,* 28–33.

Cipani, E., & McLaughlin, T. F. (1983). The effects of contingent re-checking on academic performance. *Corrective and Social Psychology, 29,* 88–93.

Cipani, E., & Schock, K. (2007). *Functional behavioral assessment, diagnosis, and treatment: A complete system for education and mental health settings.* New York: Springer Publishing.

Cipani, E., & Schock, K. (2011). *Functional behavioral assessment, diagnosis, and treatment: A complete system for education and mental health settings* (2nd ed.). New York: Springer Publishing.

Cipani, E., & Spooner, R. (1997). Treating problem behaviors maintained by negative reinforcement. *Research and Intervention in Developmental Disabilities, 18,* 329–342.

Cipani, E., & Trotter, S. (1990). Basic methods of behavioral intervention. In E. Cipani & A. F. Rotatori (Eds.), *Advances in special education, 7*(A), 137–201.

Clark, H. B., Rowbury, F., Baer, A. M., & Baer, D. M. (1973). Timeout as a punishing stimulus in continuous and intermittent schedules. *Journal of Applied Behavioral Analysis, 6,* 443–455.

Cone, J. D., & Hawkins, R. P. (1977). *Behavioral assessment: New directions in clinical psychology.* New York: Brunner/Mazel.

Cooper, J. O., Heron, T. E., & Heward, W. L. (2007). *Applied behavior analysis* (2nd ed.). Upper Saddle River, NJ: Pearson Education, Inc.

Corey, J. R., & Shamow, J. (1972). The effects of fading on the acquisition and retention of oral reading. *Journal of Applied Behavior Analysis, 4,* 311–315.

Day, H. M. (1987). Comparison of two prompting procedures to facilitate skill acquisition among severely mentally retarded adults. *American Journal of Mental Deficiency, 91,* 366–372.

Derby, K. M., Wacker, D. P., Sasso, G., Steege, M., Northrup, J., Cigrand, K., & Amus, J. (1992). Brief functional assessment techniques to evaluate aberrant behavior in an out patient setting: A summary of 79 cases. *Journal of Applied Behavior Analysis, 25,* 713–721.

Durand, V. M., & Carr, E. G. (1987). Social influences on self-stimulatory behavior. *Journal of Applied Behavior Analysis, 20,* 119–132.

Dunlap, G., Ferro, J., & DePerczel, M. (1994). Nonaversive behavioral intervention in the community. In E. Cipani & F. Spooner (Eds.), *Curricular and instructional approaches for persons with severe disabilities* (pp. 117–146.) Needham Heights, MA: Allyn & Bacon.

Dunlap, G., Kern-Dunlap, L., Clarke, S., & Robbins, F. R. (1991). Functional assessment, curricular revision, and severe behavior problems. *Journal of Applied Behavior Analysis, 24,* 387–397.

DuPaul, G. J., & Ervin, R. A. (1996). Functional assessment of behaviors related to attention deficit/hyperactivity disorder: Linking assessment to intervention design. *Behavior Therapy, 27,* 601–622.

Ervin, R. A., DuPaul, G. J., & Kern, L., P. C. (1998). Classroom-based functional and adjunctive assessments: Proactive approaches to intervention selection for adolescents with attention deficit hyperactivity disorder. *Journal of Applied Behavior Analysis, 31,* 65–78.

Fisher, W. W., Adelinis, J. D., Thompson, R. H., Worsdell, A. S., & Zarcone, J. R. (1998). Functional analysis and treatment of destructive behavior maintained by don't (and symmetrical do) commands. *Journal of Applied Behavior Analysis, 31,* 339–356.

Fleece, L., Gross, A., O'Brien, T., Kistner, J., Rothblum, E., & Drabman, R. (1981). Elevation of noise volume in young developmentally disabled children via an operant shaping procedure. *Journal of Applied Behavior Analysis, 14,* 351–355.

Foxx, R. M. (1977). Attention training: The use of overcorrection to increase the eye contact of autistic and retarded children. *Journal of Applied Behavior Analysis, 10,* 489–499.

Gardner, W. I., Cole, C. L., Berry, D. L., & Nowinski, J. M. (1983). Reduction of disruptive behaviors in mentally retarded adults: A self-management approach. *Behavior Modification, 7,* 76–96.

Goldfried, M. R., & Kent, R. N. (1972). Traditional versus behavioral assessment: A comparison of methodological and theoretical assumptions. *Psychological Bulletin, 77,* 404–420.

Gunter, P. L., Venn, M. L., Patrick, J., Miller, K. A., & Kelly, L. (2003). Efficacy of using momentary time samples to determine on-task behavior of students with emotional behavioral disorders. *Education and Treatment of Children, 26,* 400–412.

Hanley, G. P., Iwata, B. A., Thompson, T. A., & Lindberg, J. S. (2000). A component analysis of "stereotypy and reinforcement" for alternate behavior. *Journal of Applied Behavior Analysis, 33,* 299–308.

Harop, A., & Daniels, M. (1986). Methods of time sampling: A reappraisal of momentary time sampling and partial interval recording. *Journal of Applied Behavior Analysis, 19,* 73–77.

Harris, K. R. (1986). Self-monitoring of attentional behavior versus self-monitoring of productivity: Effects on on-task behavior and academic response rate among learning disabled children. *Journal of Applied Behavior Analysis, 19,* 411–424.

Hayes, L. A. (1975). The use of group contingencies for behavioral control: A review. *Journal of Applied Behavior Analysis, 8,* 341–347.

Hersen, M., & Barlow, D. H. (1976). *Single-case experimental design: Strategies in studying behavior change.* New York: Pergamon.

Hesse, B. E. (1993). The establishing operation revisited. *The Behavior Analyst, 16,* 215–217.

Holland, E. L., & McLaughlin, T. F. (1982). Use of response cost, public posting and group contingencies to manage student behavior during supervision. *Journal of Educational Research, 76,* 29.

Horner, R., & Day, H. (1991). The effects of response efficiency on functionally equivalent competing behaviors. *Journal of Applied Behavior Analysis, 24,* 719–732.

Individuals with Disabilities Education Act, Pub. L. 105-17,20 D.S.C. § 1400 et seq. (1997).

Iwata, B. A. (1987). Negative reinforcement in applied behavior analysis: An emerging technology. *Journal of Applied Behavior Analysis, 20,* 361–378.

Iwata, B. A. (May 28, 2006). On extinction. Association for Behavior Analysis Convention, Atlanta, GA.

Iwata, B. A., Dorsey, M. F., Slifer, K. J., Bauman, K. E., & Richman, G. S. (1982). Toward a functional analysis of self-injury. *Analysis and Intervention in Developmental Disabilities, 2,* 3–20.

Iwata, B. A., & Bailey, J. S. (1974). Reward versus cost token system: An analysis of the effects on students and teachers. *Journal of Applied Behavior Analysis, 7,* 567–576.

Iwata, B. A., Pace, G. M., Cowdery, G. E., & Miltenberger, R. G. (1994). What makes extinction work: An analysis of procedural form and function. *Journal of Applied Behavior Analysis, 27,* 131–144.

Iwata, B. A., & Smith, R. G. (2007). Negative reinforcement. In J. O. Cooper, T. E. Heron, & W. H. Heward (Eds.), *Applied behavior analysis* (2nd ed.) (pp. 291–303). Upper Saddle River, NJ: Prentice-Hall/Pearson.

Iwata, B. A., Vollmer, T. R., & Zarcone, J. H. (1990). The experimental (functional) analysis of behavior disorders: Methodology, applications, and limitations. In A. C. Repp & N. N. Singh (Eds.), *Current perspectives in nonaversive and aversive interventions with developmentally disabled persons* (pp. 301–330). Sycamore, IL: Sycamore Publishing Co.

Jackson, G. M. (1979). The use of visual orientation feedback to facilitate attention and task performance. *Mental Retardation, 27,* 281–304.

Kennedy, C., Meyer, K., Knowles, T., & Shulka, S. (2000). Analyzing the multiple functions of stereotypic behavior for students with autism. *Journal of Applied Behavior Analysis, 33,* 559–571.

Kennedy, C. H., & Souza, G. (1995). Functional analysis and treatment of eye poking. *Journal of Applied Behavior Analysis, 28,* 27–37.

Koegel, L. K., & Koegel, R. L. (1986). The effects of interspersed maintenance tasks on academic performance in a severe childhood stroke victim. *Journal of Applied Behavior Analysis, 19,* 425–430.

Lalli, J. S., Browder, D. M., Mace, F. C., & Brown, D. K. (1993). Teacher use of descriptive analysis data to improve interventions to decrease students' problem behaviors. *Journal of Applied Behavior Analysis, 26,* 227–238.

Laraway, S., Snycerski, S., Michael, J., & Poling, A. (2003). Motivating operations and terms to describe them: Some further refinements. *Journal of Applied Behavior Analysis, 36,* 407–414.

LaVigna, G. W., Willis, T. J., & Donnellan, A. M. (1989). The role of positive programming in behavioral treatment. In E. Cipani (Ed.), *The treatment of severe behavior problems: Behavior analysis approach* (pp. 59–83). Washington, DC: American Association on Mental Retardation.

Lennox, D. B., & Miltenberger, R. G. (1989). Conducting a functional assessment of problem behavior in applied settings. *The Journal of the Association for Persons with Severe Handicaps, 14,* 304–311.

Mace, F. C., Lalli, J. S., & Pinter-Lalli, E. (1991). Linking descriptive and experimental analyses in the treatment of bizarre speech. *Journal of Applied Behavioral Analysis, 24,* 553–562.

McLaughlin, T. F. (1983). Effects of self-recording for on-task and academic responding: A long term analysis. *Journal for Special Education Technology, 5*(3), 5–12.

McLaughlin, T. F., Burgess, N., & Sackville-West, L. (1981). Effects of self-recording and self-recording and matching on academic performance. *Child Behavior Therapy, 3,* 17–27.

McLaughlin, T. F. (1984). A comparison of self-recording and self-recording plus consequences for on-task and assignment completion. *Contemporary Educational Psychology, 9,* 185–192.

Michael, J. L. (1988). Establishing operations and the mand. *The Analysis of Verbal Behavior, 6,* 3–18.

Michael, J. L. (1993). Establishing operation. *The Behavior Analyst, 16,* 191–206.

Michael, J. L. (November, 2005). Motivating operations. Maryland Association for Behavior Analysis convention, Baltimore, MD.

Michael, J. (2007). Motivating operations. In J. O. Cooper, T. E. Heron, & W. L. Heward, *Applied behavior analysis* (2nd ed.) (pp. 374–391). Upper Saddle River, NJ: Prentice-Hall/Merrill.

O'Neill, R. E., Horner, R. H., Albin, R. W., Storey, K., & Sprague, J. R. (1990). *Functional analysis of problem behavior: A practical assessment guide.* Pacific Grove, CA: Brookes/Cole.

Plummer, S., Baer, D. M., & LeBlanc, J. M. (1977). Functional considerations in the use of time-out and an effective alternative. *Journal of Behavior Analysis, 10,* 689–705.

Powell, J., Martindale, A., & Kulp, S. (1975). An evaluation of time-sampling measures of behavior. *Journal of Applied Behavior Analysis, 8,* 463–469.

Powell, J., Martindale, B., Kulp, S., Martindale, A., & Bauman, R. (1977). Taking a closer look: Time sampling and measurement error. *Journal of Applied Behavior Analysis, 10,* 325–332.

Prater, M. A., Hogan, S., & Miller, S. R. (1992). Using self-monitoring to improve on-task behavior and academic skills of an adolescent with mild handicaps across special and regular education settings. *Education and Treatment of Children, 15,* 43–55.

Premack, D. (1959). Toward empirical behavioral laws: 1. Positive reinforcement. *Psychological Record, 66,* 219–233.

Repp, A. C., Felce, D., & Barton, L. E. (1988). Basing the treatment of stereotypic and self-injuries behaviors on hypothesis of their causes. *Journal of Applied Behavior Analysis, 21,* 281–289.

Repp, A. C., & Karsh, K. G. (1994). Hypothesis-based interventions for tantrum behaviors of persons with developmental disabilities in school settings. *Journal of Applied Behavior Analysis, 27,* 21–31.

Reynolds, G. S. (1975). *A primer of operant conditioning.* Glenview, IL: Scott Foresman.

Risley, T. R. (1968). The effects and side effects of punishing the autistic behaviors of a deviant child. *Journal of Applied Behavior Analysis, 1,* 21–34.

Roberts, M. L., & Shapiro, E. S. (1996). Effects of instructional ratios on students reading performance in a regular education program. *Journal of School Psychology, 34,* 73–91.

Robinson, P. W., Newby, T. J., & Ganzell, S. L. (1981). A token system for a class of underachieving, hyperactive children. *Journal of Applied Behavior Analysis, 14,* 307–316.

Smeets, R. M., VanLieshout, R. W., Lancioni, G. E., & Strict, R. S. (1986). Teaching mentally retarded students to tell time. *Analysis and Intervention in Developmental Disabilities, 6,* 222–232.

Smith, R. G, Iwata, B. A., Goh, H., & Shore, B. (1995). Analysis of establishing operations fore self-injury maintained by escape. *Journal of Applied Behavior Analysis, 28,* 515–535.

Solnick, J. V., Rincover, A., & Peterson, C. R. (1977). Some determinants of the reinforcing and punishing effects of timeout. *Journal of Applied Behavior Analysis, 10,* 415–424.

Speltz, M. L., Wenters-Shimamaura, J., & McReynolds, W. T. (1982). Procedural variations in group contingencies: Effects on children's academic and social behaviors. *Journal of Applied Behavior Analysis, 15,* 533–544.

Spooner, F., Spooner, D., & Uliceny, G. R. (1986). Comparisons of modified backward chaining: Backward chaining with leaps ahead and reverse chaining with leaps ahead. *Education and Treatment of Children, 9,* 122–134.

Taplin, P. S., & Reid, J. B. (1973). Effects of instructional set and experimenter influence on observer reliability. *Child Development, 44,* 547–554.

Tarnowski, K. J., & Drabman, R. S. (1987). Teaching intermittent self catheterization skills to mentally retarded children. *Research in Developmental Disabilities, 8,* 521–529.

Touchette, P. E., MacDonald, F., & Langer, S. N. (1985). A scatter plot for identifying stimulus control of problem behavior. *Journal of Applied Behavior Analysis, 18,* 343–351.

Tucker, D. J., & Berry, G. W. (1980). Teaching severely multihandicapped students to put on their own hearing aids. *Journal of Applied Behavior Analysis, 13,* 65–75.

Vaughn, M. E., & Michael, J. (1982). Automatic reinforcement: An important but ignored concept. *Behaviorism, 10,* 217–227.

Vollmer, T. (May 29, 2006). On the utility of the concept of automatic reinforcement. Association for Behavior Analysis Annual Conference, Atlanta, GA.

Walker, H. M., & Buckley, N. K. (1968). The use of positive reinforcement in conditioning attending behavior. *Journal of Applied Behavior Analysis, 1,* 245–250.

Weeks, M., & Gaylord-Ross, R. (1981). Task difficulty and aberrant behavior in severely handicapped students. *Journal of Applied Behavior Analysis, 14,* 449–463.

White, A., & Bailey, J. S. (1990). Reducing disruptive behaviors of elementary physical education students with site and watch. *Journal of Applied Behavior Analysis, 23,* 353–359.

Williams, R. L., Howard, U. F., Williams, B. F., & McLaughlin, T. F. (1994). Basic principles of learning. In E. C. Cipani & F. Spooner (Eds.), *Curriculum and instructional approaches for persons with severe disabilities* (pp. 7–30). Needham Height, MA: Allyn & Bacon.

Wolery, M., Kirk, K., & Gast, D. L. (1985). Stereotypic behavior as a reinforcer: Effects and side effects. *Journal of Autism and Developmental Disorders, 15,* 145–157.

Zarcone, J. R., & Fisher, W. W. (1996). Analysis of free-time contingencies as positive or negative reinforcement. *Journal of Applied Behavior Analysis, 29,* 247–251.

Zeilberger, J., Sampen, S. E., & Sloane, H. N. (1968). Modification of a child's problem behavior in the home with her mother as therapist. *Journal of Applied Behavior Analysis, 1,* 47–53.

ABOUT THE CD-ROM

This CD contains the following material that supplements the text.

Answer keys for:

- Fill-in-the-blank questions that appear after each chapter.
- True/False questions that appear after each chapter.

PowerPoint Presentations:

- Narrated PowerPoint presentations of answers to the discussion questions from sections in Chapters 1 and 2 appear in slideshow format.

Additional Material:

- Additional free material that complements the text, through the ERIC data base as well as a free e-text may be retrieved from www.ecipani.com/PoT.pdf

Software Requirements

- Microsoft Word
- Microsoft PowerPoint
- Adobe Acrobat Reader 9.2